Protestation

In all that I shall say in this book I submit to what is taught by Our mother, the Holy Roman Church; if there is anything in it contrary to this, it will be without my knowledge. Therefore, for the love of Our Lord, I beg the learned men who are to read it to look at it very carefully and to make known to me any faults of this nature which there may be in it and the many others which it will have of other kinds. If there is anything good in it, let this be to the glory and honor of God in the service of His most sacred Mother, our Patroness and Lady, to whom I am, though all unworthy, bound and consecrated as a slave.[1]

Timothy S. Flanders
meaningofcatholic.com/contact

---

[1] Adapted from the protestation given by St. Teresa of Avila in *Way of Perfection*

Introduction to the Holy Bible for Traditional Catholics

Timothy S. Flanders

Our Lady of Victory Press, MMXIX

Introduction to
The Holy Bible
for Traditional Catholics

*A Beginner's Guide to Reading
the Scriptures for Spiritual Profit*

Timothy S. Flanders

© Our Lady of Victory Press, MMXIX

ISBN 978-0-578-62426-6

Our Lady of Victory Press is an imprint of The Meaning of Catholic.

The Meaning of Catholic is a lay apostolate dedicated to uniting Catholics against the enemies of Holy Church. MeaningofCatholic.com

Graphic design and layout by Whitney Flanders.

Our Lady of Victory, pray for us.

Please do not copy this book without permission, unless it be for a Protestant or some other soul in need of conversion.

Dedicated to my wife.

TABLE OF CONTENTS

PART I
The Things You Need More Than Anything

1. Why Read the Holy Bible? 15
2. Guide to the Prayer Book of the Church, the Psalter 39
3. Beware: Fire from Heaven Burns up the Proud 79
4. How to Read with Humility 85
5. *Without Me, You Can Do Nothing* 101
6. Church Doctrines About the Holy Scriptures 106

PART II
History: How Theologians Seized Power with the Holy Bible

7. Oral Tradition and the Early History of the Scriptures .. 113
8. Rise of the Theologians and the Protestant Revolt 140
9. How Theologians Used Translations for Heresy 159
10. The Triumph of the Theologians 169

PART III
Everything Else You Need

11. Linguistic Analysis of English Translations 251
12. Annual Bible Reader According to Matins 273
13. Refute Protestants In Five Minutes 282
14. Typlogy: *On Pascha* by St. Melito of Sardis 303
15. Overview of the Teilhardian Heresy in History 314
16. Roman Numerals, Names and Abbreviations 329
17. List of Further Reading and Resources 333

PART ONE

THE THINGS YOU NEED
MORE THAN ANYTHING

+

The Lord Jesus Christ says *I am come to cast fire on the earth: and would that it were already kindled!* (Lk. xii. 49).

The Holy Bible is a divine fire from heaven. If you read it like the saints did—with humility, piety and prayer—it is the divine fire of charity with which the Sacred Heart of Jesus burned, cleansing your faults and bringing you to eternal life. As it is written, *he shall baptize you in the Holy Ghost and fire* (Mt. iii. 11) and again, *then shall the just shine as the sun, in the kingdom of their Father* (Mt. xiii. 43).

If you read it with pride—with the temerity to forsake the wisdom of the Fathers and reject the authority of the Church—then it is a consuming fire of divine judgment which will bring you to eternal damnation. As it is written, *he will thoroughly cleanse his floor and gather his wheat into the barn; but the chaff he will burn with unquenchable fire* (Mt. iii. 12).

Our God is a consuming fire (Heb. xii. 29) says the Blessed Apostle, and St. John says *God is charity* (I Jn. iv. 8). This fire is the charity of God Himself. Do you wish to receive the love of God, brother? All men wish to receive His love, but how many are found who will also fear Him?

The Lord Jesus says, *I will shew you whom you shall fear: Fear ye him who, after he hath killed, hath power to cast into hell. Yea, I say to you: Fear him* (Lk. xii. 5). But yet again he also says *Fear not, little flock, for it hath pleased your Father to give you a kingdom* (Lk. xii. 32).

Therefore the humble man fears the Lord, and yet hopes for His mercy as it is written *his mercy is on those who fear him* (Lk. i. 50). And again the Prophet declares *the Lord taketh pleasure in them that fear him: and in them that hope in his mercy* (Ps. cxlvi. 11).

But the proud who do not fear the Lord are burned by the fire of God as the Prophet says, *all the proud shall be stubble:*

and the day that cometh shall set them on fire (Mal. iv. 1). They seek mercy but show no mercy to their neighbor, they seek love but give no charity to God, they seek knowledge but no wisdom—for they fear neither God nor man. By their knowledge they exalt themselves up to heaven, saying *Come let us make a name for ourselves* (Gen. xi. 4). *And thou*, says Jesus Christ, *which art exalted unto heaven, thou shalt be thrust down to hell* (Lk. x. 15).

Be not burned therefore, brother, but repent and believe in Jesus Christ. Take His Word and humbly receive it. Do not forsake the wisdom of the Fathers but have piety and save your soul. This small book is meant to turn your heart to humility concerning Holy Writ, for many men have taken the fire from heaven and been burned through their pride.

Yet saints and holy men of old have been warmed at its fire and enlightened by its flame. Be not numbered among the reprobate who despise God, but *casting away all uncleanness and abundance of ill-will, with meekness receive the ingrafted word, which is able to save your souls* (Ja. i. 21). We will tell the story of the humble and proud concerning Holy Scripture, but only God knows their end.

Therefore consider these words with humility, and in your charity overlook any faults of mine contained here, but lift your mind and heart to God Who shows mercy to sinners. He will guide you into every good way which is necessary for your soul. Please say a Hail Mary for me, a sinner.

Timothy S. Flanders,
Our Lady of Guadalupe
Anno Domini MMXIX

I

WHY READ THE HOLY BIBLE?

As Catholics, there is a stereotype that is usually true: we do not know the Holy Scriptures. Especially in the English speaking cultures of Euro-America, the religious landscape is dominated by Protestants who are raised reading their bible. They often have a thorough knowledge of their scriptures by the time they meet a Catholic for the first time.

This short book is designed to make it easy for you, Catholic brother, to read the Holy Bible regularly, even the whole thing once a year. This book is your companion to guide you through this from a Traditional Catholic perspective.

This book contains many important truths that are too often neglected today, leading to errors in faith or morals. The most important thing to know in the very beginning is that the Holy Bible is not about being smart. It doesn't matter how many degrees you have or how many languages you know. In order to understand and profit from the Holy Bible you need to have humility.

We will discuss this throughout the book and elaborate more below. First, let's discuss some of the different aspects of reading the Holy Bible and what that means historically.

The Saints Devoutly Read Holy Writ

The most important reason to do anything is the greater glory of God by the salvation of your soul. Devout reading of Holy Writ is one powerful method of pious devotion and holiness. This is something practiced by all the great doctors of our faith. St. Augustine and St. Thomas and St. Alphonsus. They combatted the heresies of their day and expounded the faith of their Fathers, and thus their works are still read today. These great works would not have been possible had they not deeply and humbly studied the Sacred Scriptures. Their own writings are filled on every page with quotations from the Scriptures. The saints and doctors give us ample evidence of achieving sanctity through devotion to the Holy Scriptures.

Therefore it is absolutely false for any Catholic to think that reading the Sacred Bible is a Protestant thing to do. The saints devoutly read the Sacred Page, and believed themselves greatly bound to the Scriptures. Are we better than them? No, far worse. But let us imitate our holy Fathers as best we can by receiving the holy wisdom from the Scriptures.

St. Thomas says that the study of Scripture is one of the remedies for lust. St. Jerome wrote "study the scriptures and you will not love the vices of the flesh."[2] And in another place he writes: "ignorance of the Scripture is ignorance of Christ."[3] The saints read the Holy Text on their knees with tears, and they achieved heavenly glory. Thus we too, if only in our small way, can profit greatly from the Scriptures.

---

[2] Epis. Ad Paulin.
[3] *Commentariorum in Isaiam libri xviii* prol. PL 24,17B

What about When Our Fathers Couldn't Read?

In order to answer this question we need to discuss what life was like before literacy and even before Christianity. Literacy only became widespread after the 1500s. Thus it is reasonable to ask the question: besides the doctors of the faith, what did our fathers do with the Holy Bible if they couldn't read? The truth is, Catholics have always benefitted from the Scriptures, even when they couldn't read. This is due to the fact that before literacy, oral culture existed.

What is oral culture? An oral culture is one that transmits information primarily through speaking, hearing, and remembering. Because of false modern biases, people think that illiterate people are less intelligent. This is false. Illiterate people have the same intelligence as people who can read, they simply express it in different ways. Mostly notably, illiterate people have a much stronger capacity to memorize and remember. As Rubin puts it,

> Songs, stories, and poems are kept safe in stable form for centuries without the use of writing, whereas the literate observer has trouble remembering what happened yesterday without notes.[4]

Consider the epic poems of Homer, which fill hundreds of pages. These were recited for memory by bards and much of them remembered by people. Epic poetry and such things was not uncommon in oral cultures.

---

[4] David C. Rubin, *The Cognitive Psychology of Epic, Ballads, and Counting-out Rhymes* (Oxford University Press, 1997), 3

In recent times, oral culture has begun to receive vindication after decades of historical skepticism (which we will cover in chapter 10). In 1999, John Foley wrote:

> We are becoming ever more aware of how indebted many of our most cherished literary works...are to preliterate [i.e. oral tradition] media. The Judeo-Christian Bible reveals its oral traditional roots; medieval European manuscripts are penned by performing scribes; geometric vases from archaic Greece mirror Homer's oral style...Indeed, if these final decades of the millennium have taught us anything, it must be that oral tradition never was the "other" we accused it of being; it never was the primitive, preliminary technology of communication we thought it to be. Rather, if the whole truth is told, oral tradition stands out as the *single most dominant communicative technology of our species* as both a historical fact and, in many areas still, a contemporary reality.[5]

Concerning oral culture Walter Ong writes: "In such a society, knowledge is a tribal possession, not a matter of individual speculation."[6] Oral culture meant that the community all knew the traditions and stories by heart creating a common understanding of history, morals, and religion. In this context, oral culture can accurately remember and pass down vast amounts of information across centuries.[7] To those

---

[5] John Miles Foley, "What's in a sign," *Signs of Orality*, MacKay ed. (Brill, 1999), 1
[6] Walter J. Ong, *The Presence of the Word: Some Prolegomena for Cultural and Religious History* (Yale University Press, 1967), 231
[7] For a modern example, see Duane W. Hamacher, "Finding meteorite impacts in Aboriginal oral tradition," The Conversation

who were bards and story tellers of their culture, thousands and thousands of songs, histories and stories were memorized and passed down with accuracy. The elders and storytellers served as guardians of the oral tradition.

Given how ordinary oral was culture before 1500, the phenomenon of our modern world, where everyone reads and very few remember, is actually an odd thing indeed. It is critical for understanding the Holy Bible that we remove ourselves from our strange, modern frame of reference and consider the oral culture. Before they were written, the Scriptures existed only in oral form. Once they were written, they were delivered to an oral culture to be retained. We will return to this below.

Fulcrum of Culture: Piety for Tradition

Now we said above that humility was the key. Humility is defined by St. Thomas as conformity with the truth (II-II q161). The central truth which has governed cultures since time immemorial is the passing down of tradition from generation to generation. Tradition means a thing passed down. In both Greek and Latin the word is a verb: "to tradition" means to pass down.

Tradition is what binds a culture in unity with structures and standards of faith and morality. This is a part of the natural law, and thus pre-Christian cultures show this manifestly. In the oral cultures that predate 1500, this tradition generally consisted of two parts: an oral tradition as well as a *cultus*, which we will explain below.

<https://theconversation.com/finding-meteorite-impacts-in-aboriginal-oral-tradition-38052>. Accessed November 23, 2019

But in order to have this tradition passed down, the elders of society had to guard the tradition and the new generation had to receive it. The fulcrum upon which tradition is passed down is the virtue of piety. St. Thomas says piety is part of the virtue of justice: giving to each one what is his due (II-II q57). Piety particularly gives honor to our parents and superiors (II-II q101). Piety is what makes the whole system of cultural tradition work.

Piety means that the parents and elders reverence their own parents by guarding the tradition they have received. The younger generation must then have piety toward their parents in order to receive the tradition, guard it and pass it on to their children. It begins and ends with piety.

This of course stems from humility, which conforms a soul to the truth that he needs this wisdom from the elders. He needs to listen to his parents. This moral teaching runs throughout every pre-Christian society. *My son, hear the instruction of thy father, and forsake not the law of thy mother* (Prov. i. 8. See chapter 16 on Roman numerals).

Cultus: Oral Tradition Made Visible

Finally, to bind the generations together through piety in the oral tradition, the traditions was made manifest in signs and symbols, ancient rites passed down from ancient times. They provided a physical thing to do in order to symbolize both the passing on of tradition, and manifest piety toward the fathers. The supernatural deity was then invoked in these rites in order to bless the passing down of tradition and be the authority according to whom all were bound to the tradition. It is from the word *cultus* that we derive the English "culture," since the *cultus* manifests and informs the entire fabric of social tradition from morals to religion to customs.[8]

Oral Tradition at the Time of our Lord

At the time of our Lord, the Jews existed as an oral culture just like everyone else. What made them unique was that they not only had an oral Tradition, elders, and a *cultus*, they also had written down a great body of their oral Tradition in what would become known as the "Old Testament."

Their *cultus* consisted of a sacrificial priesthood (also common) which was all-male (not common), offering sacrifices in particular liturgical rites throughout the year. Their Scriptures served as a liturgical manual out of which the priests performed the *cultus* for the people. Alongside this, there had developed by the time of our Lord a weekly gathering (*"synagogue"*) of the Jews on Saturdays (*Sabbath*) to orally recite and listen to the Scriptures. This Saturday *cultus* of readings covered the entire Pentateuch (*Torah*) in one year (the first five books of the Holy Bible: Genesis, Exodus, Leviticus, Numbers, Deuteronomy).

An ordinary Jew in Judea grew up and learned the entire Pentateuch by heart. He would then hear this whole text read every year through successive Saturdays. Advanced students would also memorize the rest of the Old Testament: the Psalms, Prophets and wisdom books. Thus like other oral cultures, there was a great deal of memorization.[9] Thus when

---

[8] For more on the concept of *cultus* see the famous work by Josef Pieper *Leisure the Basis of Culture* (Faber & Faber: 1947)
[9] Birger Gerhardsson and Eric John Sharpe, *Memory and Manuscript: Oral Tradition and Written Transmission in Rabbinic Judaism and Early Christianity*. (Eerdmans: 1961), 64. For more on this fact of early Jewish memorization education, see the media work of scholar Ray Vander Laan.

they went to their Saturday service: they heard the words of Scripture and remembered them. The Scriptures were the earliest record of the ancient oral Tradition written down.

In addition to the Scriptures, *cultus* and elders, there were also other oral traditions not yet written down. At the time of our Lord the Jews of Judea were deeply divided with various groups of elders in the society keeping their separate oral traditions which served as their interpretation of the Old Testament. The Pharisees and Sadducees are examples of just two of these elder groups who both had differing oral traditions (cf. Acts xxiii. 8).

When our Lord came to earth, he rejected the leading elders of the society and their oral Tradition. Did he also reject oral Tradition, *cultus* and elders in themselves? No. Instead, he appointed a new office of *presbyteros* (a Greek word meaning "elder")—a new priesthood—and gave a new oral Tradition and *cultus* to be received and passed down.

Our Lord did not consign His teaching to writing. Instead, he gave a new oral Tradition for the Old Testament to a new group of elders of his choosing. The *cultus* was performed by the priests with divine authority.

Thus the faith was not primarily a "religion of the book," but rather of the Incarnate Word, spread first by an oral doctrine about the Old Testament, kept safe in a *cultus*, guarded by the priests and bishops. This was the early Church.[10] Only later did much of this oral Tradition get written

---

[10] For more history on the oral culture of the early Church, see Delbert Burkett, *An Introduction to the New Testament and the Origins of Christianity* (Cambridge University Press: 2002), 124–125, 45–46, 106–107, 129–130; Leslie Baynes, *The Heavenly Book Motif in Judeo-Christian Apocalypses 200 BCE-200 CE* (Brill: 2011), 40–41; Terence C. Mournet *Oral Tradition and Literary Dependency: Variability and Stability in the Synoptic Tradition and Q* (Mohr Siebeck: 2005), 138–141.

down into the New Testament. We will cover this further in chapter 7.

This office of presbyter also has another name — *episkopos* ("episcopus" in Latin, in English "bishop"). This is a word which means "one who oversees" or "watches over." What is the bishop watching over? The *cultus* and the oral Tradition.[11]

We see references to this oral culture in the New Testament. St. Paul explicitly tells St. Timothy to remember the oral teaching and pass it on to the bishops: *And the things which thou hast heard of me by many witnesses, the same commend to faithful men who shall be fit to teach others also* (II Tim. ii. 2). Or again St. Paul writes to all the faithful in Galatia and tells them to remember the oral teaching and reject anything contrary: *But though we, or an angel from heaven, preach a gospel to you besides that which we have preached to you, let him be anathema* (Gal. i. 8). Or again St. Paul tells the Thessalonians to remember the oral teaching and be faithful to it: *brethren, stand fast: and hold the traditions, which you have learned, whether by word or by our epistle* (II Thess. ii. 14).

One of the most notable passages about the *cultus* concerned the central *cultus* of the faith. Here I will translate the Greek literally to show the significant of this passage:

> For I have received of the Lord that which also I *traditioned* (παρέδωκα) unto you, that the Lord Jesus, the same night in which he was betrayed,

---

[11] In both the New Testament and the early Church writings, "priest" and "bishop" were often used interchangeably, since the bishop holds the fulness of the priesthood. The demarcation of deacon-priest-bishop was a terminology that arose later to make the necessary distinctions in the one priesthood of Jesus Christ

> took bread, And giving thanks, broke, and said: Take ye, and eat: this is my body, which shall be delivered for you: this do for the commemoration of me (I Cor. xi. 23-24).

This central *cultus* was the new rite where the oral Tradition of Jesus Christ was recited (as St. Paul does here) and a mystery (sacrament) was celebrated by the priest.[12] Christian *cultus* was then a combination of the *synagogue* of reading with the *cultus* of the Eucharist ("Breaking of the Bread" cf. Acts ii. 42).[13]

This must be stressed again here: *Jesus Christ wrote no books*. Instead, he taught his doctrine orally to the Apostles who transmitted it to the bishops. A great example of this is in the book of Acts, when St. Paul gives his final discourse before going to his fate in Jerusalem:

> I have shewed you all things, how that so labouring you ought to support the weak and to *remember the word of the Lord Jesus*, how he said: It is a more blessed thing to give, rather than to receive (Acts. xx. 35).

Here we have a saying of our Lord that nowhere appears in the Gospels. Did he really say it? Of course he did. This is an example of the oral Tradition which the Lord commended to the first bishops—the apostles—to pass down to the people and the next succession of bishops.

---

[12] In the Latin Church the term was "Sacrament" whereas in the Greek Church this term was more often "Mystery." They both meant the same thing. See the quote below from St. Basil.
[13] The earliest reference to this basic form of the Holy Mass is given by St. Just Martyr in his *First Apology* c. 150 A.D.

Thus before the New Testament was written, there existed an oral doctrine which interpreted the Old Testament. This oral Tradition thus became the way Catholics first understood the existing Scripture: the Old Testament. When the Gentiles started being converted, they had not memorized the Old Testament like many of their Catholic brethren among the Jews. Still, because they were also an oral culture they could take in and memorize these doctrines orally. The stories of Jesus Christ and His doctrine were given and remembered, and passed down.

Consider this: there were twelve Apostles (and more) who went to the ends of the earth spreading the Gospel. Why do we not have thousands of writings from them? Because they did not pass down the doctrine of Jesus Christ primarily through writing, but rather orally within the *cultus*.

St. Basil (d. 379) explains this in a noted passage:

> Of the dogmas and kerygma [preaching] in the Church, some we possess from written teaching and others we receive from the tradition of the Apostles, handed on to us in mystery [sacramental rites]. *In respect to piety both are the same force.* No one will contradict any of these, no one, at any rate, who is even moderately versed in matters ecclesiastical. Indeed, were we to try to reject unwritten customs as having no great authority, we would unwittingly injure the Gospel in its vitals...For instance, we take the first and most general example, who taught us in writing to sign with the sign of the cross those who have trusted in the name of our Lord Jesus Christ? What writing has taught us to turn to the East in prayer? Which of the saints left us in writing the words of the Epiclesis [prayer] at the consecration of the bread of Eucharist and of the

Cup of Benediction? ... Is it not from silent and mystical tradition? Indeed, in what written word is even the anointing with oil taught? ... Does this not come from the secret and arcane teaching which our fathers guarded in a silence[?]....In the same way, the Apostles and Fathers who, in the beginning, prescribed the Church's rites, guarded in secrecy and silence the dignity of the mysteries.[14]

Here St. Basil implicitly shows a crucial principle which will become vital in Part II of this work: there is both written and unwritten Tradition. "In respect to piety both are the same force." Both are given reverence and piety as *sources of revelation*. This shows that the early Church did not restrict inspiration to the written Scriptures alone, but also to the oral Tradition and *cultus* passed down from the Apostles.[15]

But the central *cultus* of the Holy Mass was the point where the oral Traditions were made manifest. Here the oral doctrine of Jesus Christ was explained orally and eventually written in the Gospels and Epistles. The New Testament was then eventually read at the celebrating of the *cultus*.

One issue that arose early was the Gnostic heresy, which spread their writings under false names like "The Gospel of Thomas." But the bishops used the existing oral doctrine to correctly judge which books were from the Apostles and which were not. One criteria for this was whether or not a given book was traditionally read during the *cultus*. For this reason, the book of Revelation was not generally accepted for

---

[14] *De Spiritu Sancto*, ch. 27. Emphasis mine.
[15] For more on this concept, see two Protestant sources which admit this: Craig D. Allert, *A High view of Scripture?* (Baker Academic: 2007); William J. Abraham, *Canon and Criterion in Christian Theology: From the Fathers to Feminism* (Oxford University Press, 1998).

some time, because it was not read during the *cultus*. The oral Tradition preceded, governed, and confirmed the written Scripture. The Scripture gained its own authority because it was the earliest written record of the oral Tradition.

The Holy Bible Before Literacy

It would be another 1400 years before the printing press was invented, and during this time our fathers kept and passed down the faith of the Scriptures orally, as they always had. The saints and doctors who read the Holy Bible achieved great sanctity and expounded the Scriptures to the faithful who in turn transmitted the Scripture teachings through other means than written. They organized passion plays, sacrificed and worked for decades to create great monuments of sacred art and architecture and practiced devout meditation like the Rosary or vocal prayers like the Angelus. They were given the sayings and stories of our Lord orally, and they could remember them because it was an oral culture.

Most of all, the Holy Mass was the *cultus* around which culture revolved. Other than the orations and certain hymns or antiphons, the texts of every Holy Mass and the Divine Office were simply a weaving together of many different Scripture texts.[16]

Catholic life has always revolved around Jesus Christ present in the Holy Mass, and in the devout practices of the faithful. Thus it can truly be said that Catholic life, centered always around Jesus Christ as revealed in the Scriptures, either through the Old Testament and the oral doctrine, or through the later New Testament. Even when our fathers could not

---

[16] This is true more in the Latin rite than in the Greek rite, possibly because the former is more ancient and stopped developing due to historical reasons like the Fall of Rome in 410.

read, it was Scripture stories that inspired them to holiness. During the Crusades our fathers were willing to leave their families by the hundreds and die in the Holy Land because they knew the stories of Jesus Christ.

This long explanation about oral culture is meant to help us out of our modern biases and approach the Holy Bible in the context in which it was written and passed down: within an oral culture. These thing must be kept in mind with humility and piety, in order to profit spiritually from the Text. Like St. Basil and all the saints before us, we must approach the Holy Bible reverently and with great piety toward the oral Tradition upon which it is based. We will discuss in subsequent chapters how errors about these things have affected the history of the Church.

The Bible Contains the Church's Prayer Book

Here we may discuss a crucial distinction which is absolutely vital for avoiding the errors and heresies that have led many Protestant souls to spiritual peril. It is the contrast between study and prayer. Prayer is defined as a lifting of the heart and mind to God (II-II q83 a1 ad2). Thus prayer is a supernatural activity that is connected with the divine.

Study, on the other hand, is defined as causing your intellect to adhere to the truth. As is shown by Protestant heretics and secular "scholars" of the Holy Text, a man can study the Scriptures intellectually but never become Catholic or even Christian (we will discuss this more in chapter 10). This is because he is not using the Scriptures for prayer. He is not reading with humility.

The central book in the Scriptures is designed to work against this pride. It is the book most commonly used and known by Israelites and Jews and Christians for millennia, the prayer book of the Church: the *Holy Psalter*. This book contains 150 Psalms which have formed the foundational prayer of the Church. The Church has understood these words as the most perfect expression of prayer because they mystically represent the prayer of Jesus Christ—God and Man—to God the Father.

The Church as the Mystical Body of Christ has prayed these prayers more than any other prayers. It is truly the Church's prayer book more than any other text. The ancient custom was for monks to pray all 150 psalms each day. Eventually this was relaxed by St. Benedict in his rule to be all 150 Psalms each week. Every single celebration of the Holy Mass includes numerous prayers from the Church's prayer book. Initially when it was revealed, the Rosary was known as "Mary's Psalter" since it contained 150 Hail Marys and formed a way for our fathers to join with the monks in praying the 150 Psalms.

Catholics today can greatly benefit from using the Church's prayer book as their prayer. The Psalter contains psalms for every single temperament, occasion, and purpose, making it perfect for the faithful whoever they may be. We will go over this prayer book in greater detail in the next chapter.

The Most Popular Book Besides the Holy Bible

Several generations before the Protestant revolt broke out, there was a movement among Catholics called the Brethren of the Common Life. This was a lay organization which emphasized simple devotions and Catholic piety. One of its unique qualities however, was an emphasis on humble reading of the Word of God. Like most good Catholic movements, it was not without controversy, but was protected by the popes.

The most famous member of this movement was Thomas à Kempis, author of (it is said) the most popular book of all time besides the Holy Bible: *The Imitation of Christ*.

The book, like the classic texts of the saints and doctors, is filled with quotations from the Holy Scriptures. But à Kempis knew perfectly the importance of using the Scriptures not for intellectual study alone but for prayer. In the very first chapter of *Imitation* he writes:

> What good does it do to speak learnedly about the Trinity if, lacking humility, you displease the Trinity? Indeed it is *not learning that makes a man holy and just, but a virtuous life makes him pleasing to God*. I would rather feel contrition than know how to define it. For what would it profit us to know the whole Bible by heart and the principles of all the philosophers if we live without grace and the love of God?

He says on the contrary:

> There are many who *hear the Gospel* often but care little for it because they have not the spirit of Christ. Yet whoever wishes to understand fully the words of Christ must try to pattern his whole life on that of Christ.[17]

Here we see the difference between a man who studies the Word of God for intellectual knowledge and the one who reads the Word of God for prayer. The first man studies the Scriptures so that he can take pride in his knowledge or be praised by men. *Knowledge puffeth up: but charity edifieth* (I

---

[17] Chapter I.

Cor. viii. 1). The second man reads the Word of God with humility in order to pray to God, to know Him, and most of all to love Him and imitate Him, following His commands. This is the end we must have in view when we read the Holy Scriptures.

The Saintly Theologian vs. the "Theologian"

Here we must discuss a very important distinction which will be the theme of Part II: the saint and the theologian. In the early Church, a theologian was a man of prayer. He was considered to be filled with the Holy Ghost and *because of this* he understood the Scriptures. The most famous of these was also illiterate: St. Anthony of the Desert. Around him gathered the primary theologians of the 4th century: the Desert Fathers. These men helped convert St. Augustine as we will read about in chapter 4.

However, other men, who did not follow the way of prayer but the way of study alone, ridiculed Anthony for being illiterate. They and their kind would later be known falsely as "theologians," even though they were not truly theologians, like St. Anthony. A particular scene from his life illustrates this contrast in the context of what we have said:

> And again others such as these [philosophers] met him in the outer mountain and thought to mock him because he had not learned letters. And Anthony said to them, 'What do you say? Which is first, mind or letters? And which is the cause of which — mind of letters or letters of mind?' And when they answered mind is first and the inventor of letters, Anthony said, 'Whoever, therefore, has a sound mind has not need of letters.' This answer amazed both the bystanders and the philosophers, and they

departed marveling that they had seen so much understanding in an ignorant man. For his manners were not rough as though he had been reared in the mountain and there grown old, but graceful and polite, and his speech was seasoned with the divine salt, so that no one was envious, but rather all rejoiced over him who visited him.[18]

Here St. Anthony illustrates what is the essence of a true theologian: a *sound mind*. Sin darkens our intellect, but grace and virtue enlighten it. The philosophers in this story (and the so-called "theologians" who would later follow their method) had no humility, and thus with all their learning could not reach the truth as St. Anthony did, even though he could not read. The true theologian follows the way of the saints when reading the Holy Scriptures. It is the way of prayer and humility in the study of Holy Writ. If one only studies and does not pray and have humility, he will succumb to pride and be burned.

Spiritual Reading

Therefore, when you read the Holy Bible, it should not be like normal reading. It should be spiritual reading. Reading in general simply means to understand the words on the page. *Spiritual reading* is reading in a spiritual way for a spiritual purpose. The spiritual way of reading is with humility we have mentioned: coming to the Sacred Page first on our knees before God, humbly asking His mercy for our sins and grace to know and follow His commands.

Second, it means reading in His presence. Picture yourself led into the hall of the king of the universe, Who places in your

---

[18] St. Athanasios, *Life of St. Anthony*, ch. 73

hands the words He has written to you. He bids you to read them in His presence and awaits your response to Him.

Third, this also means being very careful to read slowly and trying to understand His words, and never rushing through or disrespecting His words.

Fourth, and perhaps most importantly, it means listening to the wisdom of the Fathers, like St. Anthony. We will discuss this in detail in chapter 4.

The spiritual purpose of this reading is to know Him, imitate Him, and follow His commands. In short, it is the glory of God by saving your soul. *If you are not growing in virtue by reading the Holy Scripture then you should not read the Holy Scripture, nor anything else that prevents you from overcoming sin.* It is lamentable, but it is true: some men use even the Holy Scriptures for their own pride. But, as we have said, the Scriptures are a fire from heaven: it cleanses the just but burns up the wicked. Therefore, brethren, do not approach the Sacred Text with a wicked heart, lest you be burned.

Catholic Faith and Morals

The Scriptures give great testimony to Christian faith and morals. They do not answer every moral and doctrinal question, but their teachings provide principles and morals against the extravagance of the heretics in our own day.

For example, one of the most ubiquitous sins in our day is remarriage. When one knows the Holy Scriptures, one knows that our Lord said that he who divorces his wife and marries another commits adultery:

> Every one that putteth away his wife and marrieth another committeth adultery: and he that marrieth

her that is put away from her husband committeth adultery (Lk. xvi. 18).

The Protestant heretics, who claim to follow the Scriptures, do not follow this commandment from our Lord, as the vast majority have doctrinally permitted their adherents to divorce their spouses and then marry someone else. Thus by the Holy Scripture, 50-60% of Protestants are living in adultery. (Catholics also do not follow this command, and they will answer at the judgment).

Another example: some Catholics shortly after Vatican II began to advocate heresy by denying the Virgin Birth of our Lord. But the Scriptures say clearly: "a virgin whose name was Mary" (Lk. i. 27). Thus, knowing the Scriptures fortifies the Catholic against the wickedness of heretics in our own day.

But even more than this, the Holy Scriptures judge our own souls before God and demand our repentance. Consider this passage from St. John:

> If any man say: I love God, and hateth his brother; he is a liar. For he that loveth not his brother whom he seeth, how can he love God whom he seeth not? (I Jn. iv. 20)

This verse condemns those Catholics who are zealous for orthodoxy, yet lack charity for their neighbor. How will they stand at the judgment if they have hated their brother?

The Scriptures: Central Tradition of Tradition

We discussed above the oral Tradition, the *cultus*, the priests and the Old Testament at the beginning of the Church. Sacred Tradition refers to the whole body of the Catholic faith that is passed down to us through our fathers from the

Apostles. It includes our sacred rites of Mass, the writings of the saints and doctors, devotions/prayers and also monuments like sacred art, architecture and music. But the central piece of this Holy Tradition is the Sacred Scriptures. As we stated, it is the earliest record of the Apostolic oral Tradition. As such it forms a sacred trust from our fathers to teach and pass down to our own children.

Children greatly benefit from memorizing sacred texts as so many children of past generations have. It is profitable to display the Holy Bible in a prominent place in the home and have the father of the family read the Gospels and other stories to the children and explain it according to the oral Tradition.

Apostolic succession guarantees that a single priest was consecrated by a bishop, who was consecrated by a bishop in a long line of succession all the way back to the first bishop who was consecrated by the Apostle who was consecrated by the Hands of Jesus Christ Himself. In a similar way, the writings in the Sacred Text were written by the Apostles and saints themselves. They are the closest written historical record we have of Jesus Christ. Thus the children can see Him in a powerful way through the reading of Scripture and it forms the central inheritance of Tradition from our Fathers.

Converting Protestants to the One True Faith

As we mentioned, in the English speaking world of the UK and America, the religious landscape is dominated by Protestantism. The most dominant form of Protestantism in America is known as "evangelicalism." This sect forms a general movement of Christians who follow the pietistic revivalist ideas of the 19th century. Their spirituality revolves around reading their Protestant bibles. It is common for these

Protestants to be raised reading their bibles and to have memorized a great deal of verses.[19]

One of the most powerful barriers keeping Protestants from coming back to the Church—besides sin and pride of course—is a lie which they have been taught and passed down for centuries: Catholicism does not follow the Holy Bible. What is worse, since so few Catholics read the Scriptures, this lie seems to be confirmed when any Protestant interacts with a Catholic.

We will deal with this accusation in chapter 13 on Protestantism and show you how to clearly refute the Protestant heresy from the Scriptures. But the point here is this: you cannot expect to be able to convert a serious Protestant unless you know the Scriptures. Your Protestant friends, family, and co-workers will have questions about the Catholic faith and you need to be ready to defend the faith against erroneous accusations and give good answers for genuine seekers of truth. As St. Peter writes,

> Sanctify the Lord Christ in your hearts, being ready always to satisfy every one that asketh you a reason of that hope which is in you. But with modesty and fear, having a good conscience: that whereas they speak evil of you, they may be ashamed who falsely accuse your good conversation in Christ (I Pet. iii. 15ff).

Thankfully, more important than intellectual answers to a Protestant is the charity that you show him. It is "modesty and fear" which truly makes an impact on souls, especially those

---

[19] However, the percentage of nominally Protestant Christians in America is roughly the same as Catholics: only about 30% of them go to church every Sunday.

blinded by heresy. Even if you do not know the answer to every doctrinal riddle, if you have true charity, souls will be saved. As it is written, *By this shall all men know that you are my disciples, if you have love one for another* (Jn. xiii. 35). I can personally testify that the holiness of individual Catholics was the greatest factor which caused me to abandon my own Protestant heresies.

Help the Poor Souls

Finally, we must emphasize that the spiritual power of the Scriptures can be applied also to the souls in Purgatory. From the Manual of Indulgences:

> A plenary indulgence is granted to the faithful who read Scripture as spiritual reading from a text approved by competent authority and with the reverence due to the divine word for at least a half an hour.[20]

"Spiritual reading" is meant to contrast the purely intellectual study that we discussed above. Read the Holy Text prayerfully with humility and lift your mind and will to God. A good practice is to gain the indulgence every Sunday at your weekly Holy Communion. Fulfill the requirements of 30 minutes and offer the usual conditions for gaining an indulgence: Holy Communion, confession, and prayer for the Holy Father and his intentions.

Then your spiritual reading of the Scriptures will not only be an act of worship to God, but an act of charity for some soul still locked in the prison of Purgatory. We must not neglect

---

[20] Enchiridion Indulgentiarum Normae et Concessiones (Libreria Editrice Vaticana: 2006. Third printing USCCB, 2013), 100

and forget the pour souls, who are our brethren and our fathers. that they may soon enter into eternal life and we may one day join their company. In the next chapter we will discuss the prayer book of the Church.

II

GUIDE TO THE CHURCH'S PRAYER BOOK, THE PSALTER

The Four Senses of Scripture

The Holy Psalter, or The Book of Psalms, is a collection of 150 "Psalms" written mostly by King David but also others such as Asaph and Moses. As we stated in the last chapter, it is truly the prayer book of the Church more than any other.

But in order to discuss the significance and the meaning of the Psalter, we need to talk briefly about the senses of Holy Scripture. This applies to all of Scripture, but it is especially important to keep this in mind when praying the Psalms so that the prayers can be prayed with spiritual profit.

Some modern Catholics have forgotten these senses and have thus misunderstood the Psalter and even been scandalized by it. This of course is simply a failure to have piety toward the wisdom of the Fathers, who taught these senses.[21] We will address this issue more directly below, but

---

[21] Cf. St. Thomas, Quodl., vii, Q. vi, a. 14. See also St. Augustine (*Confessions* XII.26-31; De doctr. christ., III, xxvii; etc.), St. Gregory the Great (in Ezech., iii, 13, Lib. I, hom. x, n. 30 sq.), St. Basil, St. Chrysostom, St. Jerome, St. Bernard, and, among the Scholastics, St. Thomas(I, Q. i, a. 10; "De potent.", IV, 1; "in II sent.", dist. xii, Q. i, a. 2, ad 7um), Card. Cajetan (ad I, Q. i, a. 10), and others.

the important thing here is that we must understand that Scripture has multiple senses. It is first divided into the literal sense and the spiritual sense.

The Literal Sense

And David prevailed over the Philistine, with a sling and a stone, and he struck, and slew the Philistine (I Kng. xvii. 50).[22] The literal sense is the most obvious sense at face value. It is the meaning most commonly understood by the first writer of the passage. Here in the book of I Kings, there is an obvious historical statement. David slew Goliath of Geth, and that actually happened.

However, since literal sense means the common sense, we may also include here idioms and metaphors. For example, our Lord in a parable has a man say: *Is thy eye evil, because I am good?* (Mt. xx. 15). Here our Lord is using an idiom ("evil eye") to denote a malicious will. This phrase is not meant to be a reference to a malicious eyeball. Thus the literal meaning doesn't just mean what the words literally say, but rather the common meaning of the words. We may also call it the historical meaning: what this phrase meant when it was first said or written.

The Spiritual Sense

Once the literal, historical sense is understood, the higher spiritual sense can be understood. This may or may not be known immediately by the reader. As the Gospel says,

---

[22] Please see chapter 16 for the different names of Bible books which can sometimes be confusing.

> Then he opened their understanding, that they might understand the scriptures. And he said to them: Thus it is written, and thus it behooved Christ to suffer and to rise again from the dead, the third day (Lk. xxiv. 45).

It is shown here that the spiritual meaning is not readily apparent but requires a special illumination from the Lord. That is the reason that the true theologian is the man who prays: he who knows God Himself will understand the Scriptures. And thus the spiritual meaning of the Scripture is not accepted by modern "theologians," since they do not pray.

But because the spiritual meaning requires an extra grace, we can say that the spiritual meaning of the Scripture is the *true* meaning of Scripture according to the words of the Lord: *all things must needs be fulfilled which are written in the law of Moses and in the prophets and in the psalms, concerning me* (Lk. xxiv. 44). Our Lord flatly says that these things are written *concerning me*. One way or another, the whole of Scripture is about Christ, His Church, and eternal life in the Blessed Trinity. Since this is the end goal of the words, we can call this the true meaning.

Thus taking our example above of David, we may see an obvious spiritual meaning in the real, historical slaying of Goliath having the *true* meaning of the Death and Resurrection of our Savior. Just as David was a young man and conquered Goliath with a sling instead of a sword, so our Lord was humbled on the Cross and conquered by rising again after his apparent defeat.

Since our modern society has been so deeply shaped by "theologians" who do not pray, these spiritual senses which our fathers saw is often difficult for modern Catholics to accept. But in order to read the Holy Bible with the Church, we must do our best with God's help to overcome our modern prejudices and adhere with piety to the wisdom of the Fathers. After we distinguish between the literal sense, we see there are three different types of spiritual sense: typology, tropology, and anagogy.

Typology

Typology refers to a text being a *typos* of something. It is also known as the allegorical or mystical sense. A *typos* does not equate with the English word "type" as it is used colloquially today. It is more like the English word "archetype." In typology a *typos* is like an architectural design on paper. The *typos* points out the way in which the building should be constructed. Once the building has been constructed, the *typos* fulfills its purpose.

This spiritual sense of Scripture is the way in which the Old Testament is "fulfilled" in the new. To "fulfill" means to fill up something which should be full. Just as a cup is designed to carry liquid and does not fulfill its purpose without being full. As Augustine says: "The Old Testament is the New Testament concealed; the New Testament is the Old Testament revealed."[23]

For example, St. Peter uses typology when he speaks of the ark of Noe.

> They waited for the patience of God in the days of Noe, when the ark was a building: wherein a few, that is, eight souls, were saved by water. Whereunto baptism, being of the like form (*antitypon*) now saveth you also: not the putting away of the filth of the flesh, but the examination of a good conscience

---

[23] St. Augustine, Quaest. in Hept. 2,73: PL 34, 623; cf. DV 16.

towards God by the resurrection of Jesus Christ (I Pt. iii. 21).

Notice here that St. Peter first discusses the literal meaning, noting that in fact only eight people were saved in the ark of Noe. But then he says that this real, historical event was in fact a *typos* for the real truth of Baptism's saving grace. Here is the true meaning of the ark of Noe, even though the ark of Noe also existed in history.

Another example comes from St. Paul when he speaks concerning the Law of Moses:

> Let no man therefore judge you in meat or in drink, or in respect of a festival day, or of the new moon, or of the sabbaths, Which are a shadow of things to come, but the body is of Christ (Col. ii. 16-17).

Here St. Paul shows that a *typos* is like a shadow cast by the reality of the real thing. The shadow of course gets its whole existence from the fact that the body is casting the shadow. The shadow indicates that a body is there making the shadow. This is the meaning of what the Old Testament is. More than the other spiritual senses, typology specifically points to the coming of Christ and His Church.

Finally, it must be stressed as well that a *typos* is not a mere symbol, but has real power even at the time it first existed during the Old Testament. But it gains its efficacy from the things which it typifies. The Paschal Lamb in the Exodus was not efficacious for averting the destroying angel because it was a lamb's blood. It was efficacious because it was a *typos* of the blood of Christ. In chapter 14 we provide a translation of an ancient sermon which particularly shows typology and how the Church understood the Old Testament.

Tropology

The second spiritual sense is the tropological sense, or moral sense. This refers to the *tropos* meaning "turn, way, manner." It refers to the moral meaning of the Scripture. The passage has a literal meaning, but it also hides a moral meaning which instructs the reader in how to live a life in accord with the virtues of Christ.

A sublime example of tropology comes in St. John XIII:

> He riseth from supper, and layeth aside his garments, and having taken a towel, girded himself. After that, he putteth water into a basin, and began to wash the feet of the disciples, and to wipe them with the towel wherewith he was girded (4-5).

Then our Lord gives the tropological meaning forthwith:

> Know you what I have done to you? You call me Master, and Lord; and you say well, for so I am. If then I being your Lord and Master, have washed your feet; you also ought to wash one another's feet. For I have given you an example, that as I have done to you, so you do also. Amen, amen I say to you: The servant is not greater than his lord; neither is the apostle greater than he that sent him. If you know these things, you shall be blessed if you do them (13-17).

Thus does our Lord give to us the tropological meaning of His action: this is an act of humility and charity which our Lord wills us to imitate. It is a moral command given by means of manifested action. Indeed, the whole life of our Lord is given as an example. As the Blessed Apostle declares:

> Let nothing be done through contention, neither by vain glory: but in humility, let each esteem others better than themselves: Each one not considering the things that are his own, but those that are other men's. For let this mind be in you, which was also in Christ Jesus: Who being in the form of God, thought it not robbery to be equal with God: But emptied himself, taking the form of a servant, being made in the likeness of men, and in habit found as a man. He humbled himself, becoming obedient unto death, even to the death of the cross. For which cause God also hath exalted him, and hath given him a name which is above all names: That in the name of Jesus every knee should bow, of those that are in heaven, on earth, and under the earth: And that every tongue should confess that the Lord Jesus Christ is in the glory of God the Father (Php. ii. 3-11).

Here the Blessed Apostle draws out an immense tropological meaning from the life, death and resurrection of our Savior. It is "this mind" which must be in us: the deep humility rooted in Christ our Lord. This is the power of the tropological sense: it must convert us from sin and bring us to holiness.

Anagogy

The anagogical sense points through Christ to the life of the world to come. It is particularly concerned with union with God and prayer. It means "to lead upward." Thus we may distinguish the four senses of Scripture in terms of their direction:

Literal - points *back* to the historical events

Typology - points *forward* to Christ and the Church

Tropology - points *downward* to the mortal life of a Christian

Anagogy - points *upward* toward heaven and the world to come

With anagogy we see the historical events of the Old Testament as pointing toward eternal life. For example, the life of Joseph is instructive. From the literal sense, Joseph is sold by his brothers and sent to Egypt as a slave. He is then exalted by Pharaoh as the ruler of all Egypt who saves Egyptians and Israelites from famine. Then, through his descendent Moses, Israel is led up out of Egypt and, by Josue, into the Promised Land. This is the historical sense.

Considering the *typos*, Joseph shows Christ descending from heaven in the incarnation and being exalted to save the people, then in Moses, to lead them out of slavery to sin and, by Josue (whose name is another form for Jesus) into the freedom of the Kingdom of God.

Tropologically, we see the faith and virtue that these men held which enabled them to overcome by the grace of God. *By faith Moses... Esteeming the reproach of Christ greater riches than the treasure of the Egyptians, he looked unto the reward* (Heb. xi. 24, 26).

But anagogically, we understand the life of Joseph, Moses, and Josue to be the end of time when our Lord will descend to crush the new pharaoh (antichrist) and set up His kingdom. He will then bring His people through the Red Sea of death into eternal life, while drowning the reprobate (Egyptians) in the fires of eternal condemnation.

Another famous anagogy is said by our Lord in His end times discourses in the Gospel of St. Mark:

> And when you shall hear of wars and rumours of wars, fear ye not. For such things must needs be: but the end is not yet. For nation shall rise against nation and kingdom against kingdom: and there shall be earthquakes in divers places and famines. These things are the beginning of sorrows...And unto all nations the gospel must first be preached...And you shall be hated by all men for my name's sake. But he that shall endure unto the end, he shall be saved. And when you shall see the abomination of desolation, standing where it ought not (he that readeth let him understand): then let them that are in Judea flee unto the mountains...But pray ye that these things happen not in winter...For in those days shall be such tribulations as were not from the beginning of the creation which God created until now: neither shall be...then shall they see the Son of man coming in the clouds, with great power and glory (Mk. xiii. 7-26).

Here our Lord speaks on the one hand in the literal sense by predicting the destruction of the Second Temple. On the other hand, he speaks in the anagogical sense by discussing the end times when He will come again. There are multiple senses within this passage, but the anagogical sense leads the reader upwards toward heaven and the life of the world to come.

The Mystery of The Holy Psalter

It is with these things in mind that we must approach the Psalter. Its words are shrouded in mystery and many things are deep and mystical. As Psalm LXXVII says, *I will open my mouth in parables: I will utter propositions from the beginning.* Throughout the Psalms, the four senses of Scripture abound. The first mystery, however, is the number of Psalms.

In the language of Scripture, the number 7 means perfection or completion, whereas the number 8 represents eternity and a new covenant. Thus seven times seven represents perfection times perfection, and plus one (fifty) represents complete eternity. Thus the ancient feast of Fifty (*Pentecost*) celebrated the harvest and the giving of the Law by Moses. In the New Covenant, Pentecost is the giving of the New Law: the All-Holy Spirit. But then, when we consider three sets of fifty, we immediately recognize that the number of the Psalms is trinitarian, with each 50 representing perfection, complete eternity thrice over: the Thrice Holy Trinity. Thus the mystery begins with the number.

As we pass to the words of the Psalter, we begin to see the four senses we discussed above. The literal sense of the Psalter is sometimes obvious, as it is in reference to various historical events, such as Psalm L when David repented or Psalm CXLIII when David faced Goliath.

From the historical meaning we draw out the true meaning: Jesus Christ and His Church. The words of the Psalter are understood by the Church Fathers mystically by the Church as the words of Jesus Christ, Son of God and Son of Man, addressed to God the Father. Because of this, there is hardly any prayer more intimate, more holy, and more perfect than the Holy Psalter.

We see hints of Christ Himself praying the Psalms during his passion. In particular on the cross he cries out with Psalm XXI: *My God, My God, why hast Thou forsaken me?* The saints have also envisioned this reality. In the mystical vision of Bl. Anne Catherine Emmerich we read these words about our Lord's Passion:

> The darkness which reigned around was but symbolic of that which overspread his interior; he turned, nevertheless, to his Heavenly Father, he prayed for his enemies, he offered the chalice of his sufferings for their redemption, he continued to pray as he had done during the whole of his Passion, and *repeated portions of those Psalms* the prophecies of which were then receiving their accomplishment in him.[24]

This mystical sense is depicted in Mel Gibson's *Passion of the Christ* (which was based on Bl. Catherine's vision), where our Lord is praying Psalms through the Passion, such as immediately before the scourging.

Christ did pray Psalm XXI on the cross which was receiving its fulfillment in him at that time, and the Psalm also prophesied his resurrection. As we noted, our Lord said the Psalms were written *concerning me* (Lk. xxiv. 44). Since these are the central prayers which mystically speak of the interior life of Jesus Christ, they form the central *prayer of all prayers* within the life of the Church.

This is why the Church has always used the Psalter as the foundational piece of its public prayer life whether in the

---

[24] Bl. Anne Catherine Emmerich, *The Dolorous Passion of Our Lord Jesus Christ*, trans. the Abbe de Cazales, (London, Burns, and Lambert), Ch. 44

Divine Office (which recites the entire Psalter weekly) or in the Holy Mass (which is filled with the Psalms from beginning to end).

Laymen can greatly benefit from the use of the Psalter for private prayers. But because the Psalter is not arranged like any other prayer book, it can be confusing to try to use for private prayer. We will return to this in a moment.

The Spirituality of the Church's Prayer Book

First, we need to say a further word about the spirituality and mysticism of the Psalter. As we said, the Psalms are the words of Jesus Christ to God the Father. However, this may not be apparent in every case. For example in Ps. XXXVII we read the words, *there is no peace in my bones, because of my sins.* Why would our Lord speak of His sins, He Who was *tempted in every way, yet without sin* (Heb. iv. 15)?

This points to the mystery of the Mystical Body of Christ. Our Lord assumes into His own person the members of the Church as His Body. As it is written, *we are members of his body, of his flesh, and of his bones, this is a great mystery; but I speak in Christ and in the church* (Eph. v. 30, 32) and again *as many of you as have been baptized in Christ, have put on Christ* (Gal. iii. 27).

So the Psalter forms a mystical prayer of Christ with His Body the Church in one act of worship to the Father. This is one reason why David in the Psalms is traditionally referred to as "the Prophet." Consider this explanation from St. Augustine on this reality in the aforementioned Psalm:

> Whence then come *the sins*, but from the Body, which is the Church? Because both the Head and the Body of Christ are speaking. Why do they speak

as if one person only? Because *they twain*, as he hath said, *shall be one flesh* (Eph. v. 31). *This* (says the Apostle) *is a great mystery; but I speak concerning Christ and the Church*....For why should He not say, *my sins*, who said, *I was hungry, and ye gave Me no meat; I was thirsty, and ye gave Me no drink; I was a stranger, and ye took Me not in. I was sick and in prison, and ye visited Me not* (Mt. xxv. 42).

Assuredly the Lord was not in prison. Why should He not say this, to whom when it was said, *When saw we Thee hungry, and athirst, or in prison; and did not minister unto Thee?* He replied, that He spake thus in the person of His Body. *Inasmuch as ye did it not unto one of the least of Mine, ye did it not unto Me* (Mt. xxv. 40).

Why should He not say, "from the face of my sins," who said to Saul, *Saul, Saul, why persecutest thou Me*, (Acts ix. 4) who, however, being in Heaven, now suffered from no persecutors? But just as, in that passage, the Head spake for the Body, so here too [in this Psalm] the Head speaks the words of the Body; whilst you hear at the same time the accents of the Head Itself also. Yet do not either, when you hear the voice of the Body, separate the Head from it; nor the Body, when you hear the voice of the Head: because *they are no more twain, but one flesh*.[25]

This is the mystery of the prayer of Christ to the Father. Thus the great Doctor explains the mystery of the Psalms: our Lord

---

[25] St. Augustine, *Commentary on the Psalms*

speaks, yet with His Church to the Father. Thus the words of the Psalter manifest the mystery of Christ and His Church in a way completely unique among all prayers. As such it contains not only shades of humanity for every subjective temperament, personality, and mood, but also abundant divine wisdom and spiritual unction which provides grace in time of need. The Psalter is a treasure of sacred prayers from the depths of Jesus Christ in union with the Father, in union with the Church.

The Just Man and His Enemies

There is a theme in the Psalms between the "just man" (mostly speaking in the first person) and the "enemies." The just man of course is understood to be Christ in union with the soul of every Christian. But who are the enemies? As it is said, *I will pursue after my enemies, and overtake them: and I will not turn again till they are consumed* (Ps. xvii. 38). These aggressive passages give difficulty to modern readers because they fail to understand the different senses of Scripture.[26]

In the literal sense, David was indeed fighting against his enemies and overcoming them. However, since these passages are really about Christ, how can we understand these violent verses?

St. John Cassian explains that the primary enemies in the Psalms are the sins of a man, against which he makes war. The true enemy then becomes the *old man* as the Blessed Apostle declares, *you have been taught in him, as the truth is in Jesus, to put off, according to former conversation, the old man, who is corrupted according to the desire of error* (Eph. iv. 22).

---

[26] Many of these verses and even entire Psalms were removed from the modern Divine Office. The reformers do not appear to have accepted the senses given by the Fathers, but actually cited "psychological" reasons for removing them (Preface to *The Liturgy of the Hours*, Vol. I: Advent).

Thus Christ speaks in these verses as the just man who fights within the soul of every Christian against the enemies of our salvation in order to eradicate the *old man*. As it is written, *Labour as a good soldier of Christ Jesus* (II Tim. ii. 3).[27]

In addition, other verses appear to encourage a malicious vengeance. But this too is wrapped up into the meaning of Christ speaking. St. Thomas considers the verse *may the wicked be turned into hell* (Ps. ix. 18) and explains:

> Such like imprecations which we come across in Holy Writ, may be understood in three ways: first, by way of prediction, not by way of wish, so that the sense is: "May the wicked be," that is, "The wicked shall be, turned into hell."
>
> Secondly, by way of wish, yet so that the desire of the wisher is not referred to the man's punishment, but to the justice of the punisher, according to Ps. lvii. 11: "The just shall rejoice when he shall see the revenge," since, according to Wis. i. 13, not even God "hath pleasure in the destruction of the wicked" when He punishes them, but He rejoices in His justice, according to Ps. x. 8: "The Lord is just and hath loved justice."
>
> Thirdly, so that this desire is referred to the *removal of the sin*, and not to the punishment itself, to the effect, namely, that the sin be destroyed, but that the man may live (II-II q25 a6).

---

[27] The Desert Fathers also understood the nations of the Canaanites which God commanded to be eradicated to be the *typos* of the Seven Deadly Sins. See St. John Cassian, *Conferences* and *Institutes*

Thus in the Psalms we see the *militancy* of Jesus Christ. As St. John declares: *For this purpose, the Son of God appeared, that he might destroy the works of the devil* (I. Jn. iii. 8). Thus in this sense is our Lord a destroyer, so that He can speak concerning His enemies: *In the morning I put to death all the wicked of the land: that I might cut off all the workers of iniquity from the city of the Lord* (Ps. c. 8) and the Church can say that *in thy mercy thou wilt destroy my enemies. And thou wilt cut off all them that afflict my soul: for I am thy servant* (Ps. cxlii. 12). These are the enemies of Jesus Christ: pride, lust, wrath, sloth, gluttony, covetousness and envy. In particular, it is the pervasive and overpowering demon of lust against which the violent Psalms help the Christian soul.

Two Traditions of the Psalter

We will discuss this issue later in chapter seven. The important point here is that there are two main manuscript traditions of the Holy Bible. By "manuscript tradition" we mean a body of ancient texts which were copied and handed down to us from ancient times. The Christian manuscript Tradition comes from the ancient Jewish translation of the Hebrew Bible into Greek known as the "Septuagint." This, along with other Hebrew sources now lost, is the primary manuscript Tradition from which comes the Latin Vulgate and the Catholic Bible.

The other main manuscript tradition comes from Jews who rejected Jesus Christ. This is known as the Masoretic text, which is a collection of Hebrew manuscripts handed down by Jews. This is the primary source for the Protestant Bible.

The most conspicuous difference between the two traditions is that the Greek Septuagint contains the deutero-canonical books (Tobit, Maccabees, Judith, Ecclesiasticus, etc.) while the Hebrew Masoretic does not. We will discuss this further in the aforementioned chapter.

With the Psalms, the most conspicuous difference is that the Psalms are numbered differently. After the modern liturgical reforms, all of the Catholic texts began using the Masoretic numbering. Before this, they used the ancient numbering from the Septuagint. That is why the numbers of Psalms do not line up. For the most part, the Septuagint numbering is one less than the Masoretic. But they correspond this way:

Ancient Hebrew Numbering (Septuagint and Vulgate)	Masoretic Hebrew Numbering (Masoretic Text)
1-8	1-8
9	9-10
10-112	11-113
113	114-115
114-115	116
116-145	117-146
146-147	147
148-150	148-150

For the purpose of this book, we retain the traditional numbering given in the Septuagint and Vulgate.

Most significantly, these two traditions often reveal a great divergence in the Text, particularly at points which seem to obviously speak of our Lord Jesus. Two examples will suffice.

In Psalm XXI, the verse speaks of the crucifixion like this in verse seventeen:

Ancient Hebrew translation:
They have dug my hands and feet
(ωρυξαν χειράς μου και πόδας
Foderunt manus meas et pedes meos)

Masoretic Hebrew:
Like a lion my hands and my feet (22:16)
(Kî sĕḇāḇûnî kĕlāḇîm 'ăḏaṯ mĕrē'îm hiqqîpûnî kā'ărî yāḏay wĕraglāy).

Another example is Ps. c. 3 which has this phrase indicating the pre-existing Son who is incarnate:

Ancient Hebrew translation:
From the womb before the day star I begot thee
(ἐκ γαστρὸς πρὸ ἑωσφόρου ἐξεγέννησά σε
ex utero, ante luciferum, genui te)

Masoretic Hebrew:
From the womb of the morning: thou hast the dew of thy youth (110:3)
(mê·re·ḥem miš·ḥār; lə·ḵā, ṭal yal·ḏu·ṯe·ḵā)

Thus there is some speculation that Jews changed the words to hide the prophecies of Christ. From the Dead Sea Scrolls as we shall see, it is also apparent that there were multiple Hebrew manuscript traditions of which the Masoretic only forms one. It was the Greek Septuagint and Latin Vulgate that the Church accepted from the earliest days of the Church and meditated on these verses referring to Christ.

The Meaning of Each Psalm

Taking all of this into consideration, we now present the list of Psalms with their traditional meanings. We have provided Arabic numerals to aid in finding a Psalm. These senses are adapted from the commentaries on the Psalms from the Fathers (see chapter 17 for these). If you ever encounter a difficulty in the Psalter, read these commentaries to see how the saints saw Christ in these words. The rest of this chapter serves as a reference for the prayer book of the Church. The Latin titles are also given for each Psalm, as they were known by our fathers.

1. **Psalm i.** Beatus vir. *The happiness of the Church and the evil state of the wicked.*
2. **Psalm ii.** Quare fremuerunt. *The vain efforts of the persecutors against Christ and His Church.*
3. **Psalm iii.** Domine, quid multiplicati. *The passion and resurrection of Christ.*
4. **Psalm iv.** Cum invocarem. *Christ teaches us to flee to God in tribulation, with confidence in Him.*
5. **Psalm v.** Verba mea auribus. *Christ's prayer to God against the iniquities of men.*
6. **Psalm vi.** Domine, ne in furore. *Christ in His Body prays under the scourging of God*
7. **Psalm vii.** Domine, Deus meus. *Christ in His Body prays for God's help against His enemies.*
8. **Psalm viii.** Domine, Dominus Noster. *God is wonderful in His works; especially in mankind, singularly exalted by the incarnation of Christ.*
9. **Psalm ix.** Confitebor tibi, Domine. *The Church praises God for His protection against her enemies.*

10. **Psalm x.** In Domino confido. *The confidence of Christ in the Father in the midst of persecutions.*
11. **Psalm xi.** Salvum me fac. *Christ calls for God's help in the midst of persecutions.*
12. **Psalm xii.** Usquequo, Domine. *A prayer of the Church in tribulation.*
13. **Psalm xiii.** Dixit insipiens. *The general corruption of man before our redemption in Christ.*
14. **Psalm xiv.** Domine, quis habitabit. *What kind of men shall dwell in the heavenly sion.*
15. **Psalm xv.** Conserva me, Domine. *Christ's future victory and triumph over the world and death.*
16. **Psalm xvi.** Exaudi, Domine, justitiam. *Christ's prayer in tribulation against the malice of His enemies.*
17. **Psalm xvii.** Diligam te, Domine. *The triumph of the Christian Church over all enemies.*
18. **Psalm xviii.** Coeli enarrant. *The works of God show forth His glory: the spread of the Gospel.*
19. **Psalm xix.** Exaudiat te Dominus. *Supplication of the Christian for deliverance in Christ.*
20. **Psalm xx.** Domine, in virtute. *Praise to God for Christ's exaltation after His Passion.*
21. **Psalm xxi.** Deus Deus meus. *Christ's Passion, Resurrection, and the conversion of the Gentiles.*
22. **Psalm xxii.** Dominus regit me. *God's spiritual benefits for faithful souls.*
23. **Psalm xxiii.** Domini est terra. *Who are they that shall ascend to heaven: Christ's triumphant ascension thither.*
24. **Psalm xxiv.** Ad te, Domine, levavi. *Christ's prayer for His Church against her enemies.*
25. **Psalm xxv.** Judica me, Domine. *Christ's prayer during His passion for the triumph of his Church.*

26. **Psalm xxvi.** Dominus illuminatio. *Christ's prayer before His passion.*
27. **Psalm xxvii.** Ad te, Domine, clamabo. *Christ's prayer during His passion with confidence in his resurrection.*
28. **Psalm xxviii.** Afferte Domino. *Exhortation to worship God commemorating His mighty works.*
29. **Psalm xxix.** Exaltabo te, Domine. *Christ's thanksgiving in His resurrection.*
30. **Psalm xxx.** In te, Domine, speravi. *Christ's prayer in His passion.*
31. **Psalm xxxi.** Beati quorum. *The repentance of the Church and the words of comfort from Christ.*
32. **Psalm xxxii.** Exultate, justi. *Exhortation to praise God and trust in Him.*
33. **Psalm xxxiii.** Benedicam Dominum. *Exhortation to the praise and service of God.*
34. **Psalm xxxiv.** Judica, Domine, nocentes me. *Christ prays against His persecutors, prophesying their punishment.*
35. **Psalm xxxv.** Dixit injustus. *The malice of sinners and the goodness of God.*
36. **Psalm xxxvi.** Noli aemulari. *An exhortation to despise this world. The short prosperity of the wicked and the trust in God's providence.*
37. **Psalm xxxvii.** Domine, ne in furore. *Christ prays for the remission of sins for His Church.*
38. **Psalm xxxviii.** Dixi custodiam. *Christ in His passion before His death, intercedes for the sins His Church.*
39. **Psalm xxxix.** Expectans expectavi. *Christ's coming and redeeming mankind.*
40. **Psalm xl.** Beatus qui intelligit. *The happiness of him that shall believe in Christ; notwithstanding his humble*

poverty: the malice of Christ's enemies, especially the traitor Judas.

41. **Psalm xli.** Quemadmodum desiderat. *The prayer of the Church for union with Christ.*
42. **Psalm xlii.** Judica me, Deus. *The prayer of the Church for resurrection.*
43. **Psalm xliii.** Deus auribus nostris. *The Church commemorates former favors and present afflictions, under which she prays for deliverance.*
44. **Psalm xliv.** Eructavit cor meum. *The excellence of Christ's kingdom, the endowments of His Church and the glory of the Mother of God.*
45. **Psalm xlv.** Deus noster refugium. *The Church in persecution trusts in the protection of God.*
46. **Psalm xlvi.** Omnes gentes, plaudite. *The gentiles are invited to praise God for the establishment of the kingdom of Christ.*
47. **Psalm xlvii.** Magnus Dominus. *God is greatly to be praised for the establishment of His Church.*
48. **Psalm xlviii.** Audite, omnes gentes. *The fate of those who live on in sin without thought of death or hell.*
49. **Psalm xlix.** Deus deorum. *The coming of Christ who prefers virtue and inward purity above the blood of victims.*
50. **Psalm l.** Miserere. *David's repentance after his sin.*
51. **Psalm li.** Quid gloriaris. *Christ's prophesy of the future punishment of the wicked and exaltation of His Church.*
52. **Psalm lii.** Dixit inspiens. *The general corruption of man before the coming of Christ.*
53. **Psalm liii.** Deus in nomine tuo. *Prayer of Christ for help in distress.*

54. **Psalm liv.** Exaudi, Deus. *Christ persecuted by the Jews and betrayed by Judas.*
55. **Psalm lv.** Miserere mei, Deus. *Prayer of the Church under distress.*
56. **Psalm lvi.** Miserere mei, Deus. *Prayer in affliction and praise for deliverance.*
57. **Psalm lvii.** Si vere utique. *Christ reproves the wicked and foretells their destruction.*
58. **Psalm lviii.** Eripe me. *Christ persecuted by the Jews.*
59. **Psalm lix.** Deus, repulisti nos. *After many afflictions, the Church of Christ shall prevail.*
60. **Psalm lx.** Exaudi, Deus. *Prayer for the coming of the Kingdom of Christ which shall have no end.*
61. **Psalm lxi.** Nonne Deo. *Encouragement to trust in God and serve Him.*
62. **Psalm lxii.** Deus, Deus meus ad te. *The thirsting of the Church for Christ.*
63. **Psalm lxiii.** Exaudi Deus orationem. *Confidence of Christ that God will bring to naught the machinations of persecutors.*
64. **Psalm lxiv.** Te decet. *God is to be praised in His Church, to which all nations are called.*
65. **Psalm lxv.** Jubilate Deo. *A psalm of the resurrection of Christ.*
66. **Psalm lxvi.** Deus misereatur. *Prayer for the propagation of the Church.*
67. **Psalm lxvii.** Exurgat Deus. *The glorious establishment of the Church prefigured in Israel. The Ascension of Christ.*
68. **Psalm lxviii.** Salvum me fac, Deus. *Christ in His passion declares the greatness of His sufferings and the malice*

of His persecutors the Jews; He foretells their reprobation.
69. **Psalm lxix.** Deus in adjutorium. *Prayer of Christ in persecution.*
70. **Psalm lxx.** In te, Domine. *Prayer of the Church for perseverance.*
71. **Psalm lxxi.** Deus, judicium tuum. *The coming of Christ and His kingdom.*
72. **Psalm lxxii.** Quam bonus Israel Deus. *Christ lifts up the weak who are tempted to despair by the contemplation of His justice.*
73. **Psalm lxxiii.** Ut quid, Deus. *The prayer of the Church under grievous persecution.*
74. **Psalm lxxiv.** Confitebimur tibi. *The just judgment seat of Christ.*
75. **Psalm lxxv.** Notus in Judaea. *God is known in His Church and exerts His power in protecting her.*
76. **Psalm lxxvi.** Voce mea. *Prayer of the Church in affliction.*
77. **Psalm lxxvii.** Attendite. *Christ recalls the mercies of God to Israel, notwithstanding their ingratitude.*
78. **Psalm lxxviii.** Deus, venerunt gentes. *The Church in time of persecution prays for relief.*
79. **Psalm lxxix.** Qui regis Israel. *A prayer for the Church in tribulation, commemorating God's former favors.*
80. **Psalm lxxx.** Exultate Deo. *Exhortation to the praise of God.*
81. **Psalm lxxxi.** Deus stetit. *The words of Christ the King to the Pharisees and other leaders.*
82. **Psalm lxxxii.** Deus, quis similis. *Prayer against the enemies of Holy Church.*

83. **Psalm lxxxiii.** Quam dilecta. *Longing for eternal life; rejoicing in Holy Communion.*
84. **Psalm lxxxiv.** Benedixisti, Domine. *The coming of Christ, to bring peace and salvation to man.*
85. **Psalm lxxxv.** Inclina, Domine. *Prayer of Christ at His passion.*
86. **Psalm lxxxvi.** Fundamenta eius. *The glory of the Church of Christ.*
87. **Psalm lxxxvii.** Domine, Deus salutis. *Christ's passion, death, and burial.*
88. **Psalm lxxxviii.** Misericordias Domini. *The perpetuity of the Church of Christ, notwithstanding her most grievous afflictions.*
89. **Psalm lxxxix.** Domine, refugium. *A prayer for the mercy of God considering the shortness of life.*
90. **Psalm xc.** Qui habitat. *The just man is secure under the protection of God.*
91. **Psalm xci.** Bonum est confiteri. *God is praised for His wondrous works.*
92. **Psalm xcii.** Dominus regnavit. *The glory and stability of the Kingdom of God in Christ.*
93. **Psalm xciii.** Deus ultionum. *God shall judge and punish the oppressors of His Church.*
94. **Psalm xciv.** Venite exultemus. *Exhortation to praise God and hear His voice.*
95. **Psalm xcv.** Cantate Domino. *Exhortation to praise God for the coming of Christ.*
96. **Psalm xcvi.** Dominus regnavit. *Exhortation to rejoice at the coming of Christ.*
97. **Psalm xcvii.** Cantate Domino. *Praises for the victories of Christ.*
98. **Psalm xcviii.** Dominus Regnavit. *The reign of Christ.*

99. **Psalm xcix.** Jubilate Deo. *The Church rejoices in the mercies of God.*
100. **Psalm c.** Misericordiam et judicium. *The perfection and judgment of Christ.*
101. **Psalm ci.** Domine, exaudi. *Prayer in affliction.*
102. **Psalm cii.** Benedic, anima. *Thanksgiving to God for His mercies.*
103. **Psalm ciii.** Benedic, anima. *God is to be praised for His mighty works and wonderful providence.*
104. **Psalm civ.** Confitemini Domino. *Thanksgiving to God for His benefits to the Church.*
105. **Psalm cv.** Confitemini Domino. *A confession of the manifold sins and ingratitude of Israel.*
106. **Psalm cvi.** Confitemini Domino. *Thanksgiving to God for His mercies.*
107. **Psalm cvii.** Paratum cor meum. *Praise to God for benefits received.*
108. **Psalm cviii.** Deus, laudem meum. *Christ against His persecutors, foretelling the just punishment for the traitor Judas.*
109. **Psalm cix.** Dixit Dominus. *Christ's exaltation and everlasting priesthood.*
110. **Psalm cx.** Confitebor tibi, Domine. *God is praise for His graces to His Church.*
111. **Psalm cxi.** Beatus vir. *The happiness of the just man.*
112. **Psalm cxii.** Laudate, pueri. *God is praised for His regard for the poor and humble.*
113. **Psalm cxiii.** In exitu Israel. *God has shown His power in delivering Israel. The vanity of idols.*
114. **Psalm cxiv.** Dilexi. *Prayer of Christ in affliction with confidence in God.*

115. **Psalm cxv.** Credidi. *Christ praises the Father and confesses He is the son of Mary.*
116. **Psalm cxvi.** Laudate Dominum. *All nations praise the Lord.*
117. **Psalm cxvii.** Confitemini Domino. *Praise to God for His mercies and the coming of Christ.*
118. **Psalm cxviii.** Beati immaculati. *The perfection of Christ.*
119. **Psalm cxix.** Ad Dominum. *Prayer of Christ in tribulation.*
120. **Psalm cxx.** Levavi oculos. *The voice of Christ speaks to comfort His Church.*
121. **Psalm cxxi.** Laetatus sum in his. *The desire of the Church for union with Christ in eternal life.*
122. **Psalm cxxii.** Ad te levavi. *Prayer in affliction with confidence in God.*
123. **Psalm cxxiii.** Nisi quia Dominus. *The Church gives glory to God for deliverance from enemies.*
124. **Psalm cxxiv.** Qui confidunt. *The just are always under the protection of God.*
125. **Psalm cxxv.** In convertendo. *The Church rejoices at her deliverance from Christ.*
126. **Psalm cxxvi.** Nisi Dominus. *The absolute necessity of the grace of God.*
127. **Psalm cxxvii.** Beati omnes. *The fear of God is the way of beatitude.*
128. **Psalm cxxviii.** Saepe expugnaverunt. *The Church of God is invincible; all her enemies come to nothing.*
129. **Psalm cxxix.** De profundis. *The sinner trusting in the mercy of God.*
130. **Psalm cxxx.** Domine, none est. *The humility of Christ.*
131. **Psalm cxxxi.** Memento, Domine. *Prayer for the coming of Christ.*

132. **Psalm cxxxii.** Ecce quam bonum. *The happiness of fraternal charity in the Church.*
133. **Psalm cxxxiii.** Ecce nunc benedicite. *Exhortation to praise God continually.*
134. **Psalm cxxxiv.** Laudate nomen. *Exhortation to praise God. The vanity of idols.*
135. **Psalm cxxxv.** Confitemini Domino. *God is praised for His wonderful works.*
136. **Psalm cxxxvi.** Super flumina. *Lamentation in this valley of tears; the need to immediately banish evil thoughts against the rock of Christ.*
137. **Psalm cxxxvii.** Confitebor tibi. *Thanksgiving to God for His deliverance in tribulation.*
138. **Psalm cxxxviii.** Domine, probasti. *The providence of God governing the Church to eternal life.*
139. **Psalm cxxxix.** Eripe me, Domine. *Prayer for deliverance from the old man.*
140. **Psalm cxl.** Domine, clamavi. *Prayer of the just man against the malice of the old man.*
141. **Psalm cxli.** Voce mea. *Prayer in the extremity of danger.*
142. **Psalm cxlii.** Domine, exaudi. *Prayer of Christ in His passion.*
143. **Psalm cxliii.** Benedictus Dominus. *David against Goliath. Christ against the world, the flesh, and the devil.*
144. **Psalm cxliv.** Exaltabo te, Deus. *Praise to the infinite majesty of God.*
145. **Psalm cxlv.** Lauda, anima. *We are not to trust in man, but God alone.*
146. **Psalm cxlvi.** Laudate Dominum. *Praise God for His benefits.*

147. **Psalm cxlvii.** Lauda, Jerusalem. *The Church praises God for His graces to His people.*
148. **Psalm cxlviii.** Laudate Dominum de caelis. *Let all things praise the Lord.*
149. **Psalm cxlix.** Cantate Domino. *The Church is bound to praise the Lord and will triumph over her enemies.*
150. **Psalm cl.** Laudate Dominum in sanctis. *Let all things praise the Lord.*

Adoration – Worship God for Who He Is

8. **Psalm viii.** Domine, Dominus Noster. *God is wonderful in his works; especially in mankind, singularly exalted by the incarnation of Christ.*
28. **Psalm xxviii.** Afferte Domino. *Exhortation to worship God commemorating his mighty works.*
32. **Psalm xxxii.** Exultate, justi. *Exhortation to praise God and trust in him.*
33. **Psalm xxxiii.** Benedicam Dominum. *Exhortation to the praise and service of God.*
44. **Psalm xliv.** Eructavit cor meum. *The excellence of Christ's kingdom, the endowments of his Church and the glory of the Mother of God.*
46. **Psalm xlvi.** Omnes gentes, plaudite. *The gentiles are invited to praise God for the establishment of the kingdom of Christ.*
47. **Psalm xlvii.** Magnus Dominus. *God is greatly to be praised for the establishment of his Church.*
65. **Psalm lxv.** Jubilate Deo. *A psalm of the resurrection of Christ.*
75. **Psalm lxxv.** Notus in Judaea. *God is known in His Church and exerts His power in protecting her.*

92. **Psalm xcii.** Dominus regnavit. *The glory and stability of the Kingdom of God in Christ.*
94. **Psalm xciv.** Venite exultemus. *Exhortation to praise God and hear His voice.*
109. **Psalm cix.** Dixit Dominus. *Christ's exaltation and everlasting priesthood.*
133. **Psalm cxxxiii.** Ecce nunc benedicite. *Exhortation to praise God continually.*
134. **Psalm cxxxiv.** Laudate nomen. *Exhortation to praise God. The vanity of idols.*
144. **Psalm cxliv.** Exaltabo te, Deus. *Praise to the infinite majesty of God.*
148. **Psalm cxlviii.** Laudate Dominum de caelis. *Let all things praise to the Lord.*
150. **Psalm cl.** Laudate Dominum in sanctis. *Let all things praise the Lord.*

Confession and Penance

6. **Psalm vi.** Domine, me in furore. *Christ in His Body prays under the scourging of God.*
24. **Psalm xxiv.** Ad te, Domine, levavi. *Christ's prayer for his Church against her enemies.*
31. **Psalm xxxi.** Beati quorum. *The repentance of the Church and the words of comfort from Christ.*
37. **Psalm xxxvii.** Domine, ne in furore. *Christ prays for the remission of sins for His Church.*
38. **Psalm xxxviii.** Dixi custodiam. *Christ in his passion before his death, intercedes for the sins his Church.*
50. **Psalm l.** Miserere. *David's repentance after his sin.*
101. **Psalm ci.** Domine, exaudi. *Prayer in affliction.*
129. **Psalm cxxix.** De profundis. *The sinner trusting in the mercy of God.*

139. **Psalm cxxxix.** Eripe me, Domine. *Prayer for deliverance from the old man.*
140. **Psalm cxl.** Domine, clamavi. *Prayer of the just man against the malice of the old man.*
142. **Psalm cxlii.** Domine, exaudi. *Prayer of Christ in His Passion.*

Thanksgiving to God for His benefits

9. **Psalm ix.** Confitebor tibi, Domine. *The Church praises God for his protection against her enemies.*
17. **Psalm xvii.** Diligam te, Domine. *The triumph of the Christian Church over all enemies.*
18. **Psalm xviii.** Coeli enarrant. *The works of God show forth his glory: the spread of the Gospel*
20. **Psalm xx.** Domine, in virtute. *Praise to God for Christ's exaltation after his Passion.*
22. **Psalm xxii.** Dominus regit me. *God's spiritual benefits for faithful souls.*
29. **Psalm xxix.** Exaltabo te, Domine. *Christ's thanksgiving in his resurrection.*
62. **Psalm lxii.** Deus, Deus meus ad te. *The thirsting of the Church for Christ.*
65. **Psalm lxv.** Jubilate Deo. *A psalm of the resurrection of Christ.*
67. **Psalm lxvii.** Exurgat Deus. *The glorious establishment of the Church prefigured in Israel. The Ascension of Christ.*
75. **Psalm lxxv.** Notus in Judaea. *God is known in His Church and exerts His power in protecting her.*
80. **Psalm lxxx.** Exultate Deo. *Exhortation to the praise of God.*

83. **Psalm lxxxiii.** Quam dilecta. *Longing for eternal life; rejoicing in Holy Communion.*
86. **Psalm lxxxvi.** Fundamenta eius. *The glory of the Church of Christ.*
91. **Psalm xci.** Bonum est confiteri. *God is praised for His wondrous works.*
95. **Psalm xcv.** Cantate Domino. *Exhortation to praise God for the coming of Christ.*
96. **Psalm xcvi.** Dominus regnavit. *Exhortation to rejoice at the coming of Christ.*
97. **Psalm xcvii.** Cantate Domino. *Praises for the victories of Christ.*
98. **Psalm xcviii.** Dominus Regnavit. *The reign of Christ.*
99. **Psalm xcix.** Jubilate Deo. *The Church rejoices in the mercies of God.*
102. **Psalm cii.** Bendic, anima. *Thanksgiving to God for His mercies.*
103. **Psalm ciii.** Benedic, anima. *God is to be praised for His mighty works and wonderful providence.*
104. **Psalm civ.** Confitemini Domino. *Thanksgiving to God for His benefits to the Church.*
106. **Psalm cvi.** Confitemini Domino. *Thanksgiving to God for His mercies.*
107. **Psalm cvii.** Paratum cor meum. *Praise to God for benefits received.*
110. **Psalm cx.** Confitebor tibi, Domine. *God is praise for His graces to His Church.*
112. **Psalm cxii.** Laudate, pueri. *God is praised for His regard to the poor and humble.*
115. **Psalm cxv.** Credidi. *Christ praises the Father and confesses He is the son of Mary.*

116. **Psalm cxvi.** Laudate Dominum. *All nations praise the Lord.*
117. **Psalm cxvii.** Confitemini Domino. *Praise to God for His mercies and the coming of Christ.*
123. **Psalm cxxiii.** Nisi quia Dominus. *The Church gives glory to God for deliverance from enemies.*
125. **Psalm cxxv.** In convertendo. *The Church rejoices at her deliverance from Christ.*
135. **Psalm cxxxv.** Confitemini Domino. *God is praised for His wonderful works.*
137. **Psalm cxxxvii.** Confitebor tibi. *Thanksgiving to God for His deliverance in tribulation.*
145. **Psalm cxlv.** Lauda, anima. *We are not to trust in man, but God alone.*
146. **Psalm cxlvi.** Laudate Dominum. *Praise God for His benefits.*
147. **Psalm cxlvii.** Lauda, Jerusalem. *The Church praises God for His graces to His people.*

Supplication in Affliction

3. **Psalm iii.** Domine, quid multiplicati. *The passion and resurrection of Christ.*
5. **Psalm v.** Verba mea auribus. *Christ's prayer to God against the iniquities of men.*
7. **Psalm vii.** Domine, Deus meus. *David, trusting in the justice of his cause, prays for God's help against his enemies.*
11. **Psalm xi.** Salvum me fac. *Christ calls for God's help in the midst of persecutions.*
12. **Psalm xii.** Usquequo, Domine. *A prayer of the Church in tribulation.*

19. **Psalm xix.** Exaudiat te Dominus. *Supplication for the Christian for deliverance in Christ.*
21. **Psalm xxi.** Deus Deus meus. *Christ's Passion, Resurrection, and the conversion of the Gentiles.*
24. **Psalm xxiv.** Ad te, Domine, levavi. *Christ's prayer for his Church against her enemies.*
25. **Psalm xxv.** Judica me, Domine. *Christ's prayer during his passion for the triumph of his Church.*
26. **Psalm xxvi.** Dominus illuminatio. *Christ's prayer before his passion.*
27. **Psalm xxvii.** Ad te, Domine, clamabo. *Christ's prayer during his passion with confidence in his resurrection.*
30. **Psalm xxx.** In te, Domine, speravi. *Christ's prayer in his passion.*
34. **Psalm xxxiv.** Judica, Domine, nocentes me. *Christ prays against his persecutors, prophesying their punishment.*
43. **Psalm xliii.** Deus auribus nostris. *The Church commemorates former favors and present afflictions, under which she prays for deliverance.*
45. **Psalm xlv.** Deus noster refugium. *The Church in persecution trusts in the protection of God.*
53. **Psalm liii.** Deus in nomine tuo. *Prayer of Christ for help in distress.*
54. **Psalm liv.** Exaudi, Deus. *Christ persecuted by the Jews and betrayed by Judas.*
55. **Psalm lv.** Miserere mei, Deus. *Prayer of the Church under distress.*
56. **Psalm lvi.** Miserere mei, Deus. *Prayer in affliction and praise for deliverance.*
58. **Psalm lviii.** Eripe me. *Christ persecuted by the Jews.*
59. **Psalm lix.** Deus, repulisti nos. *After many afflictions, the Church of Christ shall prevail.*

63. **Psalm lxiii.** Exaudi Deus orationem. *Confidence of Christ that God will bring to naught the machinations of persecutors.*
66. **Psalm lxvi.** Deus misereatur. *Prayer for the propagation of the Church.*
68. **Psalm lxviii.** Salvum me fac, Deus. *Christ in His passion declares the greatness of his sufferings and the malice of his persecutors the Jews; He foretells their reprobation.*
69. **Psalm lxix.** Deus in adjutorium. *Prayer of Christ in persecution.*
70. **Psalm lxx.** In te, Domine. *Prayer of the Church for perseverance.*
73. **Psalm lxxiii.** Ut quid, Deus. *The prayer of the Church under grievous persecution.*
76. **Psalm lxxvi.** Voce mea. *Prayer of the Church in affliction.*
78. **Psalm lxxviii.** Deus, venerunt gentes. *The Church in time of persecution prays for relief.*
79. **Psalm lxxix.** Qui regis Israel. *A prayer for the Church in tribulation, commemorating God's former favors.*
82. **Psalm lxxxii.** Deus, quis similis. *Prayer against the enemies of Holy Church.*
85. **Psalm lxxxv.** Inclina, Domine. *Prayer of Christ at His Passion.*
87. **Psalm lxxxvii.** Domine, Deus salutis. *Christ's Passion, Death, and Burial.*
88. **Psalm lxxxviii.** Misericordias Domini. *The perpetuity of the Church of Christ, notwithstanding her most grievous afflictions.*
93. **Psalm xciii.** Deus ultionum. *God shall judge and punish the oppressors of His Church.*

108. Psalm cviii. Deus, laudem meum. *Christ against His persecutors, foretelling the just punishment for the traitor Judas.*
118. Psalm cxviii. Beati immaculati. *The perfection of Christ.*
119. Psalm cxix. Ad Dominum. *Prayer of Christ in tribulation.*
122. Psalm cxxii. Ad te levavi. *Prayer in affliction with confidence in God.*
136. Psalm cxxxvi. Super flumina. *Lamentation this valley of tears; the need to immediately banish evil thoughts against the rock of Christ.*
137. Psalm cxxxvii. Confitebor tibi. *Thanksgiving to God for His deliverance in tribulation.*
139. Psalm cxxxix. Eripe me, Domine. *Prayer for deliverance from the old man.*
140. Psalm cxl. Domine, clamavi. *Prayer of the just man against the malice of the old man.*
141. Psalm cxli. Voce mea. *Prayer in the extremity of danger.*
142. Psalm cxlii. Domine, exaudi. *Prayer of Christ in His Passion.*
143. Psalm cxliii. Benedictus Dominus. *David against Goliath. Christ against the world, the flesh, and the devil.*

Wisdom and Confidence in God

1. Psalm i. Beatus vir. *The happiness of the Christ and the Church and the evil state of the wicked.*
2. Psalm ii. Quare fremuerunt. *The vain efforts of the persecutors against Christ and his Church.*
4. Psalm iv. Cum invocarem. *Christ teaches us to flee to God in tribulation, with confidence in him.*

10. **Psalm x.** In Domino confido. *The confidence of Christ in the Father in the midst of persecutions.*
13. **Psalm xiii.** Dixit insipiens. *The general corruption of man before our redemption in Christ.*
14. **Psalm xiv.** Domine, quis habitabit. *What kind of men shall dwell in the heavenly sion.*
15. **Psalm xv.** Conserva me, Domine. *Christ's future victory and triumph over the world and death.*
23. **Psalm xxiii.** Domini est terra. *Who are they that shall ascend to heaven: Christ's triumphant ascension thither.*
26. **Psalm xxvi.** Dominus illuminatio. *Christ's prayer before his passion.*
27. **Psalm xxvii.** Ad te, Domine, clamabo. *Christ's prayer during his passion with confidence in his resurrection.*
30. **Psalm xxx.** In te, Domine, speravi. *Christ's prayer in his passion.*
35. **Psalm xxxv.** Dixit injustus. *The malice of sinners and the goodness of God.*
36. **Psalm xxxvi.** Noli aemulari. *An exhortation to despise this world. The short prosperity of the wicked and the trust in God's providence.*
39. **Psalm xxxix.** Expectans expectavi. *Christ's coming and redeeming mankind.*
40. **Psalm xl.** Beatus qui intelligit. *The happiness of him that shall believe in Christ; notwithstanding his humble poverty: the malice of his enemies, especially the traitor Judas.*
41. **Psalm xli.** Quemadmodum desiderat. *The prayer of the Church for union with Christ.*
42. **Psalm xlii.** Judica me, Deus. *The prayer of the Church for resurrection.*

45. **Psalm xlv.** Deus noster refugium. *The Church in persecution trusts in the protection of God.*
48. **Psalm xlviii.** Audite, omnes gentes. *The follow of those who live on in sin without thought of death or hell.*
49. **Psalm xlix.** Deus deorum. *The coming of Christ who prefers virtue and inward purity above the blood of victims.*
51. **Psalm li.** Quid gloriaris. *Christ's prophesy of the future punishment of the wicked and exaltation of His Church.*
52. **Psalm lii.** Dixit inspiens. *The general corruption of man before the coming of Christ.*
57. **Psalm lvii.** Si vere utique. *Christ reproves the wicked and foretells their destruction.*
60. **Psalm lx.** Exaudi, Deus. *Prayer for the coming of the Kingdom of Christ which shall have no end.*
61. **Psalm lxi.** Nonne Deo. *Encouragement to trust in God and serve him.*
63. **Psalm lxiii.** Exaudi Deus orationem. *Confidence of Christ that God will bring to naught the machinations of persecutors.*
64. **Psalm lxiv.** Te decet. *God is to be praised in His Church, to which all nations are called.*
71. **Psalm lxxi.** Deus, judicium tuum. *The coming of Christ and His kingdom.*
72. **Psalm lxxii.** Quam bonus Israel Deus. *Christ lifts up the weak who are tempted to despair by the contemplation of His justice.*
74. **Psalm lxxiv.** Confitebimur tibi. *The just judgment seat of Christ.*
77. **Psalm lxxvii.** Attendite. *Christ recalls the mercies of God to Israel, notwithstanding their ingratitude.*

81. **Psalm lxxxi.** Deus stetit. *The words of Christ the King to the Pharisees and other leaders.*
84. **Psalm lxxxiv.** Benedixisti, Domine. *The coming of Christ, to bring peace and salvation to man.*
88. **Psalm lxxxviii.** Misericordias Domini. *The perpetuity of the Church of Christ, notwithstanding her most grievous afflictions.*
89. **Psalm lxxxix.** Domine, refugium. *A prayer for the mercy of God considering the shortness of life.*
90. **Psalm xc.** Qui habitat. *The just man is secure under the protection of God.*
100. **Psalm c.** Misericordiam et judicium. *The perfection and judgment of Christ.*
105. **Psalm cv.** Confitemini Domino. *A confession of the manifold sins and ingratitude of Israel.*
111. **Psalm cxi.** Beatus vir. *The happiness of the just man.*
113. **Psalm cxiii.** In exitu Israel. *God has shown His power in delivering Israel. The vanity of idols.*
114. **Psalm cxiv.** Dilexi. *Prayer of Christ in affliction with confidence in God.*
115. **Psalm cxv.** Credidi. *Christ praises the Father and confesses He is the son of Mary.*
118. **Psalm cxviii.** Beati immaculati. *The perfection of Christ.*
120. **Psalm cxx.** Levavi oculos. *The voice of Christ speaks to comfort His Church.*
121. **Psalm cxxi.** Laetatus sum in his. *The desire of the Church for union with Christ in eternal life.*
122. **Psalm cxxii.** Ad te levavi. *Prayer in affliction with confidence in God.*
124. **Psalm cxxiv.** Qui confidunt. *The just are always under the protection of God.*

126. Psalm cxxvi. Nisi Dominus. *The absolute necessity of the grace of God.*

127. Psalm cxxvii. Beati omnes. *The fear of God is the way of beatitude.*

128. Psalm cxxviii. Saepe expugnaverunt. *The Church of God is invincible; all her enemies come to nothing.*

130. Psalm cxxx. Domine, none est. *The humility of Christ.*

131. Psalm cxxxi. Memento, Domine. *Prayer for the coming of Christ.*

132. Psalm cxxxii. Ecce quam bonum. *The happiness of fraternal charity in the Church.*

134. Psalm cxxxiv. Laudate nomen. *Exhortation to praise God. The vanity of idols.*

138. Psalm cxxxviii. Domine, probasti. *The providence of God governing the Church to eternal life.*

143. Psalm cxliii. Benedictus Dominus. *David against Goliath. Christ against the world, the flesh, and the devil.*

III

BEWARE: FIRE FROM HEAVEN BURNS UP THE PROUD

As we said in the introduction, the Holy Scriptures are divine fire. They cannot be handled without great care. This great care which we must bring to the Text is humility, prayer and piety. We will discuss how to read with humility in the next chapter. Here we will discuss the dangers that exist if the Holy Bible is not treated with humility.

Pride

Heretics have arisen over the centuries who have deceived many. According to intellect alone, these heretics were experts in the Holy Text. They may have memorized the whole Scripture and studied it for years. But as the *Imitation* says, what good is all this knowledge without humility?

Instead of a way to grow in holiness, reading the Scriptures with pride becomes a great snare. This snare has caught many souls and brought them to heresy, leading to eternal peril. Therefore we must be ever mindful to approach the Sacred Text with the proper disposition. The divine knowledge contained in Holy Writ has the power to lift us to heaven. But if we allow our pride to guide us, we will be brought down to hell. Let not this snare overtake you, brother, but beseech the Lord to save you from pride and grant you true humility.

Holiness Required to Understand the Scriptures

As we discussed previously, it was not until the Lord opened the minds of the Apostles that they were able to understand the Scriptures. Therefore it is simply hubris for us to approach the Sacred Scriptures thinking that we can easily understand them. The saints shed tears on their knees with the Holy Scriptures, seeking their meaning. We would expose ourselves to spiritual ruin if we do not first seek God's divine grace to aid us in this pursuit. It is for this reason that we should never dare to interpret the Holy Bible according to our own opinion, but seek the wisdom of the Fathers.

The Vice of Curiosity

One of the snares that especially affects young, single men is the vice of curiosity. St. Thomas defines curiosity as a vice wherein a man seeks intellectual knowledge more and more for its own sake, and he neglects of the duties of his state in life (II-II q167 a1). A curious man becomes attached to the pleasure he gets out of knowing more facts and knowledge, and may also take pride in himself, thinking himself better than others because of his knowledge. He may take pleasure in the praises of men for his knowledge. This is especially exacerbated on the internet where young men can display their knowledge easily without immediate consequence.

This curiosity can then lead to self-righteousness based on their knowledge. We may call it a "spirituality of being correct." It is an attachment to the pleasure of having the truth and thinking one's self better because one has the truth. One may have the truth, but this is not because one has merited it. This is a grace from Almighty God, in spite of our sins. Do not offend the divine majesty by using the true faith as a pretense for this sin of pride.

Instead, hearken to the words of the Holy Ghost:

> Great is the power of God alone, and he is honoured by the humble. Seek not the things that are too high for thee, and search not into things above thy ability: but the things that God hath commanded thee, think on them always, and in many of his works be not curious. For it is not necessary for thee to see with thy eyes those things that are hid. In unnecessary matters be not over curious, and in many of his works thou shalt not be inquisitive. For many things are shewn to thee above the understanding of men. And the suspicion of them hath deceived many, and hath detained their minds in vanity (Ecclus. iii. 21-26).

Thus we must tremble with fear when we approach the Holy Scriptures. We must give glory to God for whatever knowledge we receive from the Sacred Text, and be careful not to take pride in ourselves for this, but give credit only to God's work in us.

This rule must govern not only our reading of Scripture but also all our knowledge of the faith whether it be history, doctrine, or spirituality. Against this the Imitation again declares: *it is not learning that makes a man holy and just, but a virtuous life makes him pleasing to God.* Remember and practice this holy adage: *whatever is good within me is God's work. Whatever is evil within me is my work.*[28]

Heresy

Heresy is defined in the current code of canon law 751:

> Heresy is the obstinate denial or obstinate doubt after the reception of baptism of some truth which is to be believed by divine and Catholic faith.

Heresy has two parts, a grave error in the intellect and obstinacy in the will. Heretics are automatically excommunicated and risk their eternal salvation. This is because heresy obstinately denies a truth which is necessary for salvation.

Notice the word "obstinate." This is the key to heresy. Men can be forgiven for making an honest error or misunderstanding something. This error may be a heresy in the intellect (on the material level), but the man does not become a true heretic unless he obstinately persists in it. If his lawful superiors correct him and he refuses to amend, he becomes an obstinate heretic.

By this rule, we can say that in the beginning, Martin Luther was simply an erring theologian. Then a papal bull condemned his errors and gave him a certain number of days to recant. He refused and publicly burned the bull in defiance. At that point, and not before, Martin Luther became a heretic. He was obstinately persisting in denying some truth about the faith.

---

[28] Rule of St. Bendict, Ch. 4

To avoid the great peril of heresy, we must not become anxious and scrupulous about making an intellectual error. We should strive for precision in truth, but not be vexed in spirit with worry. Instead, follow the wise. As the Holy Ghost declares, *he that walketh with the wise, shall be wise: a friend of fools shall become like to them* (Prov. xiii. 20) and again *The way of life, to him that observeth correction: but he that forsaketh reproofs goeth astray* (Prov. x. 17).

Heed these warnings and counsels from the Holy Ghost, brother, and flee the pride of the heretics who impiously read the Text by themselves without the wisdom of the elders. In their hubris they declare themselves to know the Scriptures because of the greatness of their intellect. But because they do not know God, they do not know the Scriptures. Flee from these fools and adhere to Jesus Christ and His Church. To do this, make use of approved authorities and resources, as we will treat in the next chapter.

Above all, we must strive more and more to be humble. A humble man may make an error in his intellect, but *a humble man cannot be obstinate*. Therefore it is humility that is the *unfailing guard against heresy*. Consider these rules against intellectual pride from Fr. Chad Ripperger:

> Always:
> -Be willing to be corrected by anyone
> -Adhere to the truth no matter what the personal cost
> -Be content to be silent in a conversation - be willing to "look stupid"

-Be interested in what other people say as a source of possible truth[29]

In the next chapter we will discuss how to avoid all these dangers and read the Holy Scriptures with humility.

---

[29] Fr. Chad Ripperger, "Intellectual Pride," Dec 2018 < http://sensustraditionis.org/release/spiritual-growth/>. Accessed November 23, 2019.

IV

HOW TO READ WITH HUMILITY

We have discussed so far the reasons why a Catholic may read the Holy Bible, the Psalter, and the dangers. Before going any further to talk about reading the Text let us beseech the Lord our God to grant us the grace to read with humility. Pray the following prayer before you read any further. Get on your knees and look upon a crucifix. Pray this for the intention of humility when reading the Holy Scriptures.

> Have mercy on me, O God, according to thy great mercy. And according to the multitude of thy tender mercies blot out my iniquity. Wash me yet more from my iniquity, and cleanse me from my sin. For I know my iniquity, and my sin is always before me. To thee only have I sinned, and have done evil before thee: that thou mayst be justified in thy words and mayst overcome when thou art judged.
>
> For behold I was conceived in iniquities; and in sins did my mother conceive me. *For behold thou hast loved truth: the uncertain and hidden things of thy wisdom thou hast made manifest to me.* Thou shalt sprinkle me with hyssop, and I shall be cleansed:

thou shalt wash me, and I shall be made whiter than snow. To my hearing thou shalt give joy and gladness: and the bones that have been humbled shall rejoice. Turn away thy face from my sins, and blot out all my iniquities.

Create a clean heart in me, O God: and renew a right spirit within my bowels. Cast me not away from thy face; and take not thy holy spirit from me. Restore unto me the joy of thy salvation, and strengthen me with a perfect spirit. I will teach the unjust thy ways: and the wicked shall be converted to thee. Deliver me from blood, O God, thou God of my salvation: and my tongue shall extol thy justice. O Lord, thou wilt open my lips: and my mouth shall declare thy praise.

For if thou hadst desired sacrifice, I would indeed have given it: with burnt offerings thou wilt not be delighted. A sacrifice to God is an afflicted spirit: a contrite and humbled heart, O God, thou wilt not despise. Deal favourably, O Lord, in thy good will with Sion; that the walls of Jerusalem may be built up. Then shalt thou accept the sacrifice of justice, oblations and whole burnt offerings: then shall they lay calves upon thy altar.
Glory to the Father and to the Son and to the Holy Ghost. As it was in the beginning, is now and ever shall be, world without end, amen.

If the Holy Psalter is the foundational prayer book of the Church, this Psalm, the *Miserere* (Psalm L), is the foundational psalm of the Psalter. In the Traditional Benedictine office it is prayed every morning. In the Greek rite it is prayed more than once a day. These are the words that should define your reading of Holy Scriptures. These words are the intentions with which you must take up Holy Writ. We must get down on our knees and read the Holy Scripture with humility. This is the way of the saints. Only within such a multitude of humble petitions can we find the phrase the *hidden things of thy wisdom thou hast made manifest to me*. In the same way, humility is the key to the Scriptures.

One of the most famous examples of reading with humility is St. Augustine. Below is a passage from St. Augustine's *Confessions*. In the story of his life he had struggled for years with sins against the flesh and the errors of false philosophy. He had pursued ambitions of rhetoric and philosophy, but still struggled deeply with his sins and the search for truth. At a moment of spiritual awakening he reads the aforementioned life of St. Anthony, the illiterate theologian of the desert. When he reads this story, he becomes deeply convicted of his sins of the flesh and is moved to contrition.

> In the midst, then, of this great strife of my inner dwelling, which I had strongly raised up against my soul in the chamber of my heart, troubled both in mind and countenance, I seized upon Alypius, and exclaimed: "What is wrong with us? What is this? What did you hear? The unlearned start up and 'take' heaven (Mt. xi. 12) and we, with our learning, but wanting heart, see where we wallow in flesh and blood! Because others have preceded us, are we ashamed to follow, and not rather ashamed at not following?"
>
> ...I flung myself down, how, I know not, under a certain fig-tree, giving free course to my tears, and the streams of my eyes gushed out, an

acceptable sacrifice unto Thee. And, not indeed in these words, yet to this effect, spoke I much unto Thee—*But Thou, O Lord, how long? How long, Lord? Wilt Thou be angry for ever? Oh, remember not against us former iniquities*; for I felt that I was enthralled by them. I sent up these sorrowful cries —*How long, how long? Tomorrow, and tomorrow? Why not now? Why is there not this hour an end to my uncleanness?*

I was saying these things and weeping in the most bitter contrition of my heart, when, lo, I heard the voice as of a boy or girl, I know not which, coming from a neighbouring house, chanting, and oft repeating, *Take up and read; take up and read.* Immediately my countenance was changed, and I began most earnestly to consider whether it was usual for children in any kind of game to sing such words; nor could I remember ever to have heard the like. So, restraining the torrent of my tears, I rose up, interpreting it no other way than as a command to me from Heaven to open the book, and to read the first chapter I should light upon. For I had heard of Anthony, that, accidentally coming in while the gospel was being read, he received the admonition as if what was read were addressed to him, *Go and sell that you have, and give to the poor, and you shall have treasure in heaven; and come and follow me.* And by such oracle was he immediately converted unto Thee.

So quickly I returned to the place where Alypius was sitting; for there had I put down the volume of the apostles, when I rose thence. I grasped, opened, and in silence read that paragraph on which my eyes first fell —*Not in rioting and drunkenness, not in chambering and wantonness, not in strife and envying; but put on the Lord Jesus Christ, and make not provision for the flesh, to fulfil the lusts thereof* (Rom. xiii. 13). No further would I read, nor did I need; for instantly, as the sentence ended — by a light, as it were, of security infused into my heart — all the gloom of doubt vanished away.[30]

Here the greatest Father of the Church, St. Augustine of Hippo, is converted from a life of error and sin to Jesus Christ by reading the Holy Scriptures with humility. Learning from St. Anthony that truth does not come from great learning but by humility, he receives the gift of faith from God, and becomes the greatest philosopher and theologian of the universal Church. It is this humility that must guide your reading of the Text. It is this humility that will make the Text powerful to you and profitable for your spiritual life.

The Way of Humility

As we mentioned in the last chapter, humility is the unfailing safeguard against heresy. It is also the fount from which springs the spirit of prayer which must permeate the Scripture as spiritual reading. If you are especially prideful and have very little humility, *do not read the Holy Scriptures* but pray to God to overcome your pride. Then pray the Psalter, especially Psalm L against pride. Then read first the book of Proverbs and work to enkindle the fear of the Lord within you. Go to confession and receive the Holy Sacrament often and

---

[30] St. Augustine, *Confessions*, Book 8, ch. 8, 12

beg God to give you the fear of the Lord. Read the *Imitation* and do what it says.

As was said above, humility means conformity with the truth. The crucial truth of humility is the adage already mentioned: *whatever good within me is the work of God, whatever evil within me is my work.* From this flows a most vital spiritual axiom: *trust in God, distrust yourself.*[31] This is the place of humility from which a soul can read the Holy Scriptures with profit.

Ask your confessor when it is right for you to read more deeply into Holy Writ. If it is prudent for your spiritual life to do so, start with the Holy Gospels. As the *Imitation* says in its first sentence:

> "He who follows Me, walks not in darkness," says the Lord. By these words of Christ we are advised to imitate His life and habits, if we wish to be truly enlightened and free from all blindness of heart. Let our chief effort, therefore, be to study the life of Jesus Christ.

Once you have read the Holy Gospels and grown in humility by the grace of God, then you can read other portions of Scripture as well.

Order of Reading the Scripture for Humility

This order should be followed if you are new to the Scriptures and especially if you are afflicted with pride:

> Pray the Psalms, particularly Psalm L - *beseech the Lord for humility*

---

[31] Dom Scupoli, *Spiritual Combat*, Ch. 1

Read Proverbs - *beseech God for fear of the Lord*
Read the Holy Gospels - *fall on your knees before our Savior*
Read the Catholic Epistles (James-Jude) - *seek charity and humility*
Read the Epistles of St. Paul (Romans-Hebrews) - *seek charity and humility*
Read the "Proverbs 2.0" (Ecclesiasticus) - *seek wisdom*
Read the Pentateuch (Genesis-Deuteronomy) - *be humbled under the mighty hand of God*
Read the historical cycle (Judges-II Paralipomenon) - *be humbled under the mighty hand of God*
Read the other historical books (I Esdras-Esther) - *worship the Lord*
Read the Maccabees - *take up your cross manfully like a saint*
Read the other wisdom books (Ecclesiastes, Wisdom) - *seek wisdom*
Read the Job, Song of Songs and the Prophecies (Isaias-Malachias) - *offer God worship for His divine mysteries*

Approved Commentaries

Once you reach the point of reading the Holy Gospels, you are in particular need of approved commentaries. As we have stressed, humility is necessary to understand and make profitable use of the Scriptures. Further, we cannot understand the Scriptures without holiness. Therefore, we must consult the wisdom of the Fathers to guide us in understanding the Text. This is the foundational virtue of piety which we discussed in the first chapter. Piety causes us to have a great filial love and reverence for our fathers who came before us.

We must be devoted to them and humbly defer to their wisdom.

Of all the Scriptures, the Holy Gospels should be read the most, as Holy Mother Church already shows with a Gospel reading at every Mass. The most important work to read with the Gospels is the *Catena Aurea* compiled by St. Thomas. This is a four volume set of commentaries on the Gospels from the Holy Fathers. The entire text is free online through the iPieta app or other such websites. Other profitable and approved commentaries are the following:

> Haydock's Bible commentary (free on iPieta) - *this commentary is helpful because it covers the entire Bible and most verses*
> Lapide Commentary
> Neale's Commentary on the Psalms (4 volumes, free on archive.org) - *this is the work of an erudite Anglican who brings together multiple patristic and liturgical sources. The best overall commentary on the Psalms*
> St. Augustine's commentary on the Psalms
> St. Robert Bellarmine's commentary on the Psalms
> St. Thomas' Commentary on individual books
> Other works of the Fathers on individual books available for free on newadvent.org
> (See Chapter 17 for all details on sources)

What about more modern commentaries? There are number of issues with modern "theologians" which we will address in Part II. However, since the 19th century there has been a great deal of historical discovery which has brought about a greater understanding of the *historical* context contained in the Holy Bible. Haydock's Commentary contains some of this, but his information is limited. The best new commentary that brings together some of the historical discoveries in modern times is the Revised Standard Version 2nd Catholic Edition Study Bible. At the time of this writing this edition is only published in the New Testament. Be careful to only use the RSV 2nd Catholic Edition, as there are issues with previous versions. The text of this RSV New Testament is lacking in some areas (which we will discuss in chapter 11), but the study notes for the text have a great deal of good information from a historical and linguistic perspective.

Lectio Divina

One potent method of reading the Scriptures is called divine reading ("Lectio Divina"). This practice has a very long Catholic Tradition and has aided many souls in praying the Scriptures and with spiritual reading. There are many variations to this method but the simplest is the following.

> Select a passage of Scripture. Most of the time the shorter passages work better, such as 1-10 verses only.
>
> Find a quiet place and place yourself in the presence of God. Consider that God looks upon you.
>
> Beg God for His grace for a profitable meditation on the Holy Scriptures. Take some time to be silent before His presence.
>
> Read the Scripture passage out loud. Pay attention to any words or phrases which strike you.

Take time in silence and consider the words. Think about what they mean. Lift your mind and will to God.

Read the passage out loud again. Pay attention. Consider it.

Take time in silence and consider the passage and place it before God. Listen if there is any aspect which God wishes to bring to your attention.

Read the passage out loud a third time.

Make a firm resolution to obey God's will in some way.

If any particular thing has struck you, offer this to God in prayer. Beg Him to help you understand His will for you. Form a resolution to God to do something for Him. Otherwise, thank and praise Him for whatever was shown to you. If nothing stood out to you, offer this time in worship to God.

An important note here is to understand that while we must have the humility to always interpret the Scriptures according to the Holy Fathers, the Word of God also speaks directly to us in our circumstances today. Just as St. Augustine was converted when he read a passage from St. Paul which applied to his life directly, God may enlighten your mind or heart to understand something using a passage from Scripture.

But beware: the heretics have also vainly thought themselves "enlightened" when they read a passage in which they were sure that God spoke to them. If you are unsure whether or not an insight comes from God, tell a knowledgeable priest or pious friend. It is usually the case that another person can see objectively whether something is from

God or not. Moreover, you guard yourself from error by showing humility toward another. Obviously anything that goes against the doctrines of the Church and the teachings of the Fathers is from the Devil.

Here we may consider Mary and Martha. Our Lord commended Mary for *sitting at the feet of Jesus and listening* (Lk. x. 39). We do not seek to gain something from our Lord, but we first sit in adoration before Him. We make acts of love, worship, and adoration to Him and Who He is. If He deigns to grant us some spiritual favor, then we rejoice for His mercy to sinners. But do not expect to always have some spiritual awakening when you read the Scriptures or do *Lectio Divina*. This is an error of pride. Seek, rather, to consider yourself unworthy of inspirations or movements from the Holy Spirit, and you will be safe from any deception of the evil one. Be content to simply sit at the feet of Jesus and listen to His words.

The Deception of Emotions or Lack Thereof

Here we come to an important note that cannot be overstated: *your emotions are not God and God is not your emotions*. There is a false gospel of Psychology that has overtaken the Church in recent times. Many Catholics seek to have a positive emotional experience and consider this to be some sort of divine inspiration. On the contrary, for those who are advancing spiritually, God will very often take away all consolations in order that you may be purified through sufferings. Suffering cleanses us from our attachments to creatures so that we may have true peace in the Uncreated. Suffering is absolutely essential to the spiritual life. This truth is absolutely fundamental in the spiritual writers.

You must toil and make every effort, especially at the beginning, to embrace tribulation and adversity as your dear sisters—desiring to be despised by all, and to have no one who entertains a favorable opinion of you, or brings you comfort, but your God.[32]

Or again, the *Imitation* declares:

Dost thou expect to escape what no mortal man can ever avoid? Which of the saints was without a cross or trial on this earth? Not even Jesus Christ, our Lord, Whose every hour on earth knew the pain of His passion. "It behooveth Christ to suffer, and to rise again from the dead, . . . and so enter into his glory." *How is it that thou lookest for another way than this, the royal way of the holy cross?*

The whole life of Christ was a cross and a martyrdom, and dost thou seek rest and enjoyment for thyself? Thou errest, thou errest, if thou seekest anything but to suffer, for this mortal life is full of miseries and marked with crosses on all sides. Indeed, the more spiritual progress a person makes, so much heavier will he frequently find the cross, because as his love increases, the pain of his exile also increases.

Yet such a man, though afflicted in many ways, is not without hope of consolation, because he knows that great reward is coming to him for bearing his cross. And when he carries it willingly, every pang

---

[32] Lorenzo Scupoli, *Of Interior Peace or the Path to Paradise* contained within *The Spiritual Combat* (Scriptoria Books: 2012), 165

of tribulation is changed into hope of solace from God.

Besides, the more the flesh is distressed by affliction, so much the more is the spirit strengthened by inward grace. Not infrequently a man is so strengthened by his love of trials and hardship in his desire to conform to the cross of Christ, that he does not wish to be without sorrow or pain, since he believes he will be the more acceptable to God if he is able to endure more and more grievous things for His sake.[33]

The greater our suffering, the more we are detached from this world and adhering to Jesus Christ.

Thus when we read the Scriptures (especially regularly and once a year), there will be many times of dryness and silence before God. Do not be alarmed, but thank God that He has favored you with this suffering for the sake of your soul. He disciplines His servants (Heb. xii. 9).

In the Roman Rite, the readings are proclaimed in Latin. This is because they are offered to God in worship. It is an act of worship to chant the Sacred Scriptures in a sacred language for the adoration of God. It is not primarily so that the faithful can understand what is said or have an emotional experience with the words themselves—the readings are explained at the homily. In the same way, when you read the Sacred Text and feel dry and do not understand, offer this also to God in worship. There are also parts of the Scripture that are particularly difficult to read (the long genealogies at the beginning of I Paralipomenon for example). Read these too and offer them to God in worship.

---

[33] Book II, Chapter 12

By keeping the deception of feelings properly understood, you will be safe from the deception of the devil to use dryness to bring you down into despair or worse.

On the other hand, if God gives you consolations of some kind, you must not be attached to those either. St. John of Cross teaches that we must make use of these consolations for a greater devotion.[34] Consolations are given to us to strengthen our weak wills. When you receive consolations, use this prayer for greater humility:

> *I thank Thee, O my God, for Thou hadst granted my feeble soul these delights in Thy mercy. Thou hast spoken to Thy servant, according to Thy abundant love. Without these things, my soul would have fallen away because of my weakness. But through of Thy grace alone, I stand before Thee to give Thee worship.*

Practice the adage from St. Ignatius of Loyola: *in consolation, prepare for desolation. In desolation, remember consolation.*[35]

Thus in consolation we gather strength and prepare ourselves for the sufferings which are inevitable and are a blessing from God. In sufferings, remember the consolations of the Lord and the rewards for those who persevere to the end.

In particular, using the Holy Psalter will assist you to speak the right words on these occasions in order to unite your soul in Christ to God the Father.

---

[34] Cf. St. John of the Cross, *Ascent of Mount Carmel*, ch. 28
[35] Cf. St. Ignatius of Loyola, *The Spiritual Excercises* (Doubleday: 2015), 101, 148

Unless the Lord had been my helper, my soul had almost dwelt in hell. If I said: My foot is moved: thy mercy, O Lord, assisted me. According to the multitude of my sorrows in my heart, thy comforts have given joy to my soul (Ps. xciii. 17-19).

Using the Lectionary

Another excellent tool is the Church's lectionary. The readings usually include an Epistle and a Gospel which apply to the saint of the day. It is a pious practice to read the life of the saint and read these readings to meditate upon this saint's life.

The lectionary at the New Mass follows a different form of readings which normally do not correspond to the saint of the day. The daily Gospel readings go through most of the four Gospels every year. It is certainly a pious practice to read through the Gospels once a year. Unfortunately many of the hard sayings of our Lord were removed from the new lectionary in an attempt to appeal to "modern man."[36] In chapter 12 we will go over a yearly reading plan which includes all of the books with all their parts according to the traditional office of Matins.

Veneration of the Holy Bible

Liturgically the Church has always venerated the Holy Scripture. The Missal is incensed before the Gospel reading and proclaimed with torches. In the Greek Catholic rite, there

---

[36] For a discussion on the problems with the New Lectionary, see Peter Kwasniewski, "The Postconciliar Lectionary at 50: A Detailed Critique," < http://www.newliturgicalmovement.org/2019/05/the-postconciliar-lectionary-at-50.html#.XdmGri2ZOqQ>. Accessed November 23, 2019

is a special book containing only the Gospels which is ornately decorated, which the faithful kiss during the Divine Office.

In the same way, we should venerate the Sacred Text. Kiss your Holy Bible before and after you read it. Place it in a prominent place always, or at least on the top and never place anything on top of it.

These and another such gestures help our bodies conform to our soul and assist with the necessary humility that we bring to the Word of God.

V

"WITHOUT ME, YOU CAN DO NOTHING"

If anyone affirms that we can form any right opinion or make any right choice which relates to the salvation of eternal life, as is expedient for us, or that we can be saved, that is, assent to the preaching of the gospel through our natural powers without the illumination and inspiration of the Holy Spirit, who makes all men gladly assent to and believe in the truth, he is led astray by a heretical spirit, and does not understand the voice of God who says in the Gospel, *For without me, you can do nothing* (John xv. 5), and the word of the Apostle, *Not that we are competent of ourselves to claim anything as coming from us; our competence is from God* (II Cor. iii. 5).[37]

This truth is absolutely fundamental to our faith and especially to the Latin Fathers (see chapter 15 for more details on this). As we shall see in part II, this truth was denied by so-called theologians which eventually led to our present crisis. As a result, many in our society deny this truth unless they are

---

[37] Synod of Orange (529), Canon 7

given a special grace from God (or have a good Catholic upbringing). This chapter is devoted to prayer. Through prayer we express our need for God's grace to allow us to read the Holy Scriptures, thus it is humility. *God gives grace to the humble, but resists the proud* (Ja. iv. 6). Pray the words of the saints who knew true humility.

<u>Prayer before reading the Holy Scriptures:</u>

O King of Glory, Lord of Hosts, Who didst triumphantly ascend the heavens, leave us not as orphans, but send us the Promised of the Father, the Spirit of Truth.

We implore Thee, O Lord, that the Consoler, Who proceededth from Thee, will enlighten our souls and infuse into them all truth, as Thy Son hath promised.

O God, Father of our Lord Jesus Christ, vouchsafe to grant us, according to the riches of Thy glory that Christ by faith may dwell in our hearts, which rooted and grounded in charity, may acknowledge the love of Christ, surpassing all knowledge. Through the same Christ our Lord. Amen.

Prayer after reading the Holy Scriptures
(St. Bede)

Let me not, O Lord, be puffed up with worldly wisdom, which passes away, but grant me that love which never abates, that I may not choose to know anything among men, but Jesus, and Him crucified.

I beg Thee, dear Jesus, that s/he upon whom Thou hast graciously bestowed the sweet savor of the words of Thy knowledge, may also possess Thee, Fount of all Wisdom, and shine forever before Thy countenance. Amen.

Prayer before reading the Holy Gospel
(Liturgy of St. John Chrysostom)

Illumine our hearts, O Master who lovest mankind, with the pure light of thy divine knowledge, and open the eyes of our mind to the understanding of Thy Gospel teaching; implant in us also the fear of Thy blessed commandments, that trampling down all carnal desires, we may enter upon a spiritual manner of living, both thinking and doing such things as are well-pleasing unto Thee: for Thou art the illumination of our souls and bodies, O Christ our God, and unto thee we send up glory, together with Thy Father who is from everlasting, and Thine all-holy, good, and life-creating Spirit: now and ever, and unto the ages of ages. Amen.

Prayer before study (St. Thomas)

O ineffable Creator, Who, out of the treasure of Thy wisdom, hast ordained three hierarchies of Angels, and placed them in wonderful order above the heavens, and hast most wisely distributed the parts of the world; Thou, Who art called the true fountain of light and wisdom, and the highest beginning, vouchsafe to pour upon the darkness of my understanding, in which I was born, the double beam of Thy brightness, removing from me all darkness of sin and ignorance.

Thou, Who makest eloquent the tongue of the dumb, instruct my tongue, and pour on my lips the grace of Thy blessing. Give me quickness of understanding, capacity of retaining, subtlety of interpreting, facility in learning, and copious grace of speaking. Guide my going in, direct my going forward, accomplish my going forth; through Christ our Lord. Amen.

Prayer before study

Grant me grace O eternal God, to desire ardently all that is pleasing unto Thee; to examine it prudently, to acknowledge it truthfully, and to accomplish it perfectly to the honor of Thy Name. Amen.

Prayer before Read the Scripture
(St. John Chrysostom)

O Lord Jesus Christ, open the eyes of my heart that I may hear Thy word, and understand and do Thy will, for I am a sojourner upon the Earth. Hide not Thy commandments from me, but open my eyes, that I may perceive the wonders of Thy Law.

Speak unto me the hidden and secret things of Thy wisdom. On Thee do I set my hope, O my God, that Thou shalt enlighten my mind and understanding with the light of Thy knowledge; not only to cherish those things which are written, but to do them; that in reading the lives and sayings of the Saints I may not sin, but that such may serve for my restoration, enlightenment and sanctification, for the salvation of my soul, and the inheritance of life everlasting. For Thou art the enlightenment of those who lie in darkness, and from Thee comes every good deed and every gift. Amen

VI

CHURCH DOCTRINES ABOUT THE HOLY SCRIPTURES

Before we proceed to the historical section of this work, let us review the doctrines of the Church regarding the Holy Scriptures. The doctrines are rooted in the doctrine of revelation in general. These come almost verbatim from Denzinger, the authoritative textbook on dogma.[38]

The Possibility and Necessity of Revelation

- Revelation, or the speaking of God to man is possible and useful. It is supernatural.
- It is morally necessary regarding natural religious truths.
- It is absolutely necessary concerning the supernatural and can be made believable by visible signs.

---

[38] See Denzinger, *The Sources of Catholic Dogma*, trans. Roy J. Deferrari (Preserving Christian Publications: 2009), [9]ff.

The Facts and Objects (Mysteries) of Revelation

- The Most Holy Trinity revealed some things, through Moses, the prophets and their other servants, and finally though Christ, who spoke and performed miracles.
- Revelation is not a work of men or some philosophical discovery or a mere evolution of Christian understanding, but a determined body of doctrine applicable to all times and men.
- Besides truths accessible even to human reason, Christian revelation contains mysteries which are the eternal decrees of God. They are inaccessible to reason and they even transcend angelic understanding. Even with the progress of science they cannot be understood or demonstrated. Nevertheless, they do not contradict reason, but exceed it and always remain obscure, nor are they inventions of men contrary to the common good.
- Revelation is not imperfect nor to be made perfect through progress, nor is it to be changed in any way into another meaning; it is immutable and was complete with the Apostles.

The Acceptance of Revelation (Faith)

- Divine Revelation requires internal faith which is divine.
- Knowledge does not suffice that is only probable, nor merely subjective (as the pseudo-mystics), nor merely internal experience, or private inspiration. But there is required a sure knowledge of the fact of revelation.
- No one invited to embrace the faith is to be forced, but if revelation is once accepted under the teaching authority of the Church, one cannot dissent from it. Hence a positive

doubt is not the basis of theological investigation. All indifferentism ("all religions are equal") is to be rejected.

The Powers, Duties and Limits of Reason

- Not all certitude is founded on faith. Natural reason is sufficient for foundational principles and with evidence we know the substance of matter, the causality of things, the distinction of things from God, temporal existence, the existence of the intellect and will, that all appearances are true, and that God and creatures are something, among other things.
- Reason without grace can know some religious things before the faith is accepted, such as the existence of God, some of His attributes, the fact of creation, miracles, and the divine revelation of Moses and Christ.
- After the reception of faith reason can attain a kind of understanding of the mysteries. It cannot, however, perceive all revealed truths or prove them with evidence. Thus with the natural light it cannot attain its supernatural end.
- Human reason is not immune from all error, thus it is not to be relied upon heavily. It is not autonomous, but relies on uncreated truth, nor is it the sole norm by which truth is known, nor is it to be made equal to religion.
- Man does not have an unlimited freedom of feeling, speaking, or writing.

The Mutual Relationship Between Reason and Revelation

- Revelation and reason cannot contradict one another, nor is faith opposed to human reason.

- Reason explains, guards, and defends revealed truths.
- Revelation, on the other hand, frees reason from errors, enlightens, and strengthens it; fosters the rectitude and purity of natural knowledge; is the infallible director of philosophy and its negative norm.
- Not only the philosopher but philosophy itself is under the teaching authority of faith and ought to be ancillary to theology. Hence errors of reason are rightly and beneficially condemned by the Church, whose judgement is to be followed even with regard to things not yet expressly defined.
- Theology is to be done in a different way than natural science. The methods and principles of scholastic theology are not to be rejected. All speculation regarding revealed truths should be founded upon the teaching of the Church and the Fathers, and even a reasonable form in words is to be retained and the commonly received terminology is to be preserved.

The Sources of Revelation

- The written source of revelation is the canonical books of both Testaments of which the authentic version is the Vulgate.
- These complete books with all their parts are to be received as sacred and canonical and to be faithfully guarded as from God Who is the author of both Testaments, and as such handed down by the Church.
- They are to be judged and interpreted according to the unanimous consent of the Fathers and the sense of the Church, according to sound principles.
- True inerrancy belongs to Sacred Scripture.
- The reading of Sacred Scripture is not necessary nor fitting for all, nevertheless it is by no means forbidden. However,

any sort of vernacular translation whatsoever is not permitted, nor any without notes and approval from the bishop.
- Another source of revelation is ecclesiastical Tradition. The authority of the Fathers on faith and morals is the highest, especially of St. Augustine, likewise the common teaching of the scholastic theologians is to be held, but particularly St. Thomas Aquinas, and modern authors are not to be rashly preferred. The practices of the Church establishes a norm for belief, so that the "law of praying is the law of believing" (*lex orandi, lex credendi*).
- No other public source of revelation exists outside of the canonical books and apostolic Tradition so that as a result faith or Christian doctrine is immutable, safeguarding a progress of further knowledge of things revealed.

PART TWO

HISTORY: HOW
"THEOLOGIANS"
SEIZED POWER USING
THE HOLY BIBLE

+

VII

ORAL TRADITION AND THE EARLY HISTORY OF THE SCRIPTURES

Now that we have laid the necessary foundations in prayer and humility, we can begin to discuss the history of the Holy Bible and the ways it impacts us today. This survey will span over the next four chapters and take us into our present crisis. In many ways this history helps explain how our crisis has come about.

The important theme in this section is the contrast we drew between the true theologian and the so-called "theologian." The first man is a man of prayer and humility, which inform his studies. The second man does not pray nor have humility, but trusts in his own intellect to show him the truth. The term "theologian" today has nothing to do with prayer or humility, but only advanced degrees and intellect. As such, we will use this term in this section to denote the modern meaning contrasted with the way of the saints.

Oral Culture and Modern Textual Criticism

Before we go into some of the history, let's review some of what was said about oral culture in the introduction. As we have discussed before, before the printing press was invented in the 15th century, the world was dominated by oral culture. The oral cultures held a much more robust memory, since men generally could not read, yet were no less intelligent. Thus a great deal of cultural weight was given to oral story telling.

Eventually these stories were written down and then passed down in written form. After they were written, there still existed an extensive oral commentary on written texts which gives us their meaning. Thus the oral culture precedes the written text, and then written texts depend on the oral culture for their meaning.

Throughout modern history and especially beginning in the 19th century, historians made a great amount of linguistic and archaeological discoveries. This, along with other philosophical and political movements, made men begin to believe that they knew how to understand ancient texts much better than their ancestors. Even worse, historians asserted that if a thing was not written down, it did not happen.

Take a moment to understand how absurd this is. Throughout the history of millennia, thousands upon thousands of ancient texts were created, monuments erected, records decreed, and even more stories were told. Throughout these millennia, hundreds and hundreds of wars, natural disasters, migrations took place, which destroyed, changed, or fragmented all of these historical records. What we possess today in the historical record is a fragment of a fragment of a fragment of a fragment of the whole body of historical evidence that once existed. It is simply foolish to assert that any lack of evidence indicates that any one event did not happen.[39] But history of this kind is not interested in historical truth as we shall see below.

In this climate (which exists to this day) historians generally discount oral culture as unreliable, and attempt to understand ancient texts without it. This, however, is a mistake for several reasons. First, it is a matter of history that oral tradition dominated oral cultures until the printing press. Thus it is historically incorrect to dismiss such a dominant aspect of history and culture.

Second, by ignoring oral culture, modern historians quickly misunderstand the texts by assuming they can come to a better understanding than the ancient peoples themselves. But this can only be assumed if the ancient peoples themselves were less intelligent and could not remember the oral traditions.

But this is a tenuous claim. The oral cultures which transmitted these texts also knew their meanings better than any historian centuries removed from their cultural context. It is vital that we consider the great oral culture dominating the formation of the Holy Bible. This will become a key point later on.

The Pentateuch and Oral Tradition

As we mentioned, the Pentateuch is the term for the first five books of the Bible: Genesis, Exodus, Leviticus, Numbers and Deuteronomy. This is also known as "The Law of Moses"

---

[39] Cf. Edwin Yamauchi, *The Stones and the Scriptures* (Baker: 1981), *The Scriptures and Archaeology* (Wipf and Stock: 2013), "The Current Status of Old Testament Historiography," in *Faith, Tradition, and History*, edited by Millard, Hoffmeier, and Baker (1994).

or the *Torah*. From the first words of Genesis the Holy Bible is founded upon the authority of oral Tradition. Why is this?

Moses wrote the first five books of the Holy Bible (more on that below). From the book of Exodus onward, he was an eye witness to these events. However, the entire book of Genesis predates Moses by hundreds of years. Thus Moses himself relied on generations and generations of oral Tradition to write the book of Genesis. Thus we must understand that the Holy Scriptures are firmly grounded on a centuries-old oral Tradition. The reason the Scriptures are authoritative is because of oral Tradition: they are the earliest instance of the oral Tradition written down. Thus the oral Tradition predates, validates, and consummates the Scriptures. Oral Tradition is fundamental.

Further, as we mentioned above, it is thus understood that *inspiration is not confined to the text of the Holy Bible*. Inspiration also is understood to be guiding oral Tradition. If you believe that Genesis is inspired, then you must believe that centuries of oral Tradition upon which Moses based the book was also inspired, since it would have been preserved from error over many centuries since the beginning of the world. Thus this truth must be fundamentally known: the oral and written Traditions of the Bible are both inspired of the Holy Ghost.

First Century Versions of the Holy Bible

Eventually a great body of oral Tradition was written down by the Israelites and passed down to us. This forms what would become known as the Old Testament. However, *there exists no original text* of the Holy Bible. What we have are copies of copies of copies passed down to us over centuries. The process of translating the Holy Text and passing it down is a matter of assembling these copies and attempting to ascertain the most accurate approximation of the original text. This is known today as "Textual Criticism," meaning critically examining the manuscript copies. This is a process that has been going on from the beginning, but, as we have said, it was the oral Tradition which was the foundation of the Text itself.

We mentioned in the chapter on the Psalter that there are two main manuscript Traditions. In fact, at the time of our Lord we know of at least four different Traditions of the Old Testament:

> The Samaritan Pentateuch
> The proto-Masoretic
> The Dead Sea Scrolls
> The Septuagint (and Geniza fragments)

Of these by far the most accepted was the Septuagint, which was read by Jews across the Roman Empire. This was a Greek translation of ancient Hebrew texts completed around the year 200 B.C. The word "Septuagint" means "seventy" (thus it is sometimes written as LXX). This refers to an ancient story of seventy Rabbis who translated the entire Hebrew text separately. When they compared their translations, they found they were exactly the same, word for word.[40]

Some doubt the veracity of this story, but it points to the general belief by the Jews at the time of our Lord that the Septuagint was divinely inspired. Most Jews in the Roman Empire knew Greek more than Hebrew or Aramaic, and they used the Septuagint as Scripture.

---

[40] This story comes from a document known as the *Letter of Aristeas*, which dates to about the 2nd century B.C.

When the New Testament quotes the Old Testament, the majority of cases (about 75%) quote the Greek Septuagint, and not the other versions.[41] However, in a minority of cases the New Testament does quote the other versions, and sometimes the version is entirely unknown. For example, Matthew ii. 23 says,

> And coming he dwelt in a city called Nazareth: that it might be fulfilled which was said by the prophets: That he shall be called a Nazarene.

Here the sacred writer mentions a prophecy of our Lord regarding his home city of Nazareth. However, he quotes "the prophets," and for two thousand years no one has discovered which prophet St. Matthew referred to here. Some speculate it was a prophet's manuscript now lost, others think it refers to the Hebrew word for "branch."[42] It may indicate as well an oral tradition never written. In any case, since the exact original text of the Old Testament (nor the New) does not exist, the oral Tradition governs the Text.

Another example is instructive from the Epistle of St. Jude.

> When Michael the archangel, disputing with the devil, contended about the body of Moses, he durst not bring against him the judgment of railing speech, but said: The Lord command thee (Jd. i. 9).

Here St. Jude makes reference to an oral Tradition not written in the Holy Bible. And yet this story is taken as authoritative

---

[41] Karen H. Jobes and Moises Silva, *Invitation to the Septuagint* (Baker: 2000), 189-93
[42] Cf. Scott Hahn and Curtis Mitch, *RSV New Testament 2CE Study Bible* (Ignatius: 2010), 11

and instructive for those receiving St. Jude's epistle. His readers and hearers would have taken this oral Tradition as an authority as well.

Thus even though we do not have the original text of the Holy Bible, we do have an oral Tradition also inspired by the Holy Spirit. The oral Tradition then becomes the basis for understanding and putting together the Biblical Text, which is the earliest written record of the oral Tradition.

The Oral Tradition of the Apostles

When our Lord instituted the New Covenant in 33 A.D., he also gave to the Apostles the Apostolic Tradition, or the Deposit of Faith, which was entirely in oral form as we have discussed. We see references to this in the Gospels:

> And beginning at Moses and all the prophets, he expounded to them in all the scriptures, the things that were concerning him (Lk. xxiv. 27).

Here is a clear reference to a long oral discourse given by our Lord to the Apostles which explains the meaning of the Old Testament concerning Himself. Again another example comes from the Acts of the Apostles:

> The former treatise I made, O Theophilus, of all things which Jesus began to do and to teach, Until the day on which, giving commandments by the Holy Ghost to the apostles whom he had chosen, he was taken up. To whom also he shewed himself alive after his passion, by many proofs, for forty days appearing to them, and speaking of the kingdom of God (Acts i. 1-3).

Thus we have another clear reference to multiple discourses from our Lord for a span of forty days. We are not given the details of these words until much later when the oral Tradition begins to be written down. But consider the depth and weight of the Sermon on the Mount (Mt. v-vii), which appears from the Text to be delivered in one day and perhaps within an hour or two. Consider: how many sermons did our Lord give during the forty days after His Resurrection?

It is in this context that we hear the passage which we have already quoted above:

> Then he opened their understanding, that they might understand the scriptures. And he said to them: Thus it is written, and thus it behooved Christ to suffer, and to rise again from the dead, the third day: And that penance and remission of sins should be preached in his name, unto all nations, beginning at Jerusalem (Lk. xxiv. 45-47).

To our minds, as I have said, this meaning is not always clearly seen from the Old Testament. Thus not only is it necessary to have an illumination from God, as well as humility and prayer, we must also humbly accept the oral Tradition of the Lord.

Our Lord wrote no book. When God became man, he did not consign His words to written form but gave them in oral form. He committed them to the Apostles, who would later write them down. Thus the example of our Lord itself teaches that the oral Tradition is to be given great authority with the written Text. Both are inspired and form the "sources of revelation" for the Church.

The Incarnate Word

Ultimately the faith is not a religion of the Book or even of the oral Tradition, but of the Incarnate Word. This Word of God is the Second Person of the Trinity, Jesus Christ, and it this Word which is the authority. As it is written, *and the word became flesh and dwelt among us* (Jn. i. 14) or as St. Paul says:

> God, who, at sundry times and in divers manners, spoke in times past to the fathers by the prophets, last of all, in these days hath spoken to us by his Son, whom he hath appointed heir of all things, by whom also he made the world (Heb. i. 1-2).

The Apostles understood that God had done something entirely new. Before He had spoken His Word to us, mediated through the prophets and the Old Testament, but in the Church, the Word is incarnate in His Son.

Our Lord ascended to His throne in Heaven and grafted the Church into His Body to become one with them. Sending the Holy Spirit, He truly makes Himself present, most especially in the Blessed Sacrament—the central *cultus* of Catholic culture. But also, it is the person of the priest who, through the Apostolic Succession, has literally received the hands of Jesus Christ. It is the priest that gives the word about the Word in preaching and the Scriptures.

Thus it is manifest that the faith is not like the false religions of Muhammadanism or Rabbinic Judaism or the Protestant sects, but a real divine life. This is because only Catholicism asserts that their religion truly makes present the Divine Word of God. This is why we cannot read the Holy Scriptures without humility. This is why we cannot understand them without piety to the Tradition. Because these virtues are necessary to know the Word of God: Jesus Christ. Without knowledge of Jesus Christ in holiness, the Scriptures are only a book to be used for the purpose of man. This is why the Lord constituted His Church not only with a written and oral Word, but with a Magisterium.

The Magisterium: Safeguard of Humility

When our Lord founded the Church on St. Peter and filled the Apostles with the Holy Spirit, He also gave them the divine authority and assistance to guard and expound this Deposit of Faith. He committed it to them in oral form, they wrote it down, but were also in charge of guarding this Deposit until His return. This eventually became known as the Magisterium, which is the Pope and the Bishops and the Ecumenical Council religiously guarding the Deposit and handing it down without change.

The Lord said, *He who hears you [apostles] hears me* (Lk. x. 16). Thus the Bishops as successors of the Apostles act in the Person of Jesus Christ and Jesus Christ acts in them in a unique way. By guiding the Magisterium with divine inspiration, God has given the Church a safeguard of humility. Every man must receive the faith with piety and read the Scriptures with humility. If he doesn't, the Magisterium will come against his pride. The Church is called Holy Mother Church with good reason: she guards her children from their own pride, disciplines them if she must, and protects them from error. Without the Magisterium, there is no safeguard against pride. This is evident in the Eastern Orthodox churches, who have the written and oral Tradition, but no Magisterium.[43]

In the book of Acts we see the Magisterial prototype of the Pope of Rome and the Ecumenical Council, as well as their canonical authority over the Church. First, we need a bit of context for this.

At the time of our Lord, the Law of Moses was in force. It cannot be overstated how important this was. This law was of divine origin and the Jews were to keep it, in many cases on pain of death. The Maccabees revolted and shed their blood rather than eat pork. It was a universal, canonical, binding authority.

However, within the law itself Moses wrote that God would raise up another like Moses. What does it mean to be like Moses? There have been many prophets, but none of them were lawgivers, like Moses. Thus did Moses prophesy: *The Lord thy God will raise up to thee a Prophet of thy nation and of thy brethren like unto me: him thou shalt hear* (Dt. xviii. 15), again elsewhere it is said, *Appoint, O Lord, a lawgiver over them: that the Gentiles may know themselves to be but men* (Ps. ix. 21).

Our Lord gave many teachings and commandments which we refer to as the New Law. However, the existing canonical system of lawful authority of priests and juridical authority was not fully recreated until the book of Acts. We have discussed this in reference to the oral Tradition, but the book of Acts shows us the concrete action of the Magisterium.

Our Lord performed the sacrifice of the New Covenant as the New High priest, then ordained his apostles as priests of

---

[43] On the problem of the Eastern Orthodox churches without a Magisterium, see Vladimir Soloviev, *Russia and the Universal Church*, trans. Rees (London: Centenary Press, 1948), 49, 50

the New Covenant. But this priesthood, like the old, did not simply have sacramental authority but also juridical authority. It participated in the lawgiving of the New Moses.

We see this in the dramatic changes that happen in the book of Acts. First, Pope St. Peter receives a special vision. Only he is given the vision, and it directs him to Cornelius who is a Gentile. Because of the interaction the Pope, on his own authority abrogates the law of Moses to baptize a Gentile. He does not require that Cornelius follow the Law of Moses before he is baptized (Acts x. 47).

This action is incredibly significant, because an individual—the first pope—acted with the authority of the New Lawgiver—Christ—to abrogate the divine law of Moses. This points to the priestly power having also a juridical authority to interpret and implement the oral Tradition given by Jesus Christ, even making new laws. It also points to the unique authority which St. Peter held as the prince of the apostles.

The pope's action is then confirmed by a council of the Apostles:

> For it hath seemed good to the Holy Ghost and to us, to lay no further burden upon you than these necessary things: That you abstain from things sacrificed to idols, and from blood, and from things strangled, and from fornication; from which things keeping yourselves, you shall do well (Acts xv. 28-29).

This was then sent to the whole Church to obey (Acts xvi. 4).

This is so significant that it alters *the foundation of the entire universe* as the Jews knew it. First, the Law of Moses is abrogated. This means that the pope and bishops are claiming for themselves an authority *above* Moses to change divine law according to new revelation from God. They claim for themselves the authority of Christ.

Second, the pope and council then claim authority to bind the entire church to this law. This initiative by the pope which is confirmed by a universal council foreshadows the actions of the pope and councils in the future.[44]

Thus we have the oral and written Tradition, as well as the Magisterium which guards the Tradition, all from the words of the New Testament themselves. This is then shown in the celebration of the *cultus* which manifests all these things in worship to God. Years later the Church would describe it this way:

> Sacred Tradition and Sacred Scripture form one sacred deposit of the word of God, committed to the Church. Holding fast to this deposit the entire holy people united with their shepherds remain always steadfast in the *teaching of the Apostles, in the common life, in the breaking of the bread and in prayers* (see Acts 2, 42, Greek text), so that holding to, practicing and professing the heritage of the faith, it becomes on the part of the bishops and faithful a single common effort.
>
> But the task of authentically interpreting the word of God, whether written or handed on, has been entrusted *exclusively* to the living teaching office of

---

[44] It must be noted that this change also happened within the time of the Apostles as a new revelation. The pope and bishops after the Apostles do not have the same authority in terms of revelation, since revelation ended with the last Apostle. They do have the authority, however, to bind the entire Church to an interpretation of the Revelation as it was handed down by the Apostles.

the Church [Magisterium], whose authority is exercised in the name of Jesus Christ. This teaching office is *not above* the word of God, but serves it, teaching only what has been handed on, listening to it devoutly, guarding it scrupulously and explaining it faithfully in accord with a divine commission and with the help of the Holy Spirit, it draws from this one deposit of faith everything which it presents for belief as divinely revealed.

It is clear, therefore, that sacred Tradition, Sacred Scripture and the teaching authority of the Church, in accord with God's most wise design, are so linked and joined together that one cannot stand without the others, and that all together and each in its own way under the action of the one Holy Spirit contribute effectively to the salvation of souls.[45]

Eventually the so-called theologians would deny that the Tradition was given "exclusively" to the Magisterium, but would assert this ownership for themselves as we shall see.

The Faithful Supporting the Magisterium

Here we must pause from our historical narrative to address a crucial issue here. It is this interdependence between the Tradition and the Magisterium which must be thoroughly understood by Catholics today. The Sacred Tradition in both written and oral form is meant to be guarded by the Magisterium. The Magisterium, as this text declares, is "not above the word of God."

---

[45] Vatican II, *Dei Verbum* (1965), 10. Emphasis mine. We will discuss the problems in this document in chapter 10.

Therefore at times the Magisterium herself can go astray, because even though it forms the primary organ of God's divinely inspired guardianship, God has not taken away the free will of bishops and popes. They can still fall into sin and error.

In those times, God has also inspired all the faithful as well by virtue of their Baptism and Confirmation to guard the Tradition, especially when the Magisterium has become eclipsed or become corrupted. The faithful serve as the secondary guardians in this rare case, when most of the bishops or pope have lost their way. Thus just as God gave the prototype of the Magisterium in the book of Acts, He also gave the prototype of the faithful support of the Magisterium in the person of St. Paul rebuking the first pope, St. Peter:

> But when Cephas [Peter] was come to Antioch, I withstood him to the face, because he was to be blamed. For before that some came from James, he did eat with the Gentiles: but when they were come, he withdrew and separated himself, fearing them who were of the circumcision. And to his dissimulation the rest of the Jews consented, so that Barnabas also was led by them into that dissimulation.

> But when I saw that they walked not uprightly unto the truth of the gospel, I said to Cephas before them all: If thou, being a Jew, livest after the manner of the Gentiles, and not as the Jews do, how dost thou compel the Gentiles to live as do the Jews? We by nature are Jews, and not of the Gentiles sinners. But knowing that man is not justified by the works of the law, but by the faith of Jesus Christ; we also believe in Christ Jesus, that we may be justified by

the faith of Christ, and not by the works of the law: because by the works of the law no flesh shall be justified (Gal. ii. 11-16).

Here we see an Apostle St. Paul, rebuking his superior, the Prince of the Apostles, St. Peter, because he is going astray from the Magisterial teaching already defined in Acts xv. 28 and bound to the Church in Acts xvi. 4. Thus the Church understood from the beginning that even if a bishop (or even a pope) goes astray from the authoritative Tradition, they must be resisted.

This was particularly present during the Arian controversy when most of the bishops and even the pope were vacillating on heresy and orthodoxy. It was the laity who rose up to confess the faith, rebuke the bishops, and endure the extravagance of the heretics. Once the bishops and the pope came back to the faith and orthodox discipline, the laity could return again to their lives and submit to the Magisterium as usual.[46]

It is St. Thomas who explains the Pauline rebuke with clarity. He comments on the passage above from Galatians discussing the question: "Is a man bound to correct his prelate?"

> To withstand anyone in public exceeds the mode of fraternal correction, and so Paul would not have withstood Peter then, unless he were in some way his equal as regards the defense of the faith. But one who is not an equal can reprove privately and respectfully.

---

[46] See St. John Henry Newman *The Arians of the Fourth Century* (Wipf and Stock Publishers: 1996), 254ff.

> ...It must be observed, however, that if the faith were endangered, a subject ought to rebuke his prelate even publicly. Hence Paul, who was Peter's subject, rebuked him in public, on account of the imminent danger of scandal concerning faith, and, as the gloss of Augustine says on Galatians 2:11, "Peter gave an example to superiors, that if at any time they should happen to stray from the straight path, they should not disdain to be reproved by their subjects" (II-II q33 a4).

Here we see that St. Thomas states that piety must be observed toward superiors, so that we always show them reverence and never challenge them in public, but if they need correction to do so in private. This preserves the piety of all souls toward them so that no one else may be led astray toward sinning against piety toward superiors.

However, St. Thomas also makes a further distinction in saying that "if the faith were endangered," then even a public rebuke is warranted. Thus at certain times, a state of emergency exists making a public rebuke necessary, because of the eminent danger posed by the words or deeds of the prelate.

Now below we will see a different sort of "rebuke" made by the so-called "theologians," who do not wish to defend the faith but only their own opinions. They will deny that the Deposit has been entrusted to the Magisterium *alone*, and thus, unlike the faithful laity, when they rebuke the bishops, they will seek to retain the power for themselves. This will be the crucial distinction when considering this reality. We will discuss this further but let us return to our narrative.

The Septuagint and the Break with the Jews

As we said above, the Septuagint was the dominant form of the Old Testament in circulation at the time of our Lord, and the New Testament clearly uses the Septuagint more than any other version. If we take the New Testament as final judge of the correct version, we see that the Septuagint wins by a majority, but nevertheless it is not the original text, since other versions are sometimes utilized as noted. Nevertheless, the Septuagint was very early accepted by the Church as the standard Old Testament and believed to be inspired.

As the Church progressed the Apostles, empowered by the Holy Spirit and the oral Tradition, boldly proclaimed the truth to the Jews. Many accepted this, were baptized and became Catholics. Most Jews rejected the truth.

Through a series of revolutions, the Jewish community of Jerusalem was decimated by Roman authorities and in 70 A.D. the temple was destroyed in punishment for their sin as our Lord had prophesied (Lk. xix. 44). Still, the Catholics of Jewish descent remained close to the Jewish community and tensions remained between them (chapter 14 is a sermon from a Catholic of Jewish descent).

Around the year 90 A.D., the Pharisees were able to take control of the Jewish community. They came together and anathematized the Christians of Jewish descent. They put all Christians out of the synagogue for good by adding a text to their liturgy which cursed the Christians.[47]

They then began a new religion eventually known as "Rabbinic Judaism." This religion is distinct from the Judaism of our Lord, known as Temple Judaism. Rabbinic Judaism had no temple, no priesthood, and no sacrifice. Instead, the

---

[47] This was the curse known as the *Birkat haMinim*.

Pharisees began teaching that these things, hitherto understood to be commanded by God, were no longer needed. They did not claim to be prophets but began this new religion on their own authority. They continued to transmit their human traditions (which our Lord condemned in the Gospel) and eventually they were written down in two versions of the Talmud, which would also include blasphemies against our Lord and our Lady.[48]

Most significantly for our purposes, the Pharisees broke from the rest of the Jewish community in the Roman Empire and decided to stop using the Septuagint altogether. They instead took the existing Hebrew manuscripts (the proto-Masoretic) and transmitted these instead. These texts were then passed down among the Jews as a separate tradition of the Old Testament.

As we noted, among significant passages which prophesy our Lord there existed great discrepancies between the older Greek Septuagint and the later Hebrew transmission of the Jews. These discrepancies led some early saints to accuse the Jews of altering their Scriptures to obscure the prophecies about Christ.[49] Modern scholars have also asserted this.[50]

Whether these texts were changed by the Jews or represent another tradition is not always clear. What is clear is that the

---

[48] These blasphemes are contained in Gittin 57a, Sanhedrin 107b, Sotah 47a, Shabath 104b, Sanhedrin 106a, and Rosh Hashanah 17a. According to Madre Pascalina, a prominent Jew once confronted Ven. Pius XII and demanded that the Prayer for Jews be removed from the Good Friday service. He agreed to consider a softer translation if all of these blasphemies were removed from the Talmud. Charles Theodore Murr, *The Godmother* (2017), 153ff. For more on this, see Peter Schafer, *Jesus in the Talmud* (Princeton: Princeton University Press, 2007).
[49] See St. Justin Martyr, *Dialogue with Trypho the Jew*
[50] Cf. Margaret Barker *Temple Mysticism: An Introduction* (London: SPCK, 2011), pp. 14–39.

Greek Septuagint was believed to be inspired and predates the oldest Masoretic texts by a number of centuries. Thus neither the Hebrew nor the Greek is the "original text," since this does not exist. Rather the oral Tradition is the arbiter of these texts. Nevertheless the Greek Septuagint has generally been the most authoritative version for the Church from the beginning.

St. Augustine said in his day that the Church approaches the Septuagint version "as if it were the only one."[51] Another Church Father, Cyril of Jerusalem, says the Greek Septuagint "was no wordcraft, nor contrivance of human devices: but the translation of the Divine Scriptures, spoken by the Holy Ghost, was of the Holy Ghost accomplished."[52]

On the other hand, the Hebrew of the Jews was looked upon by the Church with caution. Did the Church Fathers hate Jews? Of course not. But the Jews who rejected Jesus Christ did not receive the guidance of the Holy Spirit in transmitting their manuscripts and oral tradition. Therefore it was foolish to place complete trust in their manuscripts since they were guided by an oral tradition of man.

The Value of the Hebrew and the Latin Vulgate

However, one Church Father took the time to learn Hebrew from the Jews and study the Hebrew manuscripts they were preserving. He accepted the Septuagint and respected its official use by the Church, but asserted that using the Hebrew was especially important. This was St. Jerome.

What St. Jerome shows us is how the Jews' Manuscripts still hold great value for the Holy Bible, even if the transmission was not guided by the Holy Spirit. Jerome's

---

[51] St. Augustine, *De Civitate Dei*, XVIII.43
[52] St. Cyril of Jerusalem, *Catecheses,* IV.34. Cf. also St. Clement of Alexandria, *Stromateis*, I.22, 149 among others

method in translating the Latin Vulgate helps us understand how.

Very early on the Greek text of the Septuagint and New Testament was translated into Latin. Latin was the other major language of the Roman Empire, used primarily for legal proceedings and such decrees. Thus it holds a vital role for translation and was later canonically affirmed by the Magisterium as we shall see.

But the Latin text as it was translated and circulated contained many discrepancies between manuscripts. In the process of dozens of copiers, differences appeared in the text due to copyist errors or their own commentary added to the text. These versions were known as the *Vetus Latina* or the "Old Latin." In the time of Pope St. Damasus (d. 384), the need was felt to create a standardized version of the Latin text to avoid the discrepancies.

This need illustrates another important aspect of the history of the Holy Bible: even though oral Tradition precedes and governs the written text, and the original text does not exist, there still is a great desire to preserve as much as possible the text as it was originally written. This goes back to the virtue of piety, which particularly causes us to reverence our fathers and their words. Thus by the virtue of piety, we preserve the Tradition of our fathers, both written and oral, from any addition, change or subtraction.

Thus did Pope St. Damasus commission a holy man who was an expert in the Text to translate a standard Latin text for use by the Roman Church. Thus was born the Vulgate of St. Jerome. St. Jerome's methods help us understand the primacy of oral Tradition within the textual Traditions and the methods that the Church approves with regard to textual criticism.

St. Jerome was an expert in Greek and Latin, but he insisted on learning Hebrew and studying the Hebrew texts of his day. Despite the dominance of the Septuagint, Jerome saw great value in the Hebrew text, even when it was transmitted by the Jews. It is important to bear in mind here that the Hebrew texts that Jerome used were over 500 years older than the oldest (complete) Hebrew Masoretic manuscripts we have now. The Hebrew that Jerome used is now lost. Thus whatever errors we may see in the Hebrew we use today may have not have been present at the time of Jerome.

Whatever the case, the Hebrew text assists us in gaining a deeper understanding with the meaning of the Greek and Latin, which is ultimately derived from the Hebrew originals. The most striking example of this greater understanding is in the Holy Name of Jesus as it appears in the Hebrew text.

As you may know the Holy Name of our Lord is a Hebrew word *(yeshua)* which simply means "salvation." Thus most of the times in the Old Testament when the word "salvation" is used this is the Holy Name of Jesus in the original Hebrew text. This comes out in only one passage of St. Jerome's Vulgate, Hab. iii. 18:

> But I will rejoice in the Lord: and I will joy in God my Jesus.
> *Ego autem in Domino gaudebo; et exsultabo in Deo Jesu meo*

In this particular case St. Jerome departs from the Greek Septuagint, which translates *yeshua* into "savior" (σωτῆρί) instead of "Jesus." Here St. Jerome is following the Hebrew text in a place where it accords perfectly with the Greek but using the original language to draw out a deeper meaning in the text. It is remarkable when one considers how often and prominent, then, is the Holy Name of Jesus in the original Hebrew. If we follow St. Jerome in this place and translate Isaias xii in this manner, it renders in English like this:

> I will give thanks to thee, O Lord, for thou wast angry with me: thy wrath is turned away, and thou hast comforted me. Behold, God is my **Jesus**, I will deal confidently, and will not fear: because the Lord is my strength, and my praise, and he is become my **Jesus**. You shall draw waters with joy out of the fountains of **Jesus**: And you shall say in that day: Praise ye the Lord, and call upon his name: make his works known among the people: remember that his name is high. Sing ye to the Lord, for he hath done great things: shew this forth in all the earth. Rejoice, and praise, O thou habitation of Sion: for great is he that is in the midst of thee, the Holy One of Israel.

Thus we see the great value that the Hebrew language can be for the understanding of the Text. When we consider how prominent is the Holy Name, the words of the Apostle become particularly poignant: *even to this day, when Moses is read [to the Jews] there is a veil over their hearts* (II Cor. iii. 15).

But since Jerome used the Hebrew, the Church has always regarded the Hebrew with reverence, although not in the same way as the Greek Septuagint.[53] Jerome translated his standard

---

[53] Virtually all other Church Fathers held that the Septuagint was itself inspired. St. Jerome doubted the extent to which this inspiration covered the text of the Septuagint, and did not translate the deutero-canonical books at all. The Church in her oral tradition and official Magisterial acts, however, accepted the majority view of the Fathers regarding the Septuagint books with all their parts, as accepted by the ordinary and universal Magisterium, then confirmed by the extraordinary Magisterium at Trent (see the next chapter).

Latin version, which became known as the "Vulgate," meaning "common standard." This text then became the version used by the Church for over a thousand years. All the great saints and doctors used this text for their theology and the Church continually used it for her liturgy.

The Importance of Variants

But despite the standardized Latin Vulgate, there still remained a number of texts which were different in the old Latin and other manuscripts. These are known as "variant" texts which include another reading also ancient but in most cases not contained in the majority of manuscripts. The Church, governed as she is by the oral Tradition, accepted and revered many of these variant texts by incorporating them into her liturgy and commentaries. These do not adhere to the Latin Vulgate of Jerome, but nevertheless these variants are held sacred in the Church's liturgy as the *cultus*.

The most prominent example is the Our Father. In the Latin, the version used is the one from St. Matthew's Gospel, but the Latin Vulgate uses a different wording in Latin than in the Liturgy (*quotidianum* vs. *superstantialem*). In the Gloria, the phrase is *Gloria in excelsis Deo*, whereas in the Vulgate it reads *Gloria in altissimis Deo* (Lk. ii. 14). Finally, the Sanctus has *Dominus Deus Sabaoth* (a Hebrew transliteration of the word "armies") whereas the Vulgate has *Dominus, Deus exercituum* (Is. vi. 3). Thus the variants form an integral part of the Tradition which testify to the governing authority of oral Tradition together with the written Tradition with piety toward the *cultus*.

On the one hand, the variants can be considered as a possible original text. They may also be the earliest commentaries on the text. For example in the Greek text of the

Our Father in the Gospel of St. Luke, there exists a variant Greek text which reads like this:

> *Our Father*
> *Hallowed be Thy Name*
> ***Let Thy Holy Spirit come upon us and sanctify us***
> *Thy will be done on earth as it is in heaven*
> *Give us this day...*

This identification of the Kingdom with the Holy Spirit points to the oral Tradition understanding that the Kingdom of God is the Holy Spirit.

Another important variant is Ps. xcv. 10:

> Say ye among the Gentiles, the Lord hath reigned **from the tree**.

This "from the tree" is an important variant which appears in some old Greek manuscripts, the Coptic Psalter and the Old Latin. It appears in the Traditional Roman liturgy and also in the office hymn *Vexilla Regis* which makes mention of it in this way:

> Fulfilled is all that David told
> In true prophetic song of old
> Amidst the nations, God, saith he
> Hath reigned and triumphed from the tree

This variant, although not a part of the official Latin Vulgate, is nonetheless accepted by the Church by the authority of her oral Tradition guiding the Church and governing the use of the canon of Scripture.

Thus the virtue of piety causes the Church to produce the best possible text of the Scriptures, and yet does not refrain from using other variants which have been sanctioned by continuous use. The texts contained in the *cultus* receive the same piety as the Word of God, since the *cultus* is a manifestation of the oral Tradition. Dom Benedict puts it this way:

> Ultimately, it matters very little, according to the church's spiritual vision, where particular constructions came from, and whether or not they are, critically speaking, the "best" readings. Liturgists and theologians simply do not have the authority to suppress elements of the liturgy that they find strange or unsettling or hard to understand. The words *Regnavit a ligno Deus* [God hath reigned from the tree] have become sacred and authoritative by virtue of their venerable liturgical use, their very adoption in the perennial Tradition of the Latin Church, and they are, in a non-technical but in a nonetheless authentic theological sense, the words "that David told, in true prophetic song of old."[54]

Thus the historical textual criticism of Jerome has always been held by the Church with the oral Tradition as guide. Since oral Tradition is the chronologically prior, the text of the Holy Scriptures need not adhere exactly with the *cultus* and vice versa, especially in places where the precise reading of the approximate original text is obscure.

---

[54] Benedict Maria Anderson, O.S.B., "'Fulfilled is All that David Told': Recovering the Christian Psalter," *Sacred Music* (Winter 2017: Vol. 144 No. 4), 22

A proper humility allows the Magisterium to revere the Sacred Tradition of our fathers, whether oral or written, and pass it down unchanged to subsequent generations. The history of this transmission is understood to be guided and sanctioned by the Holy Spirit and our Lord Himself since He left His teaching to us first in oral form. The saints were those who prayed and came to know God within this Christian culture, founded in charity and piety. They devoutly read the Scriptures and religiously held to the Tradition of the Holy Fathers. This was the understanding of what a true theologian was. But in time, a new idea about theologians would arise and challenge the whole culture, shattering society and tearing apart the Church.

VIII

THE RISE OF THE "THEOLOGIANS" AND THE PROTESTANT REVOLT

The relationship we have discussed between *cultus*, oral Tradition, Scripture and the Magisterium was a constant from the oral discourses of our Lord until the Protestant revolt.[55] First came the period of the Seven Ecumenical Councils when the doctrines of Christ and the Trinity were explained. The Church worked to convert the western pagans to the faith while the Church grew, reaching a climax in the 13th century.[56]

This century witnessed St. Thomas Aquinas, St. Bonaventure, St. Anthony of Padua and other great saints. During this time the Magisterium worked to expound the Deposit in an ever clearer way and saints and doctors defended the faith and preachers converted thousands. These days were not without evils—far from it—but the Sacred Tradition was the one universal constant, creating a growing culture of Christendom.

---

[55] Among the Greek schismatics, this relationship was also present although to a lesser degree, owing to their lack of a unified Magisterium.
[56] We are passing over the complex history of the eastern schisms for the sake of brevity. Nevertheless the basic elements of Christian culture we have discussed here existed among them, save the Magisterium.

The saints exemplified that very important truth about Biblical studies before the Protestant revolt: that a true theologian is a man who prays. At the time of St. Thomas there existed a burgeoning system of universities across Europe which taught the faith. Yet even in the 13th century, intellect alone was not the final measure of authority. As the life of St. Thomas shows, although he was perhaps the greatest intellect the Church has ever know, when he experienced God, he said famously said about his writings at the end of his life "All that I have written, is mere straw."[57]

The men of this age indeed had great learning, but the Church understood that it was really their sanctity that brought their studies true fruit. Their humility to Holy Mother Church and their piety for the Fathers made them great, not primarily their intellectual knowledge. We see particularly in St. Thomas the height of intellect with the height of sanctity, perfectly manifesting the science of the saints.

Thus we may conclude from the first 1300 years of Christianity that the intellectual life was dominated by saints. These were the men whose words carried weight and authority: Augustine, Isidore, Anselm, Aquinas—all men of fantastic intellect, but more importantly extraordinary humility.

At the very least, if a man did not perform miracles or have ecstatic visions, if he had humility and piety with great learning, this man was acceptable as an authoritative voice on doctrine. We may then say that the minimum requirement for theology was humility before the authority of the Church and the oral Tradition. We might say that such a man would be at least held to be a "scholar." Tertullian was once a scholar, but then he died a heretic. Boethius did not achieve great sanctity

---

[57] Conversation with Brother Reginald

in this life, but still, because he was a true scholar, his writings held weight.[58] St. John Cassian too, though his sanctity was barely venerated in the west, was accepted for his true scholarship.[59] This would begin to change around the year 1300.

The Birth of the "Theologian"

In the fourteenth century the Church experienced a period of decline. The papacy was dominated and fought over by the French and other powers, the Hundred Years War spilled fratricidal blood, and the Black death killed tens of thousands.

But the intellectual life also experienced a decline. It was here when a crucial change happened in the history of the Church which would eventually lead to disaster.

Kings and governments had always sought to increase their power, but in the fourteenth century they found a new way to do that. Since the pope was supreme in religious matters, kings ultimately had a check on their power through the pope. Through the pope the kings were bound to the oral and written Christian Tradition.

But in the fourteenth century, the kings found a new way to circumvent the power of the pope and increase their power: create a new definition of "theologian." Instead of a man who prays, a theologian would now be defined as simply a man

---

[58] The Roman Martyrology in fact does hold Boethius as a martyr, although his cult is very limited.
[59] St. John Cassian sided with St. Vincent of Lerins in rejecting the terminology used by St. Augustine in the Pelagian controversy, and thus his cult never gained momentum in the west as it did in the east. Nevertheless his *Conferences* and *Institutes* formed the basis for St. Benedict's rule, and were considered authorities by great saints such as St. Dominic and St. Thomas.

who studies. Sanctity and learning would be separated, and only the latter would be authoritative. Prayer and humility would no longer be a factor. This was always true for heretics, but in this new understanding of theologian this separation comes into the mainstream by the intervention of governments.[60]

This began to gain prominence particularly during a controversy involving the emperor-elect Ludwig of Bavaria (d. 1347). His election was contested by Frederick I of Austira. Pope John XXII adjudicated the dispute, but Ludwig refused to cooperate with the Magisterium. Instead, he turned to a few smart men to help justify his defiance of Church authority. These men helped him make a religious justification to disobey the Church. These men were his new theologians.

These men were Marsilius of Padua (d. 1342) and William of Ockham (d. 1347). They interpreted the Scriptures apart from the Magisterium and the oral Tradition. They asserted that the theologian could interpret the Holy Bible himself, without the Magisterium or the Tradition. Kings and princes soon made use of these ideas and promoted them. By using these new theologians, the king could then gain more power by defying the pope on religious grounds. And so they brought the role of theologians into the mainstream.

Other important movements also arose under John Wycliffe (d. 1384) and Jan Hus (d. 1415). Both of these men also claimed themselves to be theologians by asserting their own authority to interpret the Holy Bible without humility or

---

[60] The narrative given here is largely based on Scott Hahn and Benjamin Wiker, *Politicizing the Bible: The Roots of Historical Criticism and the Secularization of Scripture 1300-1700* (Herder & Herder: 2013); Jeffrey L. Morrow *Pretensions of Objectivity: Toward a Criticism of Biblical Criticism* (Pickwick: 2019). See Morrow's lecture "Deconstructing the Bible" from *Institute of Catholic Culture*.

sanctity. They rejected the fundamental authority of the oral Tradition and Wycliffe even began to make his own translation of the Holy Bible in order to justify his heresies.

But they did not work well with the political powers of the time, and thus their movements did not become a stable movement. Both of these men were declared heretics by the Council of Constance in 1415. Nevertheless, their legacy continued a shift into the 15th century of separating learning from sanctity, and thinking that intellectual knowledge is the only thing necessary for understanding the Holy Bible. This idea would have disastrous consequences.

Renaissance Humanism

In the 15th century a new movement arose which began to make this idea spread faster. This was known as Humanism. It was a flowering of linguistic and cultural knowledge as a part of what would be known as the Renaissance. Many Greeks were fleeing the attacks of the Muhammadans in the east and settled in the west, bringing their Greek language and texts to the west. Around 1450 the printing press was invented, and new knowledge was suddenly able to be mass produced. The Church was never opposed to the Renaissance in principle, and was in favor of using new knowledge and technology to spread and defend the faith. This marks the turning point, as we have said, from oral culture to literate culture.

One of the aspects of this cultural movement was the idea of *ad fontes* meaning "back to the sources." What this meant was a desire of Catholic thinkers of this time to regain some of the ancient knowledge from the early Church period in order to renew the faith in a good way. This was in effect the same thing that Jerome had done when he used the Greek and Hebrew texts to form the Vulgate.

As early as 1311 Pope Clement V had decreed that Hebrew be taught at Universities.[61] However it was not until the Renaissance—in 1506—that a comprehensive Hebrew grammar was published by the Catholic Johann Reuchlin (d. 1522). Knowledge of Greek was renewed as well, but we will return to that in a moment.

But unfortunately during this period as well, there was a great amount of corruption in the Vatican, and not a few popes led immoral lives with mistresses and led armies to conquer Italy like any secular ruler. What is worse, the Black Death had killed many of the good priests. Many of the surviving priests were those who had fled the plague instead of caring for victims, creating a general and pervasive corruption among the clergy. What exacerbated this even further was the fact that many in the clergy were very uneducated and did not even understand the Latin of the Mass.[62]

Many Catholics were critical of the hierarchy at this time of corruption but wanted to use the new knowledge to benefit the faith. The most famous of these men was Desiderius Erasmus. Using the new availability of Greek, he published his Greek New Testament in 1516. This was a very significant moment in the history of western Biblical knowledge, as it was the first time that the original language of the New Testament could be accessed and studied in the areas of western Europe since Jerome in the 5th century.

Erasmus was greatly criticized, however, by his fellow Catholics for his strong opinions about Vatican corruption. This goes back to what we discussed about public rebukes and the state of emergency in the last chapter.

---

[61] New Catholic Encyclopedia, "Hebrew Studies."
[62] At this time there was not a standardized system of seminaries and most priests were simply apprenticed.

In the spring of 1517, the Church closed the Fifth Lateran Council, which was an Ecumenical Council seeking to bring about a renewal in the Church and cleanse all of the corruption. At this council a pious laymen, Gianfrancesco Pico della Mirandola, delivered a passionate rebuke to the pope and the bishops, exhorting them to cleanse the Church of corruption of faith and morals or receive the wrath of God.[63] Erasmus' method may not have been as prudent or as pious: he openly mocked the pope and bishops in his work *In Praise of Folly*, showing their hypocrisy and sin. Thus later Catholics pointed to Erasmus' lack of piety in his words which provoked more anger instead of spreading true reform.

Martin Luther Becomes a "Theologian"

In the same year the Lateran Council closed, Martin Luther nailed his infamous 95 Theses and sparked the whole revolt. Martin Luther was an extremely intelligent Catholic priest with a bitter temper and lust for women. He had a demonic talent for writing things that set entire countries ablaze with violent rage, while quietly exonerating his own sins of fornication by his heresy of justification by faith alone. His doctrine taught that free will did not exist. In effect, God forced him to commit sins, or forced him to do good—it was not his fault.[64]

More poisonous even than Luther's temper, sins or even his heresy were his methods of using the Holy Bible. Luther is the one who truly solidified the power of the theologian, like

---

[63] Klemens Löffler, "Pope Leo X." The Catholic Encyclopedia (1910) Vol. 9.
[64] On Luther's errors influencing his personal sins, see E. Michael Jones, *Degenerate Moderns: Modernity as Rationalized Sexual Misbehavior* (Ignatius: 1993), 235ff

Ockham and Wycliffe before him. Luther and the Protestant heretics used the movement of *ad fontes* (in itself good) to justify their rejection of the uneducated clergy. Against the Magisterium and the oral Tradition of the Fathers, Luther asserted that his opinion about the Holy Bible was the only one that was correct. He wrote: "I am unwilling to submit the matter to anyone's judgment, but advise everyone to yield assent."[65]

But because Luther had strengthened the error that intellectual learning alone was necessary for the Holy Bible, the number of "theologians" with ideas of their own only multiplied. Almost overnight large areas of Europe were being led by revolutionary theologians who asserted that they knew what the Scriptures said more than anyone else. All of these theologians disagreed with each other.

The heretics hoped that Erasmus would side with them and not act like a saint, but like the new theologian. Pope Leo X approved of Erasmus' New Testament in 1519, and then excommunicated Luther in 1521. After Luther had become a definite heretic and been excommunicated, there was some question of whether Erasmus would join him. Erasmus seemed to hesitate, but two successive popes asked Erasmus to write against Luther.

In the end, Erasmus showed himself a son of the Church and duly wrote against Luther's central error: the denial of free will. Luther responded with his characteristic rancor. In his final work against Luther, Erasmus showed himself to have refused the new office of theologian in favor of humility and sanctity:

---

[65] Luther, *On the Bondage of the Will* from Rupp, E. Gordon and Philip S. Watson eds. *Luther and Erasmus: Free Will and Salvation* (Westminster Press, 1969), 334

> We are dealing with this: would a stable mind depart from the opinion handed down by so many men famous for holiness and miracles, depart from the decisions of the Church, and commit our souls to the faith of someone like you [Luther] who has sprung up just now with a few followers, although the leading men of your flock do not agree either with you or among themselves?[66]

Indeed, this is that "sound mind" with which St. Anthony disputed with the philosophers of his day. Erasmus was encountering the same thing in Luther and the other heretics. When Luther publicly broke his vows of chastity with a woman who did the same, and all the "reformers" followed him, Erasmus declare that the whole "reformation" amounted to a comedy.[67] Erasmus died a Catholic in 1536. But his use of Greek was quickly used by the Protestant heretics to try to circumvent the authority of the oral Tradition and the Magisterium.

The kings and princes saw an opportunity to gain political power against the pope, so they enthusiastically supported the "reformers." Enough of these new theologians were starting their own movements so that the kings and princes could use them for their ambitions.

Because of the widespread idea that returning to earlier sources was more accurate, the Protestant heretics were able

---

[66] Erasmus, "Hyperaspistes," *Collected Works of Erasmus, Controversies: De Libero Arbitrio / Hyperaspistes I*, Translated by Peter Macardle and Clarence H. Miller. Edited by Charles Trinkhaus (University of Toronto Press: 1999), 76, 203

[67] William Marshner, "Protestant Revolution," *Institute for Catholic Culture*. A comedy was an ancient Greek play in which everyone got married in the final scene.

to convince the masses that by ignoring oral Tradition, they could be renewing an earlier, more correct form of Christianity. This denied the governance of the Holy Spirit for a thousand years in using the Latin Vulgate and its variants with the oral Tradition as guide. It denied the authority of the Magisterium established since the book of Acts. It asserted that intellectual knowledge alone was enough to understand the Scriptures. Thus began the multiplication of Bible versions to which we now turn.

Luther's Bible Supports His Errors

Luther, as the first great new theologian in a long line of so-called theologians who would come after, immediately set to work making the Scriptures justify his errors. Luther was a disciple of Ockham, who had used his "theology" to help gain power against the pope. Luther's political ally was Prince Philip of Hesse. This allowed the prince to gain political power against the pope, while Luther gained a protector against his enemies.

Luther published the New Testament in 1522 and his full bible in 1534. This was the first full translation into German. But because Luther had turned to heresy and rejected the Church, he refused to use the Latin Vulgate as his guide but went straight to the Greek texts. In addition, he used the Masoretic Hebrew in order to circumvent the Latin. In his mind, he was just going back to the original sources, but in reality he was imposing his views on the Christian Tradition (we will discuss why this is in detail in the next chapter).

We see that Luther was a heretic when he could not find his doctrine "faith alone" in the text of the Holy Bible. So he decided to add the word "alone" (*allein*) to the text of Romans

III. 28. Here is the text in English, Greek and Latin, with brackets showing that there is no word "alone" in the text:

For we account a man to be justified by faith [ ], without the works of the law.

Arbitramur enim justificari hominem per fidem [ ] sine operibus legis.

λογιζόμεθα γὰρ δικαιοῦσθαι πίστει [ ] ἄνθρωπον χωρὶς ἔργων νόμου.

Here is the text from Luther's Bible with the word added in brackets:

So halten wir nun dafür, daß der Mensch gerecht werde ohne des Gesetzes Werke, [allein] durch den Glauben.

Now the phrase "faith alone" did not begin with Luther, but his understanding of faith alone was his own invention (we will cover this in chapter 13). It made St. Paul contradict St. James, and this is what made his choice in Romans problematic.

Later, he also removed certain books from the Old Testament which the Church had previously received as inspired, since they did not appear in the Jews' Old Testament. These books were known as "deutero-canonical" (Tobit, Maccabees, etc.) and were held in the Septuagint and by oral Tradition to be inspired along with the other books of the Old Testament. Thus instead of accepting the authority of the Fathers and the oral Tradition by the Holy Spirit, Luther became his own authority to impose his will on the Text.

Further, he considered the epistle of James to be especially bothersome to him. He said the epistle was an "epistle of straw" which had "nothing of the Gospel in it" and so he said "I will not have him in my bible."[68] It was the only time that the phrase "faith alone" appeared in the Sacred Text, but the verse says: *not faith alone* (Ja. ii. 24).

As I hope you can see here, Luther's abuse of the Sacred Scriptures was anything but humble. He was no saint, but merely a "theologian." This was the danger that the Church had already seen with letting anyone tamper with the Sacred Text. Luther wanted to impose his heresy onto the Word of God instead of allowing the Text and the Tradition to teach him. He did not read the Holy Word humbly as the saints did, but in defiance against the whole history of Christianity. This is the attitude of Protestant heretics unfortunately, who claim to follow the Holy Bible (see chapter 13 for more information).

Henry VIII and the Heretical "Anglicans"

As Luther was continuing to press his revolution in Germany, Henry VIII broke away from the Church and made himself head of his own "Anglican" Church. This was due to the fact that the Pope would not grant a declaration of nullity to his marriage, and Henry wanted to divorce his wife and remarry. His advisors wanted to take the land and riches of the Church and gain political power like Luther's Prince had done. They were strongly influenced by theologian precursors like Ockham and Wycliff. This split happened around 1534. St. Thomas More and St. John Fisher were among the few English

---

[68] Luther, *Preface to James and Jude* in *D. Martin Luthers Werke: Deutsche Bibel* (Weimar, 1906–1961), 6, 10, 33-34; 7,386, 17. Luther was not always consistent, however, as he was on other matters.

Catholic leaders who resisted and became martyrs. Eventually England adopted many of the Protestant heresies.

The English heretics endeavored to impose their heresy by creating their own Bible translation like Luther. The first version of this was the Great Bible, published shortly after Luther's in 1539. This and subsequent versions were being translated against the authority of the Church and the oral Tradition, consulting Greek, Hebrew or Latin in whatever way they pleased. This was the power of the new theologian.

Shortly thereafter, the Council of Trent, around the year 1545 dogmatically confirmed the the oral Tradition and the Latin Vulgate as the standard text of the Holy Bible:

> The sacred and holy, ecumenical, and general Synod of Trent... keeping this always in view, that, errors being removed, the purity itself of the Gospel be preserved in the Church; which [Gospel], before promised through the prophets in the holy Scriptures, our Lord Jesus Christ, the Son of God, first promulgated *with His own mouth*, and then commanded to be preached by His Apostles to every creature, as the fountain of all, both saving truth, and moral discipline; and seeing clearly that this truth and discipline are contained in the written books, and the unwritten traditions which, received by the Apostles from the mouth of Christ himself, or from the Apostles themselves, the Holy Ghost dictating, have come down even unto us, transmitted as it were from hand to hand.
>
> [The Synod,] following the examples of the orthodox Fathers, receives and venerates with *an equal affection of piety and reverence*, all the books both of the Old and of the New Testament—seeing

> that one God is the author of both—*as also the said traditions*, as well those appertaining to faith as to morals, as having been dictated, either by Christ's own *word of mouth*, or by the Holy Ghost, and preserved in the Catholic Church by a continuous succession.
>
> ...If anyone does not accept as sacred and canonical the aforesaid books in their entirety and with all their parts, *as they have been accustomed to be read in the Catholic Church* and as they are contained in the old Latin Vulgate Edition, and knowingly and deliberately rejects the aforesaid Traditions, *let him be anathema*.[69]

Thus the Church confirmed that our Lord did not write His doctrine down but gave it first in oral form and the Holy Ghost guided both the oral Tradition and that which was written down. Notice too the *cultus*, which is the manifestation of the oral Tradition becomes the arbiter of the Scriptures by the phrase "as they have been accustomed to be read." Thus like St. Basil in the 4th century, Trent also proclaimed that both sources of revelation receive "an equal affection of piety and reverence."

The reason for this anathema on the Vulgate is simple, based on the things we have already said: the Holy Spirit guided the oral Tradition and the Church to use the Vulgate for so many centuries. Therefore if the Vulgate is in error, then the Holy Spirit is in error. Thus the virtue of piety again caused the Church to reverence the governance of history by the Holy Ghost. The oral and written Traditions which centered on the Vulgate for a thousand years had been guided by the

---

[69] 4th session, Council of Trent. Emphasis mine

Magisterium and thus it could not be said that God permitted such a grievous error as the Holy Bible to be substantially flawed.

The Council of Trent continued to meet and condemn Protestant heresies until 1563, but the matter of the canon and the authoritative version of Scripture had been closed. The Council mandated that a new revision should be completed, to correct any discrepancies in the Vulgate copies as they existed at that time. It also sent a commission to the pope to create a Greek edition as well as a Hebrew edition, but this effort was never realized.[70]

Meanwhile, English Catholics were exiled from the British Isles and took refuge in Catholic territories on the continent. They founded a seminary at Douai, France in 1561 to train priests to send back to the Protestants and minister to the secret Catholics there. About one third of these seminarians were executed by the English Protestants when they went back to England. Following Jerome and Trent, they utilized the Vulgate as the standard but also utilized the Greek and Hebrew as well. They completed an English translation of the New Testament in 1582 which was published in Reims, France.

The Clementine Vulgate and the Roman Missal

Shortly after this, a new edition of the Vulgate was published by order of the Council of Trent in 1590 (Sistine Vulgate) but this edition was quickly corrected in a second edition in 1592 (Clementine Vulgate). Thus the original Douay Rheims New Testament was not based on the official Vulgate, which was published ten of years later.

---

[70] Pius XII, *Divino Afflante Spiritu* (1943), 20

In addition, a number of printing presses had begun to check the new Vulgate edition with the current Roman Missal and discovered discrepancies there. This was due to the fact that much of the Roman Missal even in the time of Jerome was based on the Old Latin as we have pointed out in chapter 7. The new printers proceeded to edit the Roman Missal to conform these things to the new Vulgate. Imagine changing the Sanctus to *Sanctus Deus exercituum*. But this was what the popular movement of *ad fontes* thought at the time. Men thought that this would be more accurate or pure. But this idea challenged the authority of the oral Tradition and the *cultus*.

In response, in 1604, Pope Clement VIII issued a decree *Cum Sanctissimum* in which he lamented this action taken in the name of the "original text."

> Although [my predecessor, Pius V] very severely forbade under many penalties that anything should be added to [the Missal], or that anything for any reason be removed from it, nevertheless, in the course of time, it has come to pass that, through the rashness and boldness of the printers, or of others, many errors have crept into the missals which have been produced in recent years.
>
> That very old (Latin) version of the Holy Bible, which even before St. Jerome's time was held in honor in the Church, and from which almost all the Introits, Graduals, and Offertories of the Masses had been taken, has been entirely removed; the texts of the Epistles and Gospels, which hitherto were read during the celebration of the Mass, have been disturbed in many places; different and utterly unusual beginnings have been prefixed to the Gospel texts; and finally many things have been

here and there arbitrarily altered. All these changes seem to have been introduced under the pretext of conforming everything to the standard of the Vulgate edition of Holy Writ.

Pope Clement then proceeded to recall all of the missals that had been altered in conformity with his new Vulgate and decreed that they be "be banned and declared null and void" and that if anyone "dare" to continue printing the altered missal, they would "incur excommunication *latae sententiae* [automatic] from which, save on the point of death, they may not be absolved except by the Roman Pontiff."

This bull perfectly illustrates the relationship of authority we have been discussing. The authority of the oral Tradition is so strong together with the piety toward the *cultus* which manifests it, that even if a more perfect "original text" of the Holy Bible is published (as Pope Clement VIII himself had done in 1592), the Church *will not* change the liturgy as a matter of grave piety to the Fathers.

The oral Tradition is what governs both the liturgy and the text of the Holy Bible. The Magisterium religiously guards both without any alteration. But because oral Tradition governs the authority of the text itself, the Church has always allowed these variants in the text in the liturgy and the Holy Bible. The variants are manifestations of one oral Tradition and find inspiration through the usage over time, just as the Vulgate version was confirmed as the authoritative version at Trent. All are centered on the *cultus* manifesting the sacred presence of God Himself and the worship of the Church.

The Douay-Rheims and the King James Version

A few years after this, the English Catholics in exile completed their full translation of the Holy Bible in 1610 published by Douai University. Together with the Rheims New Testament earlier published, this became the first complete English Catholic Bible and took the name Douay-Rheims (DR). Again, this English did not conform in all places exactly with the Clementine Vulgate since the New Testament in particular predates this Vulgate's publication. Still, this version adhered to the Vulgate on the whole as the authorized text while utilizing the Hebrew and Greek texts as well.

At the same time, the Protestants were working on their most influential Bible project yet. This was finally completed in 1611 and became known as the King James Bible (KJV). In the preface to this Bible the Protestants admitted that the early Church used the Septuagint as the standard, but the KJV instead used the Hebrew Masoretic in order to circumvent the authority of the Church, continuing, as they supposed, to go back to the original text.

This English bible, because of its influence in England, became the standard which shaped the development of the English language more than any other text. This is why the language of this bible is considered "beautiful" today: it held the cultural influence to form English culture even to our modern day.

Meanwhile, the Douay-Rheims version, being illegal for centuries, was never able to have the same cultural impact that the KJV had. Because of this, by the 18th century the English language had been shaped so much by the King James that the Douay-Rheims was extremely difficult for the average English Catholic to read. For this reason Servant of God Bishop Challoner made a significant revision of the Douay-Rheims in order make the English more readable. This happened around the year 1750. This Challoner revision was approved and accepted by the Church and this is the version that is read today as the Douay Rheims version.

Thus by the 19th century, there were generally two versions of the Holy Bible in English: the Catholic Douay Rheims and the heretical King James Version. This is the origin of the two English Bibles. In the 19th century a movement would arise which would have an even greater impact than the Protestant revolt in changing the way men looked upon the Text. But we will return to this below.

IX

HOW "THEOLOGIANS" USED TRANSLATIONS TO PROMOTE THEIR HERESIES

Before we discuss what happened in the nineteenth century we need to pause and see how the heretics used the original languages in order to circumvent the original meaning of the Text. The key here is the use of the Latin Vulgate.

As we have already seen the Latin Vulgate is not the original text but it is understood by the Church to be the closest representation of the original text and also the oral Tradition, since it has been sanctified by the use of time. Nevertheless variants are also not rejected, since they have been sanctioned in the *cultus* and also manifest the oral Tradition and other possible readings of the original text. Above all, the oral Tradition precedes, governs and guides the transmission of the written text.

Besides these things, there are a few reasons why the Latin Vulgate is so important. The first is that the Latin represents the original interpretation of the Greek and Hebrew Text. What does this mean? Every translation is an interpretation. A single word in Greek can have many different definitions. When a translator picks a Latin word to translate a Greek word, he interprets what particular meaning is most important about that word. This becomes extremely important when the heretics began to create their own bibles by translation. Because they were translating straight from the Greek or Hebrew, they claimed to represent the original meaning of the text. In reality, they were imposing their 16th century meaning onto the Ancient Text. By consulting the ancient Latin, we can know better how the early Church understood the Greek Text of the New Testament. This also applies to the Old Testament with the Septuagint, but we will cover this in a later chapter.

Translation Examples: Presbyteros

A salient example of this is the Greek word *presbyteros*. Recall that in the oral culture it is the elders who are guardians of the Tradition and who guard it and pass it down to the next generation. The word *presbyteros* in Greek means elder, as in someone who is older or in a position of authority. However, the Latin did not translate every occurrence of presbyteros as "elder" (*senior*) but often it was translated as *presbyterus*. In other words, they kept the Greek word intact and did not translate it into Latin. What does this indicate? It indicates that the term *prebyteros* did not just mean "elder" in a general sense, as in "my brother is *presbyteros* to me." Rather, it indicates a specific office within the Church with a special name. Thus the correct meaning of the Greek word in these instances, as understood by the early Church, is "presbyter" or "priest."

One of the dogmas which the Protestant heretics attacked was the doctrine of the priesthood. The Anglican heretics had "priests" to some extent but they quickly changed their ordination rites under Edward VI (d. 1553) and these were later definitively decreed as invalid by Leo XIII (*Apostolicae Curae*, 1896).

Because the overall Protestant heresy denied the Sacrament of Orders, they reflected this in their translations. They did not consult the Latin, which would have shown them that *prebyteros* was a special word with a specific meaning. Instead, in the vanity of their minds they thought that they could translate it according to the "original text." In their pride, they thought they knew better than the ancient Latin translators like St. Jerome, who lived within generations of the Apostles. In reality, they were imposing their heresy onto the text.

One of the most prominent examples of this is the epistle to Titus. The context is the Apostle St. Paul instructing St. Titus, the bishop of Crete, to ordain priests. He writes in verse five:

> For this cause I left thee in Crete: that thou shouldest set in order the things that are wanting and shouldest ordain **priests** in every city, as I also appointed thee (i. 5)

> Τούτου χάριν ἀπέλιπόν σε ἐν Κρήτῃ, ἵνα τὰ λείποντα ἐπιδιορθώσῃ καὶ καταστήσῃς κατὰ πόλιν **πρεσβυτέρους**, ὡς ἐγώ σοι διεταξάμην

> Hujus rei gratia reliqui te Cretæ, ut ea quæ desunt, corrigas, et constituas per civitates **presbyteros**, sicut et ego disposui tibi

Notice the word "presbyteros" is translating the Greek word, which the DR simply renders "priests."[71] The English also uses the word "ordain."

How did the heretics translate this verse since they were ignoring the Latin and using only the original language? The King James Version translates it this way:

> For this cause left I thee in Crete, that thou shouldest set in order the things that are wanting, and ordain **elders** in every city, as I had appointed thee.

Notice how presbyteros is simply an "elder" and not a priest. Later English translations would later obscure the word "ordain" to be "appoint," further twisting this passage to hide its reference to a bishop ordaining priests. Because of this type of mistranslation, numerous Protestant sects are led to this day by what they call "elders," basing their church government on these types of errors.

Thus the Latin shows us the meaning given to the Greek by the early Church. Besides Greek, the Latin tongue formed the universal language of the Roman Empire, and thus more than any other translation shows us the most universal understanding given to the Greek New Testament from the earliest times.

Acts XVI. 4

Another interesting example is Acts XVI. 4. Recall in chapter 7 we discussed how in the book of Acts the Magisterium first made a decision to abrogate the Mosaic law

---

[71] Note: Greek and Latin both change the endings of these words from "-us" to "-os" in different ways.

for Gentiles and bound the whole Church to this as a law. After this decision, according to the text, they decreed these decisions as dogma and canonically bound the entire Church to obey them. This verse in Acts says this explicitly:

> And as they passed through the cities, they **delivered** unto them the **decrees** for to **keep**, that were **decreed** by the apostles and ancients who were at Jerusalem.

> Ὡς δὲ διεπορεύοντο τὰς πόλεις, **παρεδίδοσαν** αὐτοῖς **φυλάσσειν** τὰ **δόγματα** τὰ **κεκριμένα** ὑπὸ τῶν ἀποστόλων καὶ πρεσβυτέρων τῶν ἐν Ἱεροσολύμοις.

> Cum autem pertransirent civitates, **tradebant** eis **custodiri dogmata** quæ erant **decreta** ab Apostolis et senioribus qui erant Jerosolymis.

A few observations here. First, the Latin text reads both "elders" (*senioribus*) and "priests" (*presbyteris*). There is a minority variant reading which is translated in the Vulgate as "ancients" yet a strong manuscript Tradition also holds "priests" as well.[72] Thus it is unclear in this case if the Text meant elders or priests in particular, but the oral Tradition resolves this question, confirming the existence of priests.

Now consider these key words:

> "Delivered" (παρεδίδοσαν) this term is the same as Tradition, but it is the verb form which

---

[72] According to *Novum Testamentum Graece et Latina* (Nestle-Aland ed. 27), *presbyteris* is the correct Latin.

does not have an English equivalent. It means literally "they traditioned to them." Since this cannot be rendered into English, it remains hidden in the English translation.

"Dogma" (δόγματα) and "decreed" (κεκριμένα). These two words were known at the time to be used as Roman legal terms when a binding law was decreed by the governing authority to make the citizens obey. Here we see the juridical authority of the Apostles and priests, pointing to a binding authority given by the Lord to the Magisterium. Thus the final word:

"To keep" (φυλάσσειν). This refers to the obedience rendered to the force of law given with binding force. An earlier Latin variant in verse XV. 41 which shows up in the Vulgate (and the DR) confirms the binding force of this law: *commanding them to keep the precepts of the apostles and the ancients.*

Thus the Vulgate and DR keep the binding force of this text through the Latin understanding of the original Greek. As we discussed above, the Magisterium claimed for itself the authority of the New Lawgiver to bind the whole Church to dogmatic decrees.

Notice what is changed in the KJV:

And as they went through the cities, they delivered them the decrees for to keep, that were **ordained** of the apostles and elders which were at Jerusalem.

Decrees are kept, but their binding force is decreased by the word "ordain" instead of decree. Notice how the KJV uses the word "ordain" as it did with Titus, even though these are different Greek words. A governing authority which intends to bind their subjects to a law does not "ordain" a law but "decrees" a law. Later Protestant translations would soften this further by changing "decreed" to "decisions." Here we have another example of the Latin showing the normative meaning for the early Church. When translators go directly to the sources without consulting Latin, they impose—consciously or unconsciously—their own interpretation on the text.

"Full of Grace"

Perhaps the most salient example of the heretics mistranslations is Luke I. 28. In this verse the Archangel Gabriel greets our Lady with these famous words:

> Hail, full of grace, the Lord is with thee: blessed art thou among women.

> χαῖρε, **κεχαριτωμένη**, ὁ κύριος μετὰ σοῦ.

> Ave **gratia plena**: Dominus tecum:

First, the DR follows a Latin and Greek variant which includes the *blessed art thou among women*. The presence of this variant in the manuscripts indicates Apostolic origins for Marian veneration. But here the Greek has the word (translated literally) "Hail, one who has been perfected in grace" (κεχαριτωμένη). All of the Latin translators rendered this as *gratia plena*, "full of grace." *There is no variant of this text in all the Latin manuscripts.* This indicates a very ancient understanding as to the meaning of this word. From this single word comes forth a multitude of devotion to and doctrine about our Lady from the very beginning of the Church.

The Protestant heretics of course, because of their pride, hated our Lady, and wished to dethrone her from her royal throne as Queen of heaven and earth. Therefore their translations from the beginning attacked this verse. Here is the King James Version:

> Hail, thou that art highly favoured, the Lord is with thee.

The singular grace given to our Lady is immediately diminished significantly to be simply "highly favored." Again, ignoring what the early Latin understood this to mean, the Protestants in their pride considered their rendering to be more accurate. But they were imposing their heresies on the Text.

Christ in the Old Testament

Finally, we will show one more example: Christ in the Old Testament. Just as we saw with the Holy Name of Jesus, the title of our Lord, "Christ," is also in the Old Testament. The word "Christ" is derived from the Greek word *Christos* which translates the Hebrew *Meshiach*, meaning "Anointed One" or "King." But because "Christ" is a title given to our Lord it gains great significance in the Old Testament.

A particular verse which bears this out is the song of Anna in I Kings I. 1-10. This song is the *typos* of the Magnificat sung by our Lady in Luke I. 46-55. But in Anna's song we see a particular verse which has strong typology for the coming of Jesus Christ in verse 10:

> The Lord shall judge the ends of the earth, and he shall give empire to his king, and shall exalt the horn of his **Christ**.
>
> *Yarem YHVH yadin apse ares weyiten oz lemalkow wayarem qeren* **Meshiaw**
>
> κύριος ἀνέβη εἰς οὐρανοὺς καὶ ἐβρόντησεν αὐτὸς κρινεῖ ἄκρα γῆς καὶ δίδωσιν ἰσχὺν τοῖς βασιλεῦσιν ἡμῶν καὶ ὑψώσει κέρας **χριστοῦ** αὐτοῦ
>
> Dominus judicabit fines terræ, et dabit imperium regi suo, et sublimabit cornu **christi** sui

Here is a clear reference to Christ and His universal dominion over the whole earth. Thus does the Greek have *Christou* which is preserved in the Latin as *Christi*. Thus did the early Church understand these Old Testament references to Jesus Christ.

But what does the King James Version do to this verse? Again, ignoring the Latin, they think they can be more accurate by translating the "original text."

> The Lord shall judge the ends of the earth; and he shall give strength unto his king, and exalt the horn of his **anointed**.

Thus the King James Version, in its efforts to reflect what they think is the original text, inadvertently ends up diminishing the

Christological significance of this verse and obscuring for the English reader its typology.

Thus in a few examples as we have seen, there is a subtle shift that happens when the Protestants tamper with the Text against the authority of the Magisterium and Tradition. The Holy Bible becomes only a tool for their own opinions and the political power of their princes. This is the sad reality that became prominent in the Protestant revolt: instead of reading the Text with humility, men took to the Word of God as a weapon against their brethren and against the Church. They became merely "theologians," not saints. Much blood was shed on account of this, and the Protestant princes and kings gained the power they sought. But this power was not enough. They wanted more. And to this we now turn.

X

THE TRIUMPH OF THE "THEOLOGIANS" IN THE TWENTIETH CENTURY

As we have discussed, the Protestant revolt brought a revolution in the understanding and use of Sacred Scripture, with the heretics freely removing books from the Bible, translating them to fit their heresy, and interpreting them against the Christian faith contained in the oral Tradition. It was the age of the theologian who held power in religious matters, backed by the government, so that the king and the theologian both could commit their sins with impunity. Crucial to this work was the use of the Hebrew Masoretic text instead of the Greek Septuagint or the Latin Vulgate in an effort to justify their readings of Scripture as the "original text." We have seen why this was a mistake from the Text but we will also discuss this further below.

But this Protestant principle of using the Holy Bible against the faith was followed by more radical Protestants still. When theologians rule without humility and no Magisterium, division and chaos is the result. Martin Luther famously lamented the rise of these "fanatics" and told his prince protector to violently suppress them.⁷³ Even worse than this, the Protestants were willing to ally with the Muhammadans to get weapons and fight against Catholics, further contributing to their political power and the fratricidal blood spilled across Christendom.⁷⁴

Eventually, however, other theologians arose who took this weaponization of the Holy Bible even further. The Protestant theologians had sought to remove the influence of the Church from society so that the government could have more power (or at least they were willing to accept such support). Still, these theologians were Christians—they did have a society which acknowledged the authority of Christ the King, like Anglican England.

The next wave of theologians were not even Christians. They were "secular theologians." They sought to remove Christ Himself from society. Since the Protestants denied that humility and sanctity were necessary to understand the Holy Bible, it was then asked, why cannot a secular man also understand what the Scriptures *really* taught? This was also a continuation of kings and governments and their thirst for absolute power without anything to challenge them. In order to do this, they had to attack the truth of the Scriptures and its inspiration from God.

We may consider one of the earliest figures in this regard to be Machiavelli (d. 1527). He used biblical interpretation for political control. In order to do this he cast doubt on the

---

[73] Cf. Martin Luther, *Against the Murderous, Thieving Hordes of Peasants* (1525) and *Against the Fanatics* (1526).

[74] One scholar writes that "the consolidation, expansion and legitimization of Lutheranism in Germany by 1555 should be attributed to Ottoman imperialism more than to any other single factor." Fischer and Galati in Jack Goody, *Islam in Europe* (John Wiley and Sons, 2013), 45

veracity of the Scriptures and the authorship and inspiration from God. He thought that religion was not a supernatural truth but should be used by politicians to control their subjects. His ideas would have lasting effects. This brings us to the first of the secular controversies surrounding the Holy Scriptures.[75]

Mosaic Authorship

One of the primary ways these thinkers sought political control was to deny that Moses wrote the Pentateuch (as we mentioned, the first five books of the Holy Bible). If one doubted that Moses wrote these books, then it was doubtful that God inspired them since they were written much later (these thinkers, like the Protestants, denied the inspiration of oral Tradition). If God did not inspire these books then the Ten Commandments did not retain their binding force. If the Ten Commandments did not retain their binding force, then the king was free to commit adultery, murder, etc., for his own political power. In the same way, murderous revolutions were not so bad. Most of all, the Pentateuch showed God's direct intervention in history and His involvement in society and politics. These secular thinkers wanted all Christian influence removed so they could be free to exercise complete political control.

---

[75] The following pages are based on the work of Jeffrey L. Morrow, *Theology, Politics, and Exegesis: Essays on the History of Modern Biblical Criticism* (Pickwick: 2017), *Alfred Loisy and Modern Biblical Studies* (Catholic University of America: 2019); Michael Gross, *The War Against Catholicism: Liberalism and the Anti-Catholic Imagination in Nineteenth-Century Germany* (Univ. of Michigan: 2005); Marvin O'Connell, *Critics on Trial: An Introduction to the Catholic Modernist Crisis* (Catholic University of America: 1995); Steven Smith, "As Moses Has Written," *Institute of Catholic Culture.*

But while the question of Mosaic authorship was raised for political purposes, it soon became the subject of intellectual questions. Without the lens of oral Tradition, the Pentateuch was a confusing set of books: it was filled with apparent contradictions, lists and repetitions that made very little sense to readers far removed from ancient oral Tradition.

As European society lost more of its oral culture and its *cultus*, the Holy Mass, society was deeply changed by its emphasis on reading and writing instead of the earlier, more universal and ordinary oral culture. Thus the doubts about the Pentateuch became more and more convincing to the average person.

Various authors discussed Mosaic authorship throughout the 17th and 18th centuries, intimately connected with political power. Isaac La Peyrère (d. 1676) and Thomas Hobbes (d. 1679) both cast doubt on Mosaic authorship and advocated that instead of Christian theologians and the Church, state-appointed professors should interpret the Holy Scriptures.

Spinoza (d. 1677) followed Machiavelli closely, doubted the Old Testament as a whole as well as Mosaic authorship. He asserted that a vast amount of historical and linguistic knowledge was necessary for biblical interpretation, asserting the idea that a theologian could be totally secular. This was of course the logical next step from the Protestant revolt: interpreting the Holy Bible only required a vast amount of intellectual knowledge, not humility and not holiness. Luther and his Protestant theologians had said anyone could read the Holy Bible, and there was no need for the saints and doctors who had holiness.

Thus even in the 17th century we see the continued shift away from the study of the Scriptures being a spiritual pursuit to a purely intellectual and rational pursuit, fueled by thinkers seeking political power. This was also the age of the Scientific Revolution, where men began to boast that their intellectual knowledge could solve every problem in society. Thus the intellectual study of the Holy Bible became a means to secularize society and control the authority of the Text. Thus an overall movement of "secular theology" was beginning.

John Locke (d. 1704), who helped form so much of modern secular thought, was an important source of secular theology in England. A French priest, Fr. Richard Simon (d. 1712), attempted to respond to the growing doubt about Mosaic authorship, but ended up casting further doubt on Mosaic authorship, and the same thing happened with Catholic Jean Astruc (d. 1766).

By the nineteenth century, Johann Gottfried Eichhorn (d. 1827) and Martin Leberecht de Wette (d. 1849) were helping to develop a theory which all but proved that Moses was not the author of the Pentateuch. This would later be known as the "Documentary Hypothesis," which we will return to below.

At the same time, political movements were arising which forcefully sought to secularize the political authority by violent revolution, beginning with the American and French revolutions at the end of the 18th century.[76] This caused the biblical controversies to gain much more prominence than ever before. Marx wrote his Communist Manifesto in 1848, the first Feminist convention was held in America in the same year, while simultaneously violent revolution was sweeping

---

[76] The American revolutionaries tolerated Catholics if they supported the secular republic, and most of the state governments had state-funded churches. However, the US federal government was secular from its founding. The French secular revolution, however, attacked Catholics and waged actual war against them, committing genocide against the Vendée Catholics with whole families and villages massacred.

Europe. In 1859, Darwin published *Origin of Species* which cast further doubt on the veracity of the Holy Bible.

The Theory of Evolution

Darwin's theories, perhaps more than any other scientific concept, came to have a lasting impact on the study and secularization of the Holy Bible. As such we must pause and address this pervasive idea. Darwin asserted that instead of the account as recorded in the Holy Bible and other ancient texts, man evolved from less sophisticated animals to the human species he is now.

In order to assert such a theory from a historical perspective, one must completely deny the authority of all oral tradition from every culture known to man. Why? Because all ancient peoples had creation stories as part of their oral Tradition. In effect, *mankind remembered a creation.* The collective memory of the planet testifies to the fact that there was a creation and not an evolution. Moreover, there are no records of evolving species over the millennia of historical records available to us.

Darwin's theory did advance certain aspects of genetic science regarding natural selection and mutation. However, his ideas came before many discoveries that have since been made on the microscopic level. Moreover, his assertion that billions of years of evolution naturally created human life was made without much evidence.

But in 1859, in the center of this secularization that was taking place, Darwin provided the politicians with the perfect way to deny the authority of the Holy Bible on scientific grounds. To them, it was a perfectly acceptable scientific assertion which undercut the authority of Moses and the Holy Bible and quickly consigned the whole Text to the museums of history. This is why evolution rapidly became a standard scientific theory, even with very little evidence to support it.

Thus, objective science was quickly abandoned in favor of using this as an *ideology* to support political power against any divine authority whatsoever. Since the time of Darwin, scientists have increasingly assumed that Darwin was correct in order to deny the authority of God in their personal lives. As a result, the scientific method—using hypotheses, observation, and evidence—has declined in this area in favor of more and more strange speculations (and evolutionists will even admit this).[77]

Moreover, over a century and a half has passed with massive scientific advances in other areas, but the hard evidence for evolution has never been found. On the contrary, more and more scientists now argue against it.[78] Perhaps even more troubling, however, Darwin's ideas helped create the eugenics movement, claiming in principle that what the Nazis would later do was not intrinsically evil. Indeed, Darwin's views on race and morality anticipated *in every way* the Nazi ideology and regime.[79]

---

[77] Christopher Ferrera, *Against Evolution: A Theory Not Worthy of Cathlic Credulity* (Latin Mass Magazine, Fall 2015) < http://www.latinmassmagazine.com/pdfs/Ferrara-Evolution-TLM-2015-Fall.pdf>. Accessed November 23, 2019. Ferrera reviews the evolutionists who admit the lack of evidence as well as their strange speculations about life's origin, including extraterrestrials.

[78] For example the movement "Dissent from Darwinism," now has over 1000 signatures from Ph.Ds in various fields. <dissentfromdarwin.org>. The most popular scientific critique of Evolutionary Theory comes from the work of Michael Behe in *Darwin's Black Box: The Biochemical Challenge to Evolution* (2006) and *Darwin Devolves* (2019). For the non-scientific reader, I recommend Ferrera, cited in note 77.

[79] On Darwin's racism and influence on the eugenics movement, see Marko and Wike, *Architects of the Culture of Death* (Ingatius: 2004), 76ff.

Protestant and Catholic Responses

But just as Darwin and the other secularists were spreading their revolutions in society, there were actual advances in the study of the Holy Bible. Archaeological and linguistic discoveries brought about many new insights into the world in which the Scriptures were remembered and written.

The Rosetta Stone was discovered in 1799 which helped unlock for the first time numerous manuscripts of antiquity. Significant Bible manuscripts were discovered such as the Codex Sinaiticus in 1844 and Hebrew fragments of Cairo in 1896. These Hebrew fragments, known as the Geniza, were at that time the oldest Hebrew texts to be discovered. They predated the Masoretic Hebrew by hundreds of years and contained a great deal from the book of Ecclesiasticus.

The cylinder of King Cyrus was discovered in 1879 (confirming the events of I Esdras i. 1-3) and the Moabite stone in 1868 (confirming the events of IV Kngs. iii. 4-6). While the secularists were attempting to use archaeology and linguistics to disprove the Holy Bible, actual discoveries were proving otherwise.[80]

As a result of this greater amount of linguistic and cultural knowledge, a group of English Protestants made a revision of

---

[80] On the historical reliability of the Holy Bible related to archaeological and other discoveries, see K.A. Kitchen, *On the Reliability of the Old Testament* (Grand Rapids: Eerdmans, 2003); James K. Hoffmeier, *Israel in Egypt: The Evidence for the Authenticity of the Exodus Tradition* (Oxford: Oxford University Press, 1996), *Ancient Israel in Sinai: The Evidence for the Authenticity of the Wilderness Tradition* (Oxford: Oxford University Press, 2005); Craig Blomberg, *The Historical Reliability of the Gospels* (IVP Academic: 2007), *The Historical Reliability of the New Testament* (B&H Academic: 2016). Be advised that some of these books are from Protestants.

the King James Version and published it in 1885, which was known as the Revised Version. A counterpart in the United States—the American Standard Version—was published in 1901. Neither of these versions gained much popularity however, and Protestants mostly continued to use the King James Version.

Meanwhile, the Church condemned in the 1864 *Syllabus of Errors* the violent efforts at secularization from their foundational principles. Among them were the basic ideas which had been put forth since Machiavelli and before: that Biblical studies could be carried out without faith and without Church authority as a purely scientific process. In short, the concept of a "secular theologian" was condemned. Among the errors singled out for condemnation were the following:

> 8. As human reason is placed on a level with religion itself, so theology must be treated in the same manner as philosophical sciences.
>
> 9. All the dogmas of the Christian religion are indiscriminately the object of natural science or philosophy, and *human reason*, enlightened solely in a historical way, *is able, by its own natural strength and principles, to attain to the true science of even the most abstruse dogmas*; provided only that such dogmas be proposed to reason itself as its object.

These condemnations went to the heart of the secular theologians' efforts to take Biblical study out of the realm of pious Christians and place it in the hands of political professors who would able to use it for secularization. It was absolutely false to assert that human reason alone was able to understand the Scriptures or the dogmas. It required the supernatural grace of God enlightened by faith and holiness. In their pride, these political professors asserted that their methods of "science" were entirely objective and completely unbiased, while they came to the conclusion that the Holy Bible was not inspired and not reliable—in order to serve their political patrons' interests.

But the Church went further in condemning this madness in 1870. This was the First Vatican Council, where further condemnations attacked the secularization efforts of the revolutionaries. Since the secularists attempted to use their "advanced" knowledge of the Holy Bible against the faith, Vatican I declared this anathema:

> If anyone shall assert it to be possible that sometimes, according to the progress of science, a sense is to be given to doctrines propounded by the Church different from that which the Church has understood and understands; let him be anathema.[81]

What the Church has proclaimed as true cannot be untrue by a greater advance in science of any kind. True scientific discovery cannot challenge what is already known to be true. True scientific discovery, as we have seen, only confirms what is true. But the secular theologians and their pseudo-science sought to only confirm their ideologies, not the truth.

The same decree also confirmed Trent that Scripture and Tradition are the sources of revelation as well as the authority of the Vulgate:

---

[81] Vatican I, *Dei Filius*, canon 3

> [This] supernatural revelation, according to the faith of the universal Church, as declared by the holy synod of Trent, is contained "in the written books and in the unwritten traditions which have been received by the apostles from the mouth of Christ Himself; or, through the inspiration of the Holy Spirit have been handed down by the apostles themselves, and have thus come to us." And, indeed, these books of the Old and New Testament, whole with all their parts, just as they were enumerated in the decree of the same Council, are contained in the older Vulgate Latin edition, and are to be accepted as sacred and canonical. These books are held by the Church as sacred and canonical, not as having been composed by merely human labour and afterwards approved by her authority, nor merely because they contain revelation without error, but because, written under the inspiration of the Holy Ghost, they have God for their author, and have been transmitted to the Church as such.[82]

Thus not only were the sources of revelation confirmed as well as the Vulgate, but also the inerrancy of the Scripture was confirmed. This will be crucial later on.

Most significant of all, Vatican I defined that the Church had infallible authority to judge matters of faith and morals — and thus the Holy Scriptures. All of the efforts of secular revolutionaries were condemned in this decree because it definitively removed the Church from any state control whatsoever. While many biblical scholars were being used for the gain of politicians, the Church proclaimed her sovereign

---

[82] Ibid., ch. 2

dominion by God's authority over all religious truth. This was merely the binding authority as explained from Acts XVI. 4.

Germany: Doubting Moses and the Gospels

But as the Church decreed the official condemnation of secular theology, those theologians were only hardening their hearts. The reaction to Vatican I in Germany had a great influence on biblical studies for years to come. Particularly in Germany, biblical professors were controlled by the state and appointed as *de facto* arms of the government. The Church had decreed at Vatican I that, on the contrary, the Church leadership was under *Church* control, not the state. Thus by this decree the Catholic professor would pledge allegiance to the pope over and against the German state. As such Catholics became political enemies of the German state.

The German ruler Otto von Bismarck (d. 1898) followed same course as Philip Hesse and Henry VIII in suppressing the faith and seizing Church land. He attacked the Catholic Church in Germany and sought to stamp out her influence. This was known as the *kulturkampf* ("Culture war") which reached its height from 1872-1878 immediately following Vatican I. A number of state-appointed secular theologians helped promote the German political program against the faith by using their biblical studies.

Heinrich Julius Holtzmann (d. 1910) created the idea that it was not St. Matthew's Gospel that was the earliest written Gospel, but rather St. Mark (before this time it was generally considered that St. Matthew was the first Gospel written). But if St. Mark was the earliest Gospel, then it could asserted that the papal passage from St. Matthew XVI was a later corruption added to the text. Thus by denying the inspiration of oral Tradition and the Magisterium, the Germans could meld their idea of the "original text" to support their political power. Once again, like Luther, the nebulous idea of the "original text" (which did not actually exist) served to justify their ideologies.

The German state employed another Biblical professor, Adolf von Harnack (d. 1930) who would later be used to defend Germany's entrance into World War I. This man also cast doubt on the historicity of the Gospel of St. John by using his historical research methods. Thus the Gospels were also doubted as to their historical value and the words of our Lord could be obscured by the pens of professors. This, of course, made all of the hard sayings of our Lord—such as his absolute condemnation of adultery—easily dismissed as corruptions of the fantasy of an "original text." You can see how tempting such an idea would be for sinful men.

Perhaps the most influential German biblical scholar of this time, however, was Julius Wellhausen (d. 1918). This man, above all, helped to firmly plant the Documentary Hypothesis as the mainstream theory which denied Mosaic authorship. He relied on the work of secular theologians going back to Machiavelli who used the Text to justify their ideology.

The Documentary Hypothesis, still prevalent today, studies the form of the Hebrew words of the Pentateuch and observes that there are different names for God used, different literary forms employed and apparent contradictions. Using only the words themselves as evidence, it then asserts that, because of these different forms, there must have been at least four different writers of the Pentateuch. After these writers wrote four different parts, these parts were later put together during the Babylonian captivity of the Jews, hundreds of years after Moses.

Welhausen, true to the pattern we have discussed, attempted to use these theories to justify his resistance to the faith. He was a liberal Protestant who hated Catholicism and was appointed by the German government to support the state's attack on the Church. As such, his theories attempted to prove that the original religion of Israel was without priests and the priesthood in the Pentateuch was only added later, corrupting the purity of the original religion. The prophets then came to call the people away from the corruption of priests. Thus like so many others before him, Welhausen sought to conform the Holy Bible to his own ideas by denying the inspiration of oral Tradition and the Magisterium.

The Documentary Hypothesis Lacks Evidence

There are a number of obvious reasons why this theory is flawed.[83] First, there existed the text of the Samaritan Pentateuch for centuries before the Babylonian captivity. It contains all five books of the Pentateuch with minor variations. How can the Pentateuch have been assembled during the Babylonian captivity if the Samaritan version already existed? It is far more plausible, from a purely historical perspective, that Moses wrote the Pentateuch and it was then copied into two versions, the Judean and the Samaritan.

Second, there is absolutely no documentary evidence that the Pentateuch was made from four different sources. No one has ever discovered these four documents from four writers, they are purely hypothetical. Rather, these theories are based solely on analyzing the Text of the Scriptures themselves.

---

[83] This analysis follows particularly the work of Steven Smith, "As Moses Has Written," *Institute of Catholic Culture*.

Thus they hinge upon the hubris of the secular theologian to claim to know vastly more about linguistics than the ancient peoples who committed them to memory. One must assert that oral cultures were gravely unintelligent to actually believe that one man wrote all five books. Much like the theory of evolution, there was no evidence that was ever discovered which substantiated this assertion in history.

Third, the theory is self-contradictory. For example, it asserts that since there are apparent contradictions in the Text, therefore it must have been written by four sources. But if the original four writers did not tolerate these repetitions and contradictions, why is it assumed that the compilers suddenly allowed it? And if the compilers allowed it, why not have one author which allowed it in the first place? Thus the application of linguistic principles is an arbitrary exercise designed to achieve a desired outcome.

Moreover, scholars are deeply divided on the number and nature of these theoretical sources. They have been debating this theory for more than a century with no consensus. In short, just like the Protestants imposing their 16th century view on the Text, the 19th century imposed its views on the Text as well. As Kennedy Hall wrote recently, "It is truly characteristic of the modern scholar to educate himself out of common sense."[84]

The Error of Limited Inerrancy

The Documentary Hypothesis leads to another error concerning the Scriptures: Limited Inerrancy. This error asserts that the Scriptures are only infallible on things that are

---

[84] Kennedy Hall, "Authorship of the Four Gospels," *The Fatima Center*, October 10th, 2019 < https://fatima.org/news-views/authorship-of-the-four-gospels/>. Accessed November 23, 2019.

written for the sake of our salvation. They do contain errors in historical and other details.

This is false. But those who deny Mosaic authorship must believe this error. This is because the Holy Bible itself states that Moses wrote the Pentateuch:

> When Moses had finished writing down in a book the words of this law to the very end, Moses commanded the Levites who carried the ark of the covenant of the LORD, "Take this book of the law, and put it by the side of the ark of the covenant of the LORD your God, that it may be there for a witness against you" (Dt. xxxi. 24-26).

Other related verses include Neh. xiii. 1, II Para. xxv. 4, Ex. xvii. 24; xxiv. 4; xxxiv. 27. More than this, our Lord Himself stated that Moses wrote the Pentateuch when he says to the Jews:

> Think not that I will accuse you to the Father. There is one that accuseth you, Moses, in whom you trust. For if you did believe Moses, you would perhaps believe me also; for *he wrote of me*. But if you do not believe *his writings*, how will you believe my words? (Jn. v. 45-47).

Thus the denial of Mosaic authorship is tied along with doubt that the Gospels contain the actual words of Jesus Christ. Other examples in the New Testament include Mt. xxii. 24; viii. 4, Jn. 1:45; v.46, Acts iii. 22, Rom. x. 5, Heb. vii. 14. Thus in order to assert that Moses did not write the Pentateuch, the advocates of the Documentary Hypothesis must further assert that when the Holy Bible itself states otherwise, it is in error.

So besides the theory of evolution which casts doubt on Genesis 1-2, the Documentary Hypothesis casts doubt on the accuracy of all these verses, leading to the error of Limited Inerrancy.

These theories lead straight to hell. If the Text cannot be trusted on historical details, how can we trust the Holy Text on matters of salvation? If we cannot trust the Holy Scriptures on matters of Salvation, then we cannot trust the Church. If the Church is not trustworthy, then Jesus Christ is not God. Thus all of this doubt of the Holy Text ultimately amounts to Atheism and the secular state with no limit to their power—exactly what their designs amount to.

For many years as we have said, these ideas were pursued by secularists and liberal Protestants. They started to become popular among Catholics, however, thanks to the work of French priest Alfred Loisy (d. 1940). In the later part of the 19th century and the early 20th, this man began to popularize the German doubts of Mosaic authorship, doubts about the Gospels and advocated the error of Limited Inerrancy. Lamentably, his errors spread among Catholics.

Holy Mother Church Against Loisy

Responding to the rise of these errors concerning the Holy Scripture, Leo XIII published his encyclical *Providentissimus Deus* in 1893. In it he confirmed Vatican I and condemned Limited Inerrancy with these words:

> Those who maintain that an error is possible in any genuine passage of the sacred writings, either pervert the Catholic notion of inspiration, or make God the author of such error (*Providentissimus Deus*, 21).

But in the same encyclical, Pope Leo also commended a proper use of the new linguistic and historical knowledge:

> For although the meaning of the Hebrew and Greek is substantially rendered by the Vulgate, nevertheless wherever there may be ambiguity or want of clearness, the "examination of older tongues," to quote St. Augustine, will be useful and advantageous (13).

This of course is what was done in the translation of the Douay Rheims when they also compared the available Hebrew and Greek manuscripts to help render the English. Moreover, Leo commended the use of a proper Biblical criticism: studying and comparing manuscripts and utilizing historical research to understand the Text and approximate the original. But he condemned the excess of the secular theologians:

> There has arisen, to the great detriment of religion, an inept method, dignified by the name of the "higher criticism," which pretends to judge of the origin, integrity and authority of each Book from internal indications alone (17).

These methods, Leo said, were simply "the reflection of the bias and the prejudice of the critics" themselves. The secular theologians had no faith, no humility, and even their intellectual method was flawed from a purely rational view point. They simply wanted to make the Holy Bible do their bidding.

In 1902 Leo XIII set up a Magisterial organization known as the Pontifical Biblical Commission. Its job was to make authoritative declarations concerning questions about the Holy Bible. In 1906 the Commission confirmed that the evidence provided by Loisy, Welhausen and others failed to prove that Moses did not author the Pentateuch. Hall sums up the decree:

> 1. There is no theological argument worthy of belief that casts doubt on the Traditional Mosaic authorship of the Books of Moses.
>
> 2. Moses was the principal author, but it is not necessary to hold that he physically wrote every single word of the books. Some he could have dictated, and some things, like his death, would have been added posthumously. However, the authorship is Mosaic throughout, and guided by the Holy Ghost.
>
> 3. It is possible that Moses consulted oral Tradition or other documents. Guided by the Holy Ghost, he did so without error in order to transmit saving truth.
>
> 4. Over the course of centuries, it is probable that some modifications have been inserted in the text, to help with explanation. Also, copyists and scribes could make errors in certain manuscripts. All of this is subject to the judgment of the Church.[85]

Thus we see that the Church held the authority of oral Tradition to govern the formation of the Text. Moses wrote it,

---

[85] Kennedy Hall, "Mosaic Authorship of the First Five Books," *The Fatima Center*, October 3rd, 2019 < https://fatima.org/news-views/mosaic-authorship-of-the-first-five-books/>. Accessed November 23, 2019.

but the Church accepts that others may have helped in certain areas. As we stated above, the whole of Genesis is simply an oral Tradition written down which predates Moses by centuries. Minor additions also could have been added after Moses, all guided by the Holy Ghost. Thus oral Tradition precedes, governs, and confirms the formation and writing of the Text.

In 1907 Pope St. Pius X issued *Lamentabili* which condemned many of the errors of the secularists with the Holy Bible. This continued to condemn the very core principles of secular theology, as his predecessor had done with the *Syllabus*. Among the condemned errors were the following:

> 1. The ecclesiastical law which prescribes that books concerning the Divine Scriptures are subject to previous examination does not apply to critical scholars and students of scientific exegesis of the Old and New Testament.

> 3. From the ecclesiastical judgments and censures passed against free and more scientific exegesis, one can conclude that the Faith the Church proposes contradicts history and that Catholic teaching cannot really be reconciled with the true origins of the Christian religion.

> 9. They display excessive simplicity or ignorance who believe that God is really the author of the Sacred Scriptures.

> 11. Divine inspiration does not extend to all of Sacred Scriptures so that it renders its parts, each and every one, free from every error.

12. If he wishes to apply himself usefully to Biblical studies, the exegete must first put aside all preconceived opinions about the supernatural origin of Sacred Scripture and interpret it the same as any other merely human document.

Thus the vain imaginings of the secular theologians about some "true origins of the Christian religion" was flatly condemned. The Church saw through their ploys and pretenses of objectivity to their true intentions: denying the saving dogmas of Jesus Christ. If these errors were not condemned, souls would be lost for eternity.

Soon after this the saint drew up an *Oath Against Modernism* (1910) "To be sworn to by all clergy, pastors, confessors, preachers, religious superiors, and professors in philosophical-theological seminaries." By thus binding the entire Church to this solemn oath, it was a supreme act of the Roman Pontiff. Contained within this oath was a condemnation of the false Biblical methods of the secular theologians:

> I reject that method of judging and interpreting Sacred Scripture which, departing from the tradition of the Church, the analogy of faith, and the norms of the Apostolic See, embraces the misrepresentations of the rationalists and with no prudence or restraint adopts textual criticism as the one and supreme norm.

The Oath bound everyone also to the condemnations from *Lamentabili*. This was particularly against Loisy, since some of the condemnations were quotations from his work. This was more direct than Leo XIII had been, but for fourteen years since that time Loisy still had not repented from his errors. Thus, after *Lamentabile*, Pius X threatened excommunication against him. When Loisy refused to recant, he was excommunicated in 1907. He never repented and later died outside the Church in 1940. But like Luther before him, his ideas were spreading.

The Magisterium Against Secular Theologians

In the same year as Loisy's excommunication, the Pontifical Biblical Commission confirmed that the Gospel of St. John was written by eyewitness St. John the Apostle, as well as its historical authenticity, condemning the idea that the words in the Gospel are not "properly and truly the words of the Lord himself."

Later that year, Pope St. Pius declared that "all are bound by the duty of conscience to submit to the decisions of the Biblical Pontifical Commission" (*Praestantia Scripturae*). From this time until World War I in 1914, the Commission pronounced judgments on all four Gospels, the Book of Acts, and the Pauline epistles including Hebrews.

In addition, it was confirmed in 1909 that the Creation account of Genesis must be held to "contain the stories of events which really happened, that is, which correspond with objective reality and historical truth." At the same time it acknowledged that there were certain interpretations possible as to the exact historical details (such as the amount of time designated by the word "day" in the first chapter) as well as further allegorical and mystical interpretations that can be drawn out, provided the historical character is maintained.

The popes Leo XIII and Pius X responded to the increased archaeological and linguistic knowledge of the time by recognizing the need for a revision of the Vulgate, whose last edition, as we have noted, was published by Pope Clement VIII in 1592. It was made clear through the further manuscript discoveries that this Clementine version appeared to contain errors which did not reflect accurately the version of St. Jerome. Even though no one had ever discovered the original manuscripts of St. Jerome, the Holy See still acted to produce a more accurate edition, as it had done following Trent. Thus the Holy See entrusted to a special commission of Benedictine Monks the revision of the Vulgate text according to the most accurate formation of the original Jerome translation. But this would be virtually the last time that Catholics paid attention to the Vulgate as we shall see.

Rise of the Teilhardian Heresy Against Fatima

But after the death of Pope St. Pius X in 1914, there would never arise another pope as holy and forceful as he in fighting against the secular theologians. From 1914 until the Second Vatican Council, the suppression of heretical tendencies was moderated by the popes Benedict XV, Pius XI, and Pius XII. Pius X's *Oath Against Modernism* remained a force of law, but it was never again enforced as it was during his pontificate. Just as he was dying in 1914, the First World War was beginning, which would be the first global violence resulting from the secularization of society. The Church had firmly and unequivocally condemned secularization in 1870. The world responded by murdering millions in the name of secularism.

Pope Benedict XV was elected right as the World War was breaking out. He spent all of his efforts attempting to bring an end to this horror—all in vain. It may be that the World Wars helped to moderate the militancy of Pius X, whose efforts admittedly caused massive opposition. Perhaps the popes during and after the World Wars chose to moderate their efforts against secularism pragmatically, since the men of their day were being provoked to mass slaughter against each other. Perhaps too, the efforts made by Leo XIII (since his 1891 French encyclical *Au milieu des solicitudes*) to reconcile with the secular Republic of France helped influence the moderation of Benedict XV through Pius XII toward secularists.[86]

Whatever the case, these popes did not hunt down the secularists in the Church and excommunicate them as Pius X had done. Benedict XV suppressed the anti-modernist organization *Soliditum Pianum*, but did uphold the excommunication of Loisy.[87]

Loisy continued to teach and publish as an excommunicated Catholic. In the same political atmosphere as Luther, the governments did not enforce what the Church had decreed, so Loisy continued to influence Catholics. The secular theologians who followed him went underground and began to pass their writings off in secret using orthodox terms and interpreting them against the faith. At the same time but at the time unknown to Benedict XV, another secular theologian began to write and spread secularization in the Catholic Church.

---

[86] It is likely that the popes' mentor, Cardinal Rampolla, helped influence their moderate approach to secular modernity. See Randy Engel, *The Rite of Sodomy: Paul VI and the Church's Paradigm Shift on Homosexuality* (New Engel: 2006)

[87] It should be noted here that the activity of this group was not always accurate and excesses existed wherein some men were condemned who perhaps should not have been, such as Marie-Joseph Lagrange. As Nichols points out, Lagrange was trying to follow the teaching of Pope Leo, but even Pope St. Pius X's commission permitted that "certain narratives thought to be properly historical have only the appearance of history" (June 23, 1905). But no one was permitted to interpret things against the consensus of the Fathers. Aidan Nichols, O.P. *The Shape of Catholic Theology* (Liturgical Press: 1991), 135.

This man was the French Jesuit Teilhard de Chardin (1881-1955). In a large way, we may ascribe the wholesale corruption of the Jesuit order to him. He wrote his first essay in 1916 during the war. His ideas sought to bring the theory of evolution into the Catholic Church and then change the Catholic faith to conform it to evolution. As his thought progressed and spread, he would describe his thought this way:

> What increasingly dominates my interests, is the effort to establish within myself and define around me, a new religion (call it a better Christianity, if you like) where the personal God ceases to be the great monolithic proprietor of the past to become the Soul of the World which the stage we have reached religiously and culturally calls for.[88]

De Chardin denied the dogma of Original Sin and taught that the whole of human history was naturally progressing toward something better—exactly in line with what evolution taught. He believed that all modern ideas and technology were to be welcomed as part of this benevolent progress. His ideas fit perfectly with the efforts of the secular theologians to wrest all power out of the hands of the Church and give it to the state, since the secular states were gaining more power in the 20th century than all governments had had for centuries before them.

But in the year after De Chardin began writing, our Lady of Fatima appeared in 1917 to exhort all to recite the Rosary every day and offer penance for the sins of men. Her message was completely contrary to that of Teilhard de Chardin: the

---

[88] Pierre Teilhard de Chardin, *Letters to Léontine Zanta,* trans. Bernard Wall (New York: Harper & Row, 1965), 114 (letter dated 26 January 1936)

world was not progressing naturally toward something better. On the contrary, the world was getting much worse. At the time, the First World War had already killed millions and was still raging. Incredibly, our Lady stated in stark terms that if men did not repent, another war would happened which would be even worse:

> You have seen hell, where the souls of poor sinners go. It is to save them that God wants to establish in the world devotion to my Immaculate Heart. If you do what I tell you, many souls will be saved, and there will be peace.
>
> This war will end, but *if men do not refrain from offending God, another and more terrible war will begin* during the pontificate of Pius XI. When you see a night that is lit by a strange and unknown light, you will know it is the sign God gives you that He is about to punish the world with war and with hunger, and by the persecution of the Church and the Holy Father.
>
> To prevent this, I shall come to the world to ask that Russia be consecrated to my Immaculate Heart, and I shall ask that on the First Saturday of every month Communions of reparation be made in atonement for the sins-of the world. If my wishes are fulfilled, Russia will be converted and there will be peace; if not, then Russia will spread her errors throughout the world, bringing new wars and persecution of the Church; *the good will be martyred* and the Holy Father *will have much to suffer*; *certain nations will be annihilated*. But in the end my Immaculate Heart will triumph. The Holy Father will consecrate Russia to me, and she will be converted, and the

world will enjoy a period of peace. In Portugal the faith will always be preserved...[89]

Instead of the rejoicing in the "stage we have reached" in the evolution of "better Christianity," Fatima completely repudiated the Teilhardian dream. The world was corrupted with the sins of men, and God was punishing it with wars because men refused to repent. Teilhard wanted to join the world in all its false glory; Fatima called the world to fall on its knees and repent. These two visions of the universe and the modern world were irreconcilable. During the subsequent years, these contrary visions both vied for influence over the hearts of the faithful and the popes. But it was the theologians who finally tipped the scales.

The Theologians within the Church

As Europe was still smoldering from the flames and death of the World War, it became clear that the secular theologians were still at work. In 1920, Benedict XV issued another encyclical on Biblical studies: *Spiritus Paraclitus*. He confirmed the condemnation of Limited Inerrancy in these words:

> Although these words of our predecessor [Leo XIII] leave no room for doubt or dispute, it grieves us to find that not only men outside, but even children of the Catholic Church—nay, what is a peculiar sorrow to us, even clerics and professors of sacred learning—who in their own conceit either openly repudiate or at least attack in secret the Church's teaching on this point....For while conceding that

---

[89] From the text of the Third Apparition, July 13th. Emphasis mine.

inspiration extends to every phrase—and, indeed, to every single word of Scripture—yet, by endeavoring to distinguish between what they style the primary or religious and the secondary or profane element in the Bible, they claim that the effect of inspiration—namely, absolute truth and immunity from error—are to be restricted to that primary or religious element.

Their notion is that only what concerns religion is intended and taught by God in Scripture, and that all the rest—things concerning 'profane knowledge,' the garments in which Divine truth is presented—God merely permits, and even leaves to the individual author's greater or less knowledge. Small wonder, then, that in their view a considerable number of things occur in the Bible touching physical science, history and the like, which cannot be reconciled with modern progress in science! (*Spiritus Paraclitus*, 19)

From 1920-1941, the Pontifical Commission continued to censure and condemn erroneous biblical study methods by Catholics. However, the number of condemnations and documents released were greatly reduced. The secular theologians still had some power at many universities keeping their doctrines secret, and they were not happy with the restrictions placed upon them by the Holy See and the Biblical Commission. Because of the moderation of the subsequent popes after St. Pius X, these Catholics were able to gain greater influence with the Holy See over time.

In 1922, Pius XI was elected. He opened the door to the secular theologians in the universities by condemning *Action Française* in 1926, a political organization which promoted Catholicism in France. In many ways this began to tip the balance of power away from Fatima and toward Teilhardianism. Especially from this point the influence of the secular theologians began to increase significantly in the Church, particularly among the Jesuits and Dominicans of northern Europe. Meanwhile Teilhard's ideas had become so popular among the Jesuits that the superior general took notice and censured him for his denial of Original Sin in 1926.

At the same time, another Jesuit was rising in the ranks of the Church, this one from Germany: Augustin Bea. By 1930, he was made rector of the Pontifical Biblical Institute. Under his leadership, he was able to secure permission to attend a Protestant biblical conference 1935. Fr. Bea was particularly interested in Jewish studies and advocated for dialogue with Jews while favoring the Masoretic Hebrew text. To his credit, he did defend Mosaic authorship. His influence would end up changing the course of Biblical studies in the Catholic Church as we shall see.

In the same year 1935, the "theologians" began to make their views public. An essay was written by a French Dominican named Yves Congar entitled "The Deficiency of Theology," critiquing the Thomism which was promoted by the Magisterium of Pius X.[90] This essay followed along the (indirect) suppression of French Thomism by Pius XI nine years earlier.

This essay and the French Dominicans who followed it (Chenu in 1937 and Charlier in 1938), argued that the secularization of Europe had not come about because of secular theology and modern man's trust in himself as the

---

[90] Jürgen Mettepenningen, *Nouvelle Théologie - New Theology: Inheritor of Modernism, Precursor of Vatican II* (T&T Clark International: 2010), 31

papacy had condemned since Pius IX and Fatima had proclaimed, but rather that the Church through Thomism had been disconnected from the every day life of individual souls.

To be fair, they had a point. During the 19th century while secularization was raging, many poor families were displaced in the cities and moved into the factories. The Church did much to alleviate their suffering, and this social crisis even prompted the first encyclical on the justice of society (*Rerum novarm*, 1891). But the Church's response had arguably been slow and not sufficient to meet the needs of many common families, and they were persuaded instead by the rhetoric of secular revolutionaries and Communists. As a result by 1900, much of Europe had been secularized.[91]

But the solution of these French Dominicans was not to call men to repentance and turn to Christ as Fatima had commanded, nor to piously pass down the Tradition as the Magisterium had promoted, but rather to form their own new ideas which they believed, like Teilhard, would be a "better Christianity."

During this period, these French Dominicans argued that in order to bring about their new era of piety, they would return to St. Thomas and ignore the centuries of saints who had been commenting on his works since his death in 1274. In their mind, they were "returning to the sources," for a more accurate picture of what St. Thomas *really said*. In reality, they were imposing their 20th century thought onto St. Thomas.

Why is this? As we have stated, the inspiration of the Holy Ghost is not restricted only to the Scripture, nor just the oral Tradition and the *cultus*, but the Magisterium was guided as well. The saints down through the centuries since St. Thomas

---

[91] See Own Chadwick, *The Secularization of Europe in the Nineteenth Century* (Cambridge University Press: 1990)

had developed the doctrine of the Church to understand it properly and to expound it faithfully to the people of every age. God guided the Church, and thus He would not allow the whole of the Church's authorities to fall into error. For this reason, the Church had already condemned the ideas of Congar in 1864:

> [Condemned]: The method and principles according to which the ancient scholastic doctors treated theology are by no means suited to the necessity of our times and to the progress of the sciences.[92]

Bl. Pius IX had said that by this idea "the authority of the Church herself is called into danger," since God would not allow all the scholastics since St. Thomas to fall into error together.[93] Instead, this pontiff declared that the consensus of the scholastics was also a source of infallible teaching of the Church, due to working together with the universal and ordinary Magisterium. These men had piously handed down the oral Tradition in union with the elders and understood it, therefore their consensus also must be held to be without error.[94] Thus piety and humility demanded a Catholic consent also to these Fathers—many of whom were saints and doctors—as a necessary inheritance of the faith.

But Congar, Chenu and the other Dominicans wanted to circumvent their obligations to this piety, and go back to the "original text" of St. Thomas. They implicitly asserted, then, that their advanced learning *was superior* to the erudition and sanctity of St. Robert Bellarmine, St. Charles Borromeo, St.

---

[92] *Syllabus of Errors* (1864), 13
[93] *Tuas Libenter* (1863) Denzinger 1681
[94] Ibid., Denzinger 1683

Alphonsus Liguori, and other such men like Francisco Suárez, Thomas Cajetan or Juan de Torquemada.

They truly believed that the modern world needed to ignore all these men. Their efforts ended up imposing 20th century philosophy onto the Angelic Doctor. This was the beginning of the movement known as *Nouvelle théologie*, which would ultimately produce the triumph of the "theologian" in the Church.

This movement is known to history by the French for "New Theology." During the final years of Pius XI, the movement was particularly evident among the Dominicans, while Teilhard's ideas were slowly spreading among the Jesuits. Too many men were thirsting for new ideas, not for penance, humility, and piously passing down the Tradition of our fathers.

And so the warning of Fatima from World War I was left unheeded:

> If men do not refrain from offending God, another and more terrible war will begin during the pontificate of Pius XI... When you see a night that is lit by a strange and unknown light, you will know it is the sign God gives you that He is about to punish the world with war and with hunger, and by the persecution of the Church and the Holy Father.

In the night of January 25-26 of 1938, as the press reported at the time, something like the Northern Lights appeared in the night and was seen as far as Italy. Men were frightened by this bizarre light and ran into the streets in a panic. Firemen were called out thinking the buildings were on fire.[95]

In the Spring of 1938, having mobilized and slowly grown their army, the Nazis quietly annexed Austria. Later that year, Pius XI suffered a heart attack and in February of 1939, while uttering the words "Peace, peace, peace," he passed to his eternal reward. In the fall of that year, the Nazis invaded Poland. Again another Pope Pius died and again another world war began.

Venerable Pius XII: Cracks in the Vanguard

Pius XII was elected to face the worldwide horror of the Second World War. During the global slaughter of millions of men, women, and children, major cracks would develop in the vanguard of the Church, leading directly to the modern crisis we now find ourselves.

As the conflict raged for two long years, the Dominicans' *Nouvelle théologie* efforts were finally noticed by the Holy See. Rome saw these errors, like Bl. Pius IX had, as a danger to "the authority of the Church herself." In 1942, these Dominicans' works were put on the index of forbidden books. This quickly slowed the growth of the movement among the Dominicans. In the next period of the growing *Nouvelle théologie*, as World War II raged on, the Jesuits now pressed for "better Christianity."

Perhaps more than any other Jesuit, Augustin Bea was able to gain a great amount of influence during the pontificate of Pius XII. He gained so much of the trust of Pius XII that he eventually became his confessor. Even as the Dominicans'

---

[95] *New York Times,* January 26, 1938 as referenced by Taylor Marshall, *Infiltration: The Plot to Destroy the Church from Within* (Crisis: 2019), 99

books were being forbidden, Bea was advocating for a new scholarly freedom for the theologians.

As we mentioned, Bea was an advocate of the Masoretic text and a great lover of Jewish and Hebrew studies. He would eventually become influential at Vatican II. After some time he convinced Pius XII to issue a new encyclical which became the largest crack in the defenses of the Church against overturning the authority of the oral Tradition and the Fathers. In September of 1943, the Allies invaded the Italian mainland. Later that month, this encyclical was released on the feast of St. Jerome: *Divino Afflante Spiritu*.

This encyclical is considered a revolution in biblical studies. It was seen by many as opening the door for scholars to take their research in any direction. Before this the Magisterium held a very strong grip on the freedom of scholars, watching over them to keep them safe from the errors of secular theology. The Church did this because it was understood that historical research and intellectual thought was not enough to understand the Holy Bible. Humility, piety and sanctity were the essential foundations. Modern historical research was seen as helpful but easily corrupted by ideology and sinful bias. In short, it was not progressing in a benevolent Teilhardian evolution.

Pius XII's innovation was to change the opinion of the Magisterium to this modern research and adopt a Teilhardian optimism toward its progress:

> Today [biblical studies] has rules *so firmly established and secure*, that it has become a most valuable aid to the purer and more accurate editing of the sacred text and that *any abuse can easily be discovered*...

Today therefore, since this branch of science has attained to *such high perfection*, it is the honorable, though not always easy, task of students of the Bible to procure by every means that as soon as possible may be duly published by Catholics editions of the Sacred Books and of ancient versions, brought out in accordance with these standards, which, that is to say, unite the greatest reverence for the sacred text with an exact observance of all the rules of criticism.

And let all know that this prolonged labor is *not only necessary for the right understanding of the divinely-given writings*, but also is *urgently demanded* by that piety by which it behooves us to be grateful to the God of all providence, Who from the throne of His majesty has sent these books as so many paternal letters to His own children.[96]

Thus Pius XII seems to reverse here (if only in emphasis and optimism), the condemnations made by Pius IX and X against the purely scientific study of the Holy Bible. As we said, Leo XIII had permitted such historical study, but emphasized its susceptibility to corruption and bias. Pius XII seems to indicate here that the biblical study—promoted for so long by secularists as being truly objective based solely on intellectual knowledge—can in fact be objective because of the "high perfection" of its discipline. Its errors are immediately rooted out by rules "firmly established and secure" and thus its use to understand the Scriptures is not only "necessary" but "urgently demanded" by "piety" itself! This was a remarkable claim coming from the Holy See, which had long held in suspicion

---

[96] *Divino Afflante Spiritu*, 18-19. Emphasis mine.

these secularists and their assertions of objectivity. Thus does Pius XII call for translations from what he calls "the original text."

> The original text...having been written by the inspired author himself, has more authority and greater weight than any even the very best translation, whether ancient or modern; this can be done all the more easily and fruitfully, if to the knowledge of languages be joined a real skill in literary criticism of the same text (16).

He mentions "original text(s)" eight times in the encyclical, but never states what this is exactly. It would become clear soon, however, that he meant the Masoretic Hebrew. Unfortunately he made an error thinking this was the original text, which seems to have come from Bea's influence. Even in this year the only thing that existed were copies of copies of copies.

Still, Pius XII was careful to condemn Limited inerrancy (1-3) and affirm the inerrancy of the Vulgate:

> [The] special authority or as they say, authenticity of the Vulgate was not affirmed by the Council [of Trent] particularly for critical reasons, but rather because of its legitimate use in the Churches throughout so many centuries; by which use indeed the same is shown, in the sense in which the Church has understood and understands it, to be free from any error whatsoever in matters of faith and morals; so that, as the Church herself testifies and affirms, it may be quoted safely and without fear of error in disputations, in lectures and in preaching; and so its

authenticity is not specified primarily as critical, but rather as juridical (21).

Hence, Pius XII qualified the decree of Trent to state that the Vulgate was not the authentic text in the sense that there could never be any improvements to more accurately approximate the original text. This in itself was not controversial, as we have seen how the Church has dealt with variants in her liturgy as well as revised editions to the Vulgate even through Pius X. The innovation, rather, besides placing such great faith in the modern historical methods, was in asserting that there existed an "original text."

Thus for the first time ever, the Holy See authorized translations from the Jews' manuscript tradition, the Masoretic Hebrew, thinking it to be the "original text." Fr. Bea immediately set to work with the Masoretic and produced a Hebrew translated version in 1945 known as the Pian Psalter. In following the Masoretic text, many of the Christological references were removed, and the entire Latin liturgical Tradition based on the Vulgate translation was cast into doubt. Pius XII made this Psalter optional for clerics to recite. This action called into question the entire history of the Church which, despite Jerome's and others' use of the Hebrew, never placed *complete trust* in Jews for their manuscripts, since they were not guided by the Holy Ghost as the Church was. The shift to the Masoretic challenged the confidence which had been placed in the Church's Tradition as inspired and guided to hand down the Scriptures. The emphasis on the necessity of humility, piety, and reverence to the Fathers was immediately swallowed up in the flood of new optimism toward "objective" modern research.

This was indeed a watershed moment in the history of the Church, since the Scriptures were the central piece of Sacred

Tradition. By calling into question the central piece of Tradition, Pius XII was moving a foundation stone, as it were, of an entire edifice of Catholic thought, faith, and liturgy for centuries. Catholic scholars everywhere took it as *carte blanche* to begin translating the Holy Scriptures in whatever way they wished from the Hebrew. The local bishop had to give approval, but the gate was now open for the influence of secular theologians on the Text as we shall see. From this time on, Catholic English translations of the Holy Bible ignored the Holy See and even the New Vulgate which was later published.

Less than two years later, Germany surrendered and the war was soon over. All of Europe and much of the world lay in ruins with unburied bodies strewn across globe. The Roman Pontiff had just reversed centuries of Church Tradition regarding the Sacred Word of God. Then suddenly something happened that changed everything.

The Dead Sea Scrolls

Beginning in 1946, a number of ancient scrolls were discovered in caves near the Dead Sea. They were ancient texts translated by the Essenes, a group of schismatic Jews living around the time of our Lord. For the first time since the Geniza discoveries in 1896, Hebrew texts had been discovered which predated the Masoretic text by centuries. But whereas the Geniza copies were mostly fragments, the Dead Sea Scrolls were numerous, including a complete copy of Isaias. This radically altered the conversation about the Holy Bible and immediately challenged the Holy See's decision to approve the Masoretic Hebrew as the "original text." This happened in many ways but in particular we will mention two.

First, the Dead Sea Scrolls contained some of the Deutero-Canonical books pointing to their canonical status against the Masoretic which removed them. (This had already been shown to some extent in the Geniza discoveries with Ecclesiasticus). Second, the Dead Sea Scrolls also matched with the Septuagint and Vulgate in a number of significant places, particularly the Historical books and the Psalms (this is also true of the Samaritan Pentateuch). However, in other places, particular the book of Isaias, the Scrolls matched the Masoretic. Summarizing these conclusions, Dom Benedict writes:

> This discovery witnesses to a vast multiplicity of Hebrew readings, some favoring the MT [Masoretic], some the Samaritan Pentateuch, and others the LXX [Septuagint]. It is no longer possible, then, blithely to assume that the MT is more or less "the Hebrew original," and that its differences with the LXX are due to defects in the latter. Any search therefore, for "the original Hebrew," is a dead end. We have only what has been mediated to us by the Tradition in which we stand.[97]

Thus the Dead Sea Scrolls immediately showed that the Holy See's decision to favor the Masoretic as the original text was flawed. The Masoretic could not be considered the original text because *there was no* original text. Only a multitude of copies of copies and, as the Dead Sea Scrolls showed, a number of copying traditions that followed different readings, sometimes vastly different in the case of the Psalter. This discovery should have altered the course of biblical

---

[97] Benedict Maria Anderson, "Fulfilled is All that David Told," op. cit., 11

studies at that point, but the massive change it brought was restricted to the historical evidence available.

Because of the Encyclical of Pius XII, the authority of the Vulgate and Septuagint were still cast into doubt, and with them the whole oral Tradition. The words of the encyclical too, as we have seen, appeared to give approval to scholarly study in itself as a perfected science, so that Catholic scholars felt freed from the restrictions previously given by the Pontifical Biblical Commission. Thus began the proliferation of Catholic translations and the meteoric rise of the theologian to power in the Church, supporting the rise of *Nouvelle théologie*.[98] It was a time about which Ratzinger would one day lament, that biblical studies "had gotten off to so optimistic a start."[99] Men thought that if they just studied hard enough, they could understand the Holy Bible.

Nouvelle théologie Grows under Pius XII

Following *Divino Afflante Spiritu* and its German Jesuit patron Bea, the *Nouvelle théologie* movement received a new boost among the Jesuits: Bouillard in 1944, Danielou, and De Lubac in 1946.[100] At the same time the Dominicans had not fully stopped their efforts either.

The movement was deeply inspired by the errors of Teilhard de Chardin, and believed that through their learning, they could bring about a new era in the Church. It was the works of Teilhard, as Schönborn says, that created a

---

[98] Mettepenningen, 120
[99] Josef Ratzinger, "Biblical Interpretation in Crisis" 1988 Erasmus Lecture < https://www.firstthings.com/web-exclusives/2008/04/biblical-interpretation-in-crisis>. Accesssed November 23, 2019.
[100] Mettepenningen, 34

"fascination...for an entire generation."[101] The excitement was building among these men for a new ear of "better Christianity."

Joseph Ratzinger as a German academic under the influence of these new ideas, would later describe how he felt in those days:

> We were lucky that we lived in a time in which both the youth and liturgical movements had opened up new horizons, new paths. Here we wanted to press forward with the Church, so that, in precisely this way, she would be young again.
>
> At that time we all had a certain contempt for the nineteenth century; it was fashionable then. somewhat kitsch piety and over-sentimentality – *we wanted to overcome all that*. We wanted a *new era of piety*, which formed itself from the liturgy, its sobriety and its greatness, which drew on the *original sources* – and was *new and contemporary* precisely because of this.[102]

Notice what is missing in order to bring about the new era: prayer and humility, and the penance of Fatima.

At the same time as Ratzinger and his peers felt this enthusiasm for an imaginary future, when they considered the then current Magisterium, the feeling was different:

> [A] slight anti-Roman resentment had been imparted to us by our studies. Not in the sense that

---

[101] Christoph Cardinal Schönborn, *Change or Purpose?* (Ignatius: 2007), 142
[102] Pope Benedict XVI, *Last Testament: In His Own Words* (Bloomsbury: 2017), 66. Emphasis mine.

we would have denied the primacy, denied obedience to the Pope, but that one had a certain inner reserve towards the theology that was done in Rome. In this sense there was a certain distance.

I wanted out of classical Thomism[.] ... Thomas's writings were textbooks, by and large, and impersonal somehow[.] ... I didn't want to operate only in a *stagnant and closed philosophy*, but in a philosophy understood as a question — what is man, really? — and particularly to enter into the *new, contemporary philosophy*.[103]

By 1946, the New Theology had become so dominant that Pius XII appeared personally before the authorities of the Jesuit order and condemned the movement.[104] He had a meeting with the authorities of the Dominicans a few days later and did the same thing. In 1947, a true theologian and man of prayer, Reginald Garrigou-Lagrange, condemned the New Theology as a revival of the Modernist secular theology. In the same year the Holy See forbade Teilhard from writing and teaching on philosophy and others were silenced.

But the movement continued. The flood of academic freedom set loose in part by *Divino Afflante Spiritu* was not to be stopped. But in 1950, the Venerable Pontiff did two important things. First, in August of that year, Pius XII issued the encyclical *Humani Generis* with the subtitle "Concerning some false opinions threatening to undermine the foundations of Catholic doctrine." Without naming names, it was clearly directed against *Nouvelle théologie*.

---

[103] Ibid., 65-67, 96
[104] Mettepenningen, 4

He included moderate, fatherly words for the *Nouvelle* theologians:

> Everyone is aware that the terminology employed in the [scholastic] schools and even that used by the Teaching Authority of the Church itself is capable of being perfected and polished; and we know also that the Church itself has not always used the same terms in the same way. It is also manifest that the Church cannot be bound to every system of philosophy that has existed for a short space of time. Nevertheless, the things that have been composed through common effort by Catholic teachers over the course of the centuries to bring about some understanding of dogma *are certainly not based on any such weak foundation*. These things are based on principles and notions deduced from a true knowledge of created things.
>
> ...We may clothe our philosophy in a more convenient and richer dress, make it more vigorous with a more effective terminology, divest it of certain scholastic aids found less useful, prudently enrich it with the fruits of progress of the human mind. But *never may we overthrow it, or contaminate it with false principles, or regard it as a great, but obsolete, relic.*[105]

It must be stated that the concept of "returning to the sources" is not wrong in itself. As we have tried to show, the Church has always been improving its Biblical Text for instance, and also approved Erasmus' Greek Text as well. But the dominant thrust of *Nouvelle théologie* was not to enrich the Church and

---

[105] *Humani Generis* (1950), 16, 30. Emphasis mine.

stay loyal to the Tradition like Erasmus had done, but rather to "overthrow" the "obsolete, relic" of the scholastics since St. Thomas. Some of these men even advocated the Protestant notion of "Only Scripture" (*Sola Scriptura*) and wanted the oral Tradition to bow to the Scripture that is based on it. Despite some minority thinkers who kept a more moderate approach, the general ideology of the movement was revolution.[106]

But with the power of the Roman See, Pius XII cut to the core of the growing power of the theologians:

> This deposit of faith our Divine Redeemer has given for authentic interpretation not to each of the faithful, *not even to theologians*, but *only* to the Teaching Authority of the Church.[107]

Thus it was not true what Ockham or Luther or Welhausen said about the "theologian" who could simply use his great learning to understand the Holy Bible. The Sacred Tradition was entrusted "only" to the Magisterium, *not* the theologians.

---

[106] Yves Congar would triumphantly state after Vatican II, "The Church did peacefully its October Revolution." *Le Concile au jour le jour deuxieme session* (Paris: 1964), 115. The October Revolution was the Communist revolution of Russia which Fatima had condemned. Foremost among the minority of new thinkers who opposed revolution was Dietrich von Hildebrand, who utilized the new phenomenological philosophy but adhered strictly to Sacred Tradition. He would later become a staunch critic of the New Mass and privately of Vatican II. His approach never gained prominence except among the Traditionalists. Nevertheless, Ratzinger wrote: "I am personally convinced that, when, at some time in the future, the intellectual history of the Catholic Church in the twentieth century is written, the name of Dietrich von Hildebrand will be most prominent among the figures of our time." *The Soul of a Lion: Dietrich Von Hildebrand, A Biography* (Ignatius: 2000), 12

[107] *Humani Generis*, 21. Emphasis mine.

Pius XII then condemned Limited Inerrancy again and censured the theologians' purely rationalistic Biblical methods:

> For some go so far as to pervert the sense of the Vatican Council's definition that God is the author of Holy Scripture, and they put forward again the opinion, *already often condemned*, which asserts that immunity from error extends only to those parts of the Bible that treat of God or of moral and religious matters...In interpreting Scripture, *they will take no account of the analogy of faith and the Tradition of the Church*. Thus they judge the doctrine of the Fathers and of the Teaching Church *by the norm of Holy Scripture, interpreted by the purely human reason of exegetes*, instead of explaining Holy Scripture according to the mind of the Church which Christ Our Lord has appointed guardian and interpreter of the whole deposit of divinely revealed truth.
>
> Further, according to their fictitious opinions, the literal sense of Holy Scripture and its explanation, carefully worked out under the Church's vigilance by so many great exegetes [saints and scholastics], should yield now to a new exegesis, which they are pleased to call symbolic or spiritual...
>
> It is not surprising that novelties of this kind have already borne their deadly fruit in almost all branches of theology.[108]

---

[108] Ibid., 22-25

Thus did Pius XII reverse the optimism he once decreed in 1943 during the war. The methods were clear and their result was already showing. These men of *Nouvelle théologie* were questioning the guidance and authority of the Holy Ghost in the oral Tradition and refusing humility toward the Magisterium. They wanted all to submit to their opinion of Scripture, "interpreted by the purely human reason of exegetes." By their methods they imitated Luther in making themselves into theologians instead of humble scholars and saints of the Word of God, accepting the doctrines of their Fathers the saints.

A few months after this the Venerable Pontiff forever confirmed the authority of oral Tradition by dogmatizing a teaching found nowhere in Sacred Scripture: the Bodily Assumption of the Blessed Virgin Mary. By raising this doctrine and feast to the level of dogma, Pius XII—at least on a dogmatic and liturgical level—slowed the advance of *Nouvelle théologie* and their efforts to impose their own opinions against the Tradition.

Nevertheless, just as his immediate predecessors, he did not renew the vigor of Pius X, although he did canonize him. He suffered a major illness beginning in 1954, which seemed to allow others to take control. In his old age he permitted the theologians to begin to take apart the liturgy, and approved a radical change to the Holy Week rite based on modern opinions of theologians in 1955.

In that same year Teilhard died, but his book *The Phenomenon of Man* was published later that year, against the previous warnings and censures. In 1957, the Curia took action and renewed the ban on Teilhard's works. But few paid any attention, and the translations were already begun to spread his errors. In October 1958, Pius XII passed to his eternal reward.

John XXIII, Fatima, and the "Theologians"

Under St. John XXIII, the *Nouvelle théologie* only continued growing, but with more momentum. They continue pushing their ideas to reinterpret the Holy Scriptures without Tradition and without the Magisterium. Yves Congar wrote in 1960: "The idea of an exclusively oral Tradition, by personal contact, of revealed truths never written down is a figment of the imagination."[109] When the Second Ecumenical Council was announced, the theologians of *Nouvelle théologie* immediately began organizing. Excitement builded as they descended on Rome for the council, eager to begin their new era of piety and "better Christianity."

On the other hand, the seer of Fatima, Lucia, had stipulated that the so-called "Third Secret of Fatima" was to be opened by the pope in 1960. Pope St. John read this document and according to what the Vatican released in 2000, the pope read these words:

> [Pointing] to the earth with his right hand, the Angel cried out in a loud voice: '*Penance, Penance, Penance!*' ... the Holy Father passed through a big city half in ruins and half trembling with halting step, afflicted with pain and sorrow, he prayed for the souls of the corpses he met on his way...on his knees at the foot of the big Cross he was killed by a group of soldiers who fired bullets and arrows at him, and in the same way there died one after another the other Bishops, Priests, men and women Religious, and various lay people of different ranks and positions. Beneath the two

---

[109] Yves Congar, *Tradition and Traditions* (English Translation Burns and Oates: 1966), 167

arms of the Cross there were two Angels each with a crystal aspersorium in his hand, in which they gathered up the blood of the Martyrs and with it sprinkled the souls that were making their way to God.[110]

In the shadow of the ruins of the Second World War, the pope read these words of doom and their cry for penance. But he refused to release them, nor accept Fatima's vision of the modern world. Instead, he accepted the optimism that had been spread by Teilhard.

As Ratzinger would later recall, Teilhard's words "exerted a wide influence" on the Council with its "daring vision" providing a "concrete hope."[111] Echoing the optimism shown by Ven. Pius XII toward modern scholarship, Pope St. John XXIII stated at the beginning of Vatican II that mankind was progressing toward "new order" so much that "men of themselves are inclined to condemn [their own errors]."[112]

But the original documents for Vatican II, prepared by the Roman Curia, were not influenced by Teilhard, *Nouvelle théologie*, or any new, contemporary ideas. They were written by men formed in the Tradition, looking with skepticism on the secularist world. It was the secular world whose hopes and dreams had just scattered millions of bodies of men, women, and children across the globe over two world wars. It was the secularist dream that had created innumerable widows and orphans for whom the Church was now caring. They sought to

---

[110] Congregation of the Doctrine of the Faith, *The Message of Fatima* (2000)
[111] Joseph Cardinal Ratzinger, *Principles of Catholic Theology* (San Francisco: Ignatius Press, 1987), 334
[112] *novum rerum ordinem...Hodie homines per se ipsi ea damnare incipere videantur*. Pope John XXIII, Address *Gaudet Mater Ecclesia* (Oct. 11, 1962)

call on the modern world to repent of its errors. Thus the view of the Curia was more that of Fatima, than Teilhard: a world fallen under the sin of Adam, inclined to evil, and in desperate need of conversion to Jesus Christ.

The Original Vatican II Document on Revelation

Thus from the first days of the Council the battle lines were quickly drawn between the Curia and their allies on the one hand, and the *Nouvelle théologie* and their allies on the other. The latter, more in number and very organized, quickly took control of the council.[113] They took aim at the documents from the Curia.

One of the early documents presented to the Council was on Revelation: *De Fontibus Revelationis* "On the Sources of Revelation." The document cogently explained the authority of oral Tradition with the written Scriptures forming the authoritative sources of Revelation:

> Instructed by the commands and examples of Christ and of the Apostles, therefore, Holy Mother Church has always believed and believes still that the complete revelation is not contained in Scripture alone but in Scripture and in Tradition as in a twofold source, although in different ways.
>
> Besides containing what was revealed, the books of the Old and New Testaments were also written under the inspiration of the Holy Spirit, so that they have God as their author. But truly divine Tradition,

---

[113] On the takeover of the council by the German "Rhine group," see two sources favorable to Vatican II: *The Rhine Flows into the Tiber* by Ralph Wiltgen (TAN, 1991) and *What Happened at Vatican II* by John O'Malley (Harvard University Press, 2010).

preserved in the Church by a continuous succession, contains all the matters of faith and morals which the Apostles received either from the mouth of Christ or from the suggestions of the Holy Spirit and which they transmitted outside Holy Scripture as it were by hand to the Church so that in it they might be handed on further by the Church's preaching. Therefore the things which divine Tradition contains by itself are drawn not from books, but from the Church's living preaching, from the faith of believers, and from the Church's practice. As for things belonging to the past, many are known from various written, although not inspired, documents.

Let no one, therefore, dare to consider Tradition to be of inferior worth or refuse it his faith. For although Holy Scripture, since it is inspired, provides a divine instrument for expressing and illustrating the truths of faith, still its meaning can be clearly and fully understood or even presented only by means of the apostolic Tradition. Indeed, Tradition and it alone is the way in which some revealed truths, particularly those concerned with the inspiration, canonicity and integrity of each and every sacred book, are clarified and become known to the Church.[114]

Here the Curia defined the faith very clearly and in contradiction to the Protestant heretics. Both Scripture and oral Tradition were "sources of revelation."

---

[114] *De Fontibus Revelationis*, English Translation by Fr. Joseph A. Komonchak (2012) < https://jakomonchak.files.wordpress.com/2012/09/de-fontibus-1-5.pdf> (Accessed November 16th, 2019), articles 4, 5

This document also firmly condemned Limited Inerrancy, following the recent papal encyclicals on Scripture we have discussed:

> Because divine Inspiration extends to everything, the absolute immunity of all Holy Scripture from error follows directly and necessarily. For we are taught by the ancient and constant faith of the Church that it is utterly forbidden to grant that the sacred author himself has erred, since divine inspiration of itself necessarily excludes and repels any error in any matter, religious or profane, as it is necessary to say that God, the supreme Truth, is never the author of any error whatever.[115]

Not surprisingly, this document caused an uproar from the *Nouvelle théologie* theologians. They found this document so offensive that they strenuously campaigned for the entire document to be scrapped and an entirely new document written. The *Nouvelle théologie* partisans argued this document was too rigid, too confrontational, and too much like the Magisterium had been for the past century and a half. They wanted revolution.

Ratzinger was one of the leaders of the opposition to this document. He particularly objected to the phrase "sources of revelation." He would write later that he wanted to impose his own interpretation of the Fathers and try to remove the Magisterium's influence on it:

> The basic orientation was there, but on the other hand there was much to improve. Primarily, that it

---

[115] *De Fontibus Revelationis*, 12

be less dominated by the current Magisterium, and had to give greater voice to the Scriptures and the Fathers.[116]

Of course, the Scriptures and Fathers would need an interpreter. If he wanted the document "less dominated" by the Magisterium, who would then interpret the Tradition? The theologians.

Thus was the council dominated by the theologians crying out for their new ideas to be accepted and imposed on the Church. They had a conscious intention to break with the Magisterium of the recent past and force the Magisterium to move in a different direction than before. The *Nouvelle théologie* did not want to call the world to repentance, but thought that the modern world would accept their new ideas instead.

The Original Trashed, Ambiguities Created

One of the aspects of the dispute over the document on Revelation was on the concept of a "pastoral" Council. The Curia and their allies argued that being pastoral meant presenting to the world the clear teachings of the Catholic Church. The *Nouvelle théologie* partisans asserted that being pastoral meant obscuring things that were offensive to the secular Modernists and Protestants, and trying to cooperate with the enemies of the Church.

Some of them believed that they should simply join the enemies of the Church, since the Church (they asserted) had made serious errors in condemning the modern world and secular theologians. Other *Nouvelle théologie* thinkers

---

[116] Benedict, *Last Testament*, 99

actually *did* want to convert the world, but wanted to be very gentle about it and only convert by example, not condemnation or calls for conversion. These two opinions (later known as "liberal" and "conservative"), however, were able to ally *against* the Curia in order to overturn all of their documents (save one). They then rewrote them all with a strong Teilhardian, positive optimism toward the world, and almost none of the message of Fatima.

The Council Fathers fought over the document on Revelation so much that even though it was introduced at the very beginning of the Council, it was not completed until the very end of the three year meeting and promulgated just before close in November of 1965. Like all the documents of Vatican II, the final document created at the Council, *Dei Verbum*, had a great deal of excellent teaching, as we have quoted it above in chapter seven. Nevertheless, on certain key points the document was vague and left the door open to secular theologians which had previously been closed by the Magisterium.

For example, in articles 9, 21, and 24, the authority of oral Tradition is not clearly stated, but appears to take a second place to Scripture, even though in other places like article 9 or article 10, this authority appears to be equal. In addition, the traditional phrase used in the original draft, taking both Scripture and Tradition as "sources of revelation" was entirely removed. As we have seen in chapter 6, this phrase was the normal way of speaking about them before the Council. Why do these different areas of the text seem contradictory? Cardinal Kasper explains:

> In many places, [the Council Fathers] had to find compromise formulas, in which, often, the positions of the majority are located immediately

next to those of the minority, designed to delimit them. Thus, the conciliar texts themselves have a huge potential for conflict, open the door to a selective reception in either direction.[117]

Thus during the immediate years after the documents' promulgation the pope himself asserted that "the whole of the Dogmatic Constitution *Dei Verbum* is an apologia of the Holy Scriptures as the supreme rule of faith" (March 26, 1969). It is impossible that a reasonable mind could take this meaning out of the *original* draft, but the final document of *Dei Verbum* does not make the authority of Tradition explicitly clear. In effect, this makes the teaching more palatable for Protestant heretics, but ultimately unclear as to whether the Tradition is another source of Revelation. This was what Pius XII had feared in *Humani Generis*.

Ratzinger would write later about their work at the Council that:

> We handled things correctly, even if we certainly did not correctly assess the political consequences and the actual repercussions. One thought too much of theological matters then, and did not reflect on how these things would come across.[118]

Indeed, it was this document which would further open the way for Biblical scholars to begin spreading chaos which Ratzinger himself would condemn and provoke serious action by John Paul II as we shall see.

---

[117] Cardinal Walter Kasper, *L'Osservatore Romano*, April 12, 2013
[118] Benedict, *Last Testament*, 105

Opening the Door to Limited Inerrancy

Another area of debate at the Council was the question of Limited Inerrancy. As we have seen, this question had been firmly settled by the Magisterium over a number of encyclicals. Pius XII had even condemned the *Nouvelle théologie* because they asserted questions like this were still open for discussion.[119]

But at Vatican II on the Council floor some of the bishops openly asserted the error of Limited Inerrancy. Franz Cardinal Konig of Vienna stated openly that the Holy Word contains errors (*a veritate deficere*), based on the recent archaeological discoveries.[120]

Further, on a purely historical level, this type of conclusion can be made when one assumes, like Pius XII, that the modern historical method is absolutely objective making it difficult for scholars to err, and also that the historical data we have available is not a fragment of a fragment of a fragment. Both of these assertions had been shouted by the secular theologians for centuries, in an attempt to undermine the faith. On the contrary, as we have seen, numerous discoveries vindicated the authenticity of the Text (see the final list of resources for more information).

Nevertheless, the *Nouvelle théologie* party battled forcefully for Limited Inerrancy. In the end, like Kasper noted,

---

[119] "If the Supreme Pontiffs in their official documents purposely pass judgment on a matter up to that time under dispute, it is obvious that that matter, according to the mind and will of the same Pontiffs, cannot be any longer considered a question open to discussion among theologians" Pius XII, *Humani Generis* (1950), 20

[120] Denis Farkasfalvy, O. Cist. "Inspiration and Interpretation," *Vatican II: Renewal within Tradition*, Oxford University Press, 2008, 86

a compromise was struck, and an ambiguous phrase was promulgated:

> Therefore, since everything asserted by the inspired authors or sacred writers must be held to be asserted by the Holy Spirit, it follows that the books of Scripture must be acknowledged as teaching solidly, faithfully and without error that truth which God wanted put into sacred writings *for the sake of salvation*.[121]

Thus again, like the authority of Tradition, the original draft left no room for question whereas the final draft opened the door to this error.

As a result of this, Limited Inerrancy was permitted to spread among the Catholic scholars. For example, years later during the pontificate of Benedict XVI, who was attempting to correct the crisis by his "Hermeneutic of Continuity" concept, a book was published in 2008 called *Vatican II: Renewal within Tradition*. The purpose of this book was ostensibly to apply this continuity to the Council in order to set the record straight and pave a way through the crisis. It brought together numerous scholars who wrote essays on the documents of Vatican II.

Two luminaries of Scripture were brought forward to write essays on *Dei Verbum*. They both disagreed as to whether the document taught Limited Inerrancy. In the first place,

---

[121] Emphasis mine. *Dei Verbum* 11: *Cum ergo omne id, quod auctores inspirati seu hagiographi asserunt, retineri debeat assertum a Spiritu Sancto, inde Scripturae libri veritatem, quam Deus nostrae salutis causa Litteris Sacris consignari voluit, firmiter, fideliter et sine errore docere profitendi sunt.*

accomplished Scripture scholar Fr. Francis Martin writes that *Dei Verbum* 11

> eliminates many of the problems of the inerrancy debate and allows a simple acknowledgement of the inaccuracies (historical, textual, and so forth) that appear in the sacred text.[122]

Whereas on the other hand the Catholic Scripture scholar, Fr. Farkasfalvy in the same book says that *Dei Verbum* 11 "ultimately provided...no significant insights or true advancement for the issue [of inerrancy] under debate." He further asserts that in some mistranslations,

> *Dei Verbum* misleadingly appears to teach that inerrancy covers only those statement that regard *our salvation*. One may say that this misinterpretation caught on early in the reception of the council and is being propagated even by recognized and first-rate scholars.

In the footnotes he mentions the work of Fr. Raymond Brown, who helped edit the *Jerome Biblical Commentary* (1968) in the wake of the Council. Ratzinger himself as Benedict XVI would also deal with Limited Inerrancy, but let us return to our narrative.

The Triumph of the Theologians in the Church

When the Council closed on 1965, it was already evident to many reasonable minds that the Church was being thrown

---

[122] Lamb and Levering, eds., *Vatican II: Renewal within Tradition* (Oxford, 2008), 67

into chaos. Just as the theologians of *Nouvelle théologie* took over the Council and bent it to their own ends, theologians throughout the world began to take over the Church.

One prominent scholar of the day, Dietrich Von Hildebrand, begged Pope St. Paul VI in 1965 to condemn heresies but the pope refused.[123] He removed the Oath Against Modernism which bound theologians to reverence the Text as Pius X had ordered, and stripped the Pontifical Biblical Commission of Magisterial authority. All of their pronouncements from that time had no binding force.

As the situation continued to unravel with heretical bishops openly publishing heresy Paul VI seemed to realized that the extensive documents of Vatican II were not enough. Thus he promulgated an orthodox creed in 1968 and condemned contraception in the same year in *Humanae Vitae*. But he refused to enforce orthodoxy and a worldwide rebellion of priests, bishops and faithful, led by theologians, continued under Paul VI until his death in 1978.

During this time the revision of the Vulgate was being completed, but because of Pius XII's ruling, the English translations ignored even the New Vulgate and made their own translations. As a result they were influenced by Protestant heretics and secular theologians (we will cover this in detail in the next chapter).

The Pontifical Biblical Commission relented on their earlier strong stances on the Holy Bible. Even during the council they put forth an instruction indicating that the Gospels did not contain direct reports of the actual words and deeds of

---

[123] Interview with Dr. Alice von Hildebrand, Latin Mass Magazine, Summer 2001 < http://www.latinmassmagazine.com/articles/articles_2001_su_hildebran.html>. Accessed November 23, 2019.

Jesus Christ.[124] The Documentary Hypothesis and doubts about the Gospels began to be taught in Catholic seminaries throughout the world, in addition to a growing assumption that the theory of evolution was *absolutely true*. This was the direct result of the ambiguities of *Dei Verbum* and Paul VI's refusal to discipline heretics.

It was the triumph of the "theologian" in the Church. Just as Ockham had once argued centuries before that the theologian had authority to interpret the Holy Scriptures without the oral Tradition and without the Magisterium, such theologians arose to dominate the Church and the seminaries. Contrasted with the faithful laity we discussed in chapter seven, who must resist the Magisterium during a state of emergency but give power back to the bishops, the theologians seized power and kept it for themselves. One such "theologian" would later describe it this way:

> In the postconciliar years the phrase [from *Dei Verbum*] "for the sake of our salvation" became a critical principle militating against any literal interpretation of those parts of the Bible that legitimated sexual or social oppression.[125]

Thus the theologians could now take the Holy Bible in whatever direction they pleased. The optimistic confidence that Pius XII had placed in modern methods was now revealed for what it was. Feminist, materialist, Marxist and liberationist

---

[124] New Catholic Encyclopedia (2nd Ed.), "Pontifical Biblical Commission," 467-477
[125] John R. Donahue, S.J., "Biblical Scholarship 50 years After Divino Afflante Spiritu," *America* (September 18, 1993) <www.americamagazine.org/issue/100/biblical-scholarship-50-years-after-divino-afflante-spiritu>. Accessed November 23, 2019.

"theologies" arose which did "not even claim to be an understanding of the text itself in the manner in which it was originally intended."[126] This kind of error was taught in seminaries throughout the world.

In 1978, John Paul I was elected and then suddenly died, provoking speculation as to the cause of his death. Soon after in the same year, John Paul II was elected. During his pontificate, he changed the course of Paul VI and began to discipline some of the theologians from Vatican II like Hans Küng and Edward Schillebeeckx.

Nevertheless, almost as soon as he became pope, St. John Paul II did not call the Church back to the Tradition or even enforce the creed of Paul VI, but immediately began proclaiming his own ideas that he had been studying.

He spent the first years of his pontificate publicly proclaiming his own interpretation of Holy Scripture on the conjugal act in what would become known as the "Theology of the Body." For whatever good was in these teachings, it was nevertheless his own views on the Scripture. He was not simply passing down the teachings of Augustine and Aquinas (whom he only mentioned in passing). He also assumed the Documentary Hypothesis within this teaching. The teaching was firmly based on his new philosophical ideas being used to interpret the Scriptures with little reference to the authorities on these matters.

During this time in 1981 he also published an encyclical (*Familiaris Consortio*) which refused to quote the prior two papal documents on this subject (*Arcanum* and *Casti Connubii*) and based itself instead on new philosophy,

---

[126] Josef Ratzinger, "Biblical Interpretation in Crisis," op. cit.

reversing as well moral theology on gender roles.[127] Thus by the pope's own example, the office of the "theologian" was firmly planted in the Church.[128] These theologians continued to spread their ideas, imitating the methods of the pope himself. Particularly in the area of moral theology, John Paul's ideas were not the only ones becoming popular. Many theologians were using the pope's method of theology—ignoring the Tradition and utilizing new philosophy—to promote contraception and divorce.

Ratzinger-Wojtyła Attempt to Dam the Flood

By 1988, the situation was critical. Josef Ratzinger delivered a famous speech entitled "Biblical Interpretation in Crisis." In this talk he implicitly repudiated the optimism of Pius XII by saying the theologians' claim to research the Holy Bible and find "pure objectivity" was "an absurd abstraction." These theologians "are no longer interested in ascertaining the

---

[127] *Familiaris Consortio* 23: "[W]omen have the same right as men to perform various public functions." This reversed the rights and duties traditionally understood within the moral theology of marriage referenced in *Casti Connubii* 74ff. See also Fr. Chad Ripperger on Marriage <http://sensustraditionis.org/release/marriage/>
[128] The Theology of the Body is not without merit, especially in confessing the dignity of the conjugal act. Nevertheless, its magisterial authority is on the lowest level of binding authority, which means that it certainly *can* contain errors. Indeed, there have been a number of issues in the moral life directly tied to this teaching. These include: in 700 pages failing to mention the primary purpose of the conjugal act (children), leading to the use of NFP as *de facto* contraception (grave matter); undermining the headship of the husband, leading to New Feminism; enlarging the definition of validity for marriage, leading to the annulment crisis; and redefining the conjugal act, overturning the moral theology regarding the marital debt (grave matter). For a critical look at these issues, see Randy Engel, *The Theology of the Body: A Study in Modernism* (New Engel Publishing: 2008).

truth, but only in whatever will serve their own particular agendas."[129] Ratzinger saw the folly where Pius XII had not:

> Underneath the existing sources—that is to say, the biblical books themselves—we are supposed to find more original sources, which in turn become the criteria for interpretation. No one should really be surprised that this procedure leads to the sprouting of ever more numerous hypotheses which finally turn into a jungle of contradictions. In the end, one no longer learns what the text says, but *what it should have said*[.]

Instead, Ratzinger called for a return to the use of the Scriptures which had obtained before the Council (and indeed, centuries before that). He called for theologians to stop trying to interpret the Text without the wisdom of the Fathers and have faith in God. And this did not require them to abandon historical research.

This, of course, was the program promoted since Leo XIII but opposed by Ratzinger himself at the Council decades before. In order to overturn the prior Magisterium, Ratzinger and the conservative *Nouvelle théologie* theologians had to ally with the liberal heretics like Küng and Schillebeeckx. Now they were faced with the fruit of their decision.

Nevertheless, Ratzinger and Papa Wojtyła seemed to believe that they could still save the Council from itself without serious action against their heretic allies. Küng and Schillebeeckx were never fully condemned, even though they were manifest heretics. The most vocal opponent of *Humanae*

---

[129] Ratzinger, "Biblical Interpretation in Crisis." Emphasis mine.

Vitae—Bishop Martini—had been given the cardinal's hat by John Paul II, but he too was not condemned.

Ratzinger would later admit that it was the Council's own Constitution on Revelation that helped provoke the crisis. At the time of Vatican II and immediately afterward, he wrote,

> Catholic moral theology suffered a collapse that rendered the Church defenseless against [the sexual revolution.]...Until the Second Vatican Council, Catholic moral theology was largely founded on natural law, while Sacred Scripture was only cited for background or substantiation. In the Council's struggle for a new understanding of Revelation, the natural law option was largely abandoned, and a moral theology based *entirely on the Bible* was demanded.[130]

Thus as we said above, *Dei Verbum* was understood as removing the authority of oral Tradition and proclaiming that the Holy Bible was the supreme rule of faith. But, it was soon discovered that "from the Bible alone morality could not be expressed systematically," and thus contemporary philosophy was imposed on the Sacred Text in order to produce a moral system.[131] John Paul II had already done this, but in a way that defended *Humanae Vitae*. But the other theologians, following the same method, could object to *Humanae Vitae*. They pushed for the Church to approve what would be known as "the culture of death." John Paul II was aware of this and

---

[130] Benedict XVI, "The Church and the Scandal of Sexual Abuse," translated by *Anian Christoph Wimmer* (National Catholic Register: 2019) <https://www.ncregister.com/daily-news/the-church-and-the-scandal-of-sexual-abuse>. Accessed November 23, 2019.
[131] Ibid.

sought to come against this, but by using the same theological method.

But by the 1990s as the crisis was reaching a climax, it was clear to the theologians in the Church that John Paul II now intended to take doctrinal action against these heresies. Ratzinger would recall this time as the crisis "reached dramatic proportions" that the theologians' opposition

> very rapidly grew into an outcry against the Magisterium of the Church and mustered, audibly and visibly, the global protest potential against the expected doctrinal texts of John Paul II.[132]

It took a few years, but John Paul II's action finally came. Did he excommunicate the heretics as Pius X had done and drive them out of the vineyard of the Lord? No. Just as Teilhard de Chardin never received the penalty of excommunication from Pius XI or Pius XII, neither did the heretics under John Paul II.[133]

Instead, John Paul II issued more documents. The documents of Vatican II—more numerous than any Council before—were meant to bring the faith to "modern man" and help him understand the faith like never before. Instead, as Paul VI had also seen, the chaos had only increased after the council. The verbose documents of Vatican II had failed to prevent heresy. Unfortunately Paul VI and John Paul II believed that issuing more documents would produce a different result.

John Paul II issued a new universal Catechism in 1992. This was the first of its kind since Pius X. Ostensibly, the new

---

[132] Ibid.
[133] Lefebvre and De Castro Mayer and their bishops were the only ones excommunicated under John aPaul II. Marshall, *Infiltration*, 191

Catechism never once quoted Pius X, who was the last sainted pontiff. Instead, it was filled with words from Vatican II.

Still, there was a heavy use of Denzinger and St. Thomas, which was directed against the liberal theologians.[134] Thus they lamented that this Catechism "ignores the results of biblical scholarship. The code for reading the Gospels is the same used by Augustine and Aquinas."[135] John Paul II had ignored Augustine and Aquinas as authorities in his "Theology of the Body," but now he brought them in as authorities in the new Catechism.

In the next year, the Pontifical Biblical Commission released a very large document in which Ratzinger admitted that the historical critical method had contained "hidden dangers" which started a "struggle." Unfortunately he asserts that all of the secular theologians' errors "could not have been envisioned 30 years ago [at the Council]."[136] In reality it was the Curia and their allies who had warned of these dangers at the council, which Ratzinger and his allies had rejected in their excitement and optimism about a "new era of piety."

Nevertheless, the document makes a great attempt to moderate the excesses of the theologians by actively critiquing their errors in twisting the Word of God to support materialism, Marxism, and Feminism. Unfortunately its affirmation of the authority of oral Tradition and the Fathers

---

[134] Denzinger as we noted refers to an authoritative source book called *Enchiridion Symbolorum* which is simply a collection of papal and conciliar texts over the history of the Church.
[135] This was Luke Johnson (*Commonweal*, May 7th, 1993) quoted in Donahue "Biblical Scholarship 50 Years After Divino Afflante Spiritu," *America*
[136] Pontifical Biblical Commission, "The Interpretation of the Bible in the Church," < http://www.catholic-resources.org/ChurchDocs/PBC_Interp-FullText.htm>. Accessed November 23, 2019.

was tepid, and its confidence in the power of historical research was vast. The word "historical" appears 107 times in the document, the word "study" 54 times. The word "pray" appears 13 times and the word "humility" appears once.

But later that year, John Paul II released perhaps the greatest document of his pontificate: *Veritatis Splendor*. It took note and condemned (albeit gently) the "theological thinking" that was "incompatible with revealed truth."[137] It then implicitly condemned the power of the theologians with these words:

> Within Tradition, *the authentic interpretation* of the Lord's law develops, with the help of the Holy Spirit. The same Spirit who is at the origin of the Revelation of Jesus' commandments and teachings guarantees that they will be reverently preserved, faithfully expounded and correctly applied in different times and places. This constant "putting into practice" of the commandments is the sign and fruit of a deeper insight into Revelation and of an understanding in the light of faith of new historical and cultural situations.
>
> Nevertheless, it can only confirm the permanent validity of Revelation and follow in the line of the interpretation given to it by the great Tradition of the Church's teaching and life, as witnessed by the teaching of the Fathers, the lives of the Saints, the Church's Liturgy and the teaching of the Magisterium.
>
> In particular, as the Council affirms, "the task of authentically interpreting the word of God, whether

---

[137] St. John Paul II, *Veritatis Splendor* (1993), 27

in its written form or in that of Tradition, has been entrusted only to those charged with the Church's living Magisterium, whose authority is exercised in the name of Jesus Christ."[138]

Here, St. John Paul II refuses to use the ambiguous phrase from *Dei Verbum* that Doctrine develops through the "study made by believers...through a penetrating understanding of the spiritual realities which they experience" which obviously affirmed the power and authority of the theologians.[139] Instead, he uses the better phrase given in article 10 where the Tradition's interpretation is committed "only" to the Magisterium, and he adds in this encyclical, this development can "only confirm" the Revelation as contained in the whole of Sacred Tradition, not contained only in Scripture.

With this more solid basis of Scripture and Tradition, Papa Wojtyła then condemned moral relativism, confirmed the Natural Law, properly framed questions of conscience and, most notably, re-confirmed the intrinsic evil in contraception, abortion, euthanasia, and especially adultery. The Roman Pontiff confirmed with clear teaching that these acts are always evil and can never be committed at any time for any reason because the "the negative commandments [i.e. against adultery] oblige always and under all circumstances."[140]

Further in 1998, John Paul II sought to bring the Church in line with an orthodox profession of faith, but with stronger force than Paul VI had. This was *Ad Tuendam Fidem*, in which the pope added further stipulations in canon law that all were bound to recite a profession of faith which included being bound by Tradition, and those who persisted in heresy were to

---

[138] Ibid., 27
[139] *Dei Verbum*, 8
[140] *Veritatis Splendor*, 27

be punished "with a just penalty." Notably, in the commentary on this document from Ratzinger's Holy Office it was declared that "the absence of error in the inspired sacred texts" is a *De Fide* doctrine which is infallible and must be believed.[141]

Thus John Paul II and Ratzinger sought to place emphasis back on the Tradition as was done before the Council, but without abandoning the same methods that had spawned the crisis at the Council—relaxation of all ecclesiastical discipline. Like Paul VI, John Paul II implicitly saw that the ambiguous loquaciousness of Vatican II was not effective and a clear and concise profession of faith was necessary, but without truly enforcing it. Thus these creeds from Paul VI and John Paul II confirmed Pius X's *Oath Against Modernism* was the correct approach, even though Vatican II attempted to reverse this. But only Pius X was able to drive the heretics underground because only he was willing to enforce it.

The Dam Does Not Hold

The theologians continued their rebellion because they received no real penalty. They were given freedom to continue to teach their heresies to seminarians and write books with harmful ideas. As Dietrich von Hildebrand had written in the seventies, the Church had abandoned the anathema: "an act of the greatest charity toward all the faithful."[142] Excommunications and discipline were rare, if they were decreed at all. And so the leading heretical bishop in the Church, Cardinal Martini, helped lead the St. Gallen Mafia

---

[141] Congregation for the Doctrine of the Faith, "Commentary on the Concluding Formula of the 'Professio fidei,'" (1998) < https://www.catholicculture.org/culture/library/view.cfm?recnum=439>
[142] Dietrich von Hildebrand, *The Charitable Anathema* (Roman Catholic Books: 1993), 5

during these years in the 1990s to plan (eventually) for the election of Pope Francis.

In 2000, Ratzinger released his most forceful document, *Dominus Iesus*, which condemned the errors of indifferentism promoted by the theologians. But no theologians were bound to accept it. In 2001, St. John Paul II made McCarrick a Cardinal. And in 2002, the first abuse scandal broke, shattering the Catholic Church in America and the world.

In 2005, Benedict was elected. As a Scripture scholar who critiqued the theologians, he was in a position, as pope, to deal with the theologians like no one else. In 2010, a Synod on the Scripture was held. The *Instrumentum Laboris* explicitly taught Limited Inerrancy by inserting the word "only" into the text of *Dei Verbum*.[143] Clearly the theologians were tirelessly at work. The synod fathers submitted a *propositio* to Pope Benedict regarding Limited Inerrancy with these words:

> The synod proposes that the Congregation for the Doctrine of the Faith clarify the concepts of "inspiration" and "truth" in the Bible, along with their reciprocal relationship, in order to better understand the teaching of Dei Verbum 11. In particular, it's necessary to emphasize the specific character of Catholic Biblical hermeneutics in this area.[144]

---

[143] "The following can be said with certainty...with regards to what might be inspired in the many parts of Sacred Scripture, inerrancy applies only to 'that truth which God wanted put into sacred writings for the sake of salvation'"(Ch. 2, 15.c)
<http://www.vatican.va/roman_curia/synod/documents/rc_synod_doc_20080511_instrlabor-xii-assembly_en.html>
[144] "Synod: Final Propositions of the Synod of Bishops on the Bible," by John Allen < https://www.ncronline.org/news/synod-final-propositions-synod-bishops-bible>. Proposition 12

If the synod fathers read the encyclicals of Leo XIII, Benedict XV and even Pius XII, inerrancy would have been much clearer. Instead, the focus was on Vatican II.

But instead of clarifying, Pope Benedict said this in *Verbum Domini*, the post-synodal exhortation released two years later:

> A deeper study of the process of inspiration will doubtless lead to a greater understanding of the truth contained in the sacred books. As the Council's teaching states in this regard, the inspired books teach the truth: [quotes the phrase from Dei Verbum 11]... one must acknowledge the need today for a fuller and more adequate study of these realities, in order better to respond to the need to interpret the sacred texts in accordance with their nature. Here I would express my fervent hope that research in this field will progress and bear fruit both for biblical science and for the spiritual life of the faithful.[145]

Astonishingly, instead of exercising his authority as Roman Pontiff to give clarity on this subject, he placed a "fervent hope" in "research." Certainly a bewildering course of action, unless Pope Benedict thought that Limited Inerrancy was not an error or an urgent issue.

It appears, sadly, that one of these may have been the case. In *Jesus of Nazareth*, published the next year, writing as Josef Ratzinger, he wrote concerning the Gospel of St. John:

> If 'historical' is understood to mean that the discourses of Jesus transmitted to us have to be

---

[145] Benedict XVI, *Verbum Domini* (2010), 19

something like a recorded transcript in order to be acknowledged as 'historically' authentic, then *the discourses of John's Gospel are not 'historical.'*

But the fact that *they make no claim to literal accuracy* of this sort by no means implies that they are merely 'Jesus poems' that the members of the Johannine school gradually put together, claiming to be acting under the guidance of the Paraclete. What the Gospel is really claiming is that it has correctly rendered the substance of the discourses, of Jesus' self-attestation in the great Jerusalem disputes, so that the readers really do encounter the decisive content of this message and, therein, the authentic figure of Jesus.[146]

He develops this to assert that the Gospels were produced by the Holy Spirit by the "we" of the Church's memory: "Because the personal recollection that provides the foundation of the Gospel is purified and deepened by being inserted into the memory of the Church, it does indeed transcend *the banal recollection of facts.*"[147]

Thus it appears all but certain that Ratzinger in this writing holds to the error of Limited Inerrancy. Why? Because the Gospel of St. John itself declares that it was written by the eyewitness, St. John himself:

> This is that disciple who giveth testimony of these things, and hath written these things; and we know that his testimony is true (Jn. xxi. 24).

---

[146] Joseph Ratzinger, *Jesus of Nazareth* (Ignatius Press: 2011), 229. Emphasis mine.
[147] Ibid., 231

Thus in order for the assertion of Ratzinger to be true, this verse must be false. Therefore, Ratzinger wrote here, censuring "the banal recollection of facts," of Limited Inerrancy in so many words.

Against this, the Pontifical Biblical Commission answered this question over a century earlier:

> Can [it] be said that the deeds related in the fourth Gospel are totally or partially so invented that they are allegories or doctrinal symbols; [and] that the words of the Lord are not properly and truly the words of the Lord himself, but theological compositions of the writer, although placed in the mouth of the Lord?
> Answer: in the negative.

Despite all of the obfuscation since the pontificate of Pius XII, this ruling has never been altered by an equal or higher Magisterium.

Lamentably, we see in the person of Ratzinger especially the failure of the hermeneutic of continuity. By successfully overcoming the prior Magisterium at Vatican II and allying with the liberal heretics, the Conservative wing of *Nouvelle théologie* was never able to overcome the seeds, as it were, of their own destruction. By refusing to suppress the heretics, the heretics eventually gained enough power to elect a pope after their own designs. Unfortunately after fifty years of Conservative *Nouvelle théologie* popes, it seems they have not shown themselves to be saints toward the Holy Bible, but theologians.

Francis, James Martin, and the Theologians

After Benedict resigned in 2013, the liberal heretics were able to elect their chosen successor to Cardinal Martini: Pope Francis I. Under this pope, not only have the theologians remained in power, but they have also gained more bishoprics and congregational posts than ever before. As a result they have been able to push forward the original intentions of Küng and Schillebeeckx and their allies: Vatican III. In their mind, the Second Vatican Council was only the beginning, and the liberal theologians had been pushing for the next steps in a logical progression: women priests, contraception, divorce and remarriage, etc.

To his credit, St. John Paul II had firmly opposed many of these moral errors in his encyclicals and official pronouncements. But because, like St. Paul VI, he would not enforce this with the heretics and follow the example of St. Pius X, the theologians were able to take their vengeance, as it were, under pope Francis. They took the over-population myth accepted by Paul VI, and began to push the climate change agenda beginning with *Laudato Si.'* Then they rigged the family synods which "abrogated" the moral law on adultery. Pope Francis has also "abrogated" *Veritatis Splendor* on contraception, stating that it can be practiced licitly in extreme circumstances. And besides all this and more, at the time of this writing [December of 2019], the theologians are now pushing for women priests and Francis is giving them more power for it, while causing a pagan idol to receive adoration.

Perhaps more than any other public figure, though, the reign of the theologians shows itself in the work of James Martin, personally favored by Pope Francis. This Jesuit appears to be thoroughly instructed in the ways of the "theologians." So much so, that he openly uses emotional manipulation in order to undermine the faith and push his heresies. His book promoting his primary heresy is called *Building a Bridge*, which uses psychological manipulation and emotional provocations to push poison for souls. Of course, he does not rely on the moral theology of the Church to say this, but his chosen group of Biblical theologians.

A recent statement of his is a perfect example of the methods of this Jesuit and the theologians for decades before him, which will bring our narrative to a close. In a Tweet on October 23, 2019, Martin wrote this:

James Martin, SJ
@JamesMartinSJ

Interesting: "Where the Bible mentions [same-sex sexual] behavior at all, it clearly condemns it. I freely grant that. The issue is precisely whether the biblical judgment is correct. The Bible sanctioned slavery as well and nowhere attacked it as unjust..

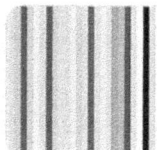
A Deeper Tenor — Center for Action and Contemplation
Gender and Sexuality A Deeper Tenor Wednesday, October 23, 2019 My deceased friend Walter Wink (1935-2012), a ...
cac.org

3:35 PM · Oct 23, 2019 · Twitter Web App

175 Retweets **1.1K** Likes

This link that was shared by Martin contained these blasphemous words against God's Holy Word:

> [W]omen are pressing us to acknowledge the sexism and patriarchalism that pervades Scripture and has alienated so many women from the church. The way out, however, is not to deny the sexism in Scripture, but to *develop an interpretive theory that*

> *judges even Scripture* in the light of the revelation in Jesus. What Jesus gives us is a critique of domination in all its forms, *a critique that can be turned on the Bible itself.* The Bible thus contains the principles of its own correction. We are freed from bibliolatry, the worship of the Bible. It is restored to its proper place as witness to the Word of God. And that Word is a Person, not a book.[148]

The reader will pardon me for quoting this filth in full in order to illustrate the depth to which these heretical theologians descend. A few important points about this. First, this theologian is a Protestant which, to a Catholic, already discredits his authority. Second, the theologian is advocating for a Marxist "critique of domination," thus like all theologians, is imposing his own philosophy on the ancient Text against the oral Tradition and the Magisterium. Third, and most importantly, he uses a truth in order to advocate a heresy: the Word of God is indeed a person, not the Holy Bible itself. But by using this truth, the heretic then denies the inerrancy of the Holy Bible, forming the principle upon which he can dare to challenge the moral code in the Scriptures themselves.

Thankfully, His Excellency, Bishop Strickland took a stand against the powerful Martin:

---

[148] Walter Wink, "Homosexuality and the Bible," in *Homosexuality and Christian Faith: Questions of Conscience for the Churches,* ed. Walter Wink (Fortress Press: 1999), 47-48 < https://cac.org/a-deeper-tenor-2019-10-23/> Accessed November 18th, 2019. Emphasis mine.

Tweet

Bishop J. Strickland @Bishopoftyler · Oct 23
Thank you for acknowledging that you question scripture. If we go down that road where do we stop? I know you have lots of support but you are challenging the Deposit of Faith that I promised to defend. As a bishop I'll keep defending it.

> **James Martin, SJ** @JamesMartinSJ · Oct 23
> Interesting: "Where the Bible mentions [same-sex sexual] behavior at all, it clearly condemns it. I freely grant that. The issue is precisely whether the biblical judgment is correct. The Bible sanctioned slavery as well and nowhere attacked it as unjust.. cac.org/a-deeper-tenor...
> Show this thread

💬 442   🔁 1.1K   ♡ 5.3K   ↑

James Martin, SJ
@JamesMartinSJ

Replying to @Bishopoftyler

Dear Bishop: Apparently, you believe that this quote is from me. It is not. It is from Walter Wink, the Protestant Scripture scholar and theologian. Also, as you know, Catholics are not fundamentalists when it comes to Scripture, as "Dei Verbum" clearly states. Many thanks.

12:52 PM · Oct 24, 2019 · Twitter Web App

On a side note, we see one of the tactics of James Martin: he indirectly supports the blasphemies quoted above, then exonerates himself by saying he did not say it. But to our point, Martin brings it back to *Dei Verbum* 11. He then further developed his defense by mocking the intelligence of the bishop:

244

Thus although Mr. Wink may be a "heretic," he is so smart and has authored so many books about Scripture, this accusation is ultimately "puerile." Based on what we have said about a "theologian" contrasted with a true theologian as a man of prayer and humility, Mr. Wink fits the definition in Martin's mind: he only needs great learning to understand the Holy Bible. He does not need piety to the Fathers or humility toward the Magisterium. His knowledge is so great that he knows more than everyone else. Finally Martin puts "inerrancy" in quotation marks and mocks those who think Catholics are "fundamentalists." The implication, of course, is that *Dei Verbum* teaches Limited Inerrancy.

If the Holy Scriptures only hold limited inspiration, then everything can be doubted. The brazen of Mr. Wink can be touted by a Catholic priest as a brilliant mind. In reality, he is only a false theologian, who will be forgotten tomorrow compared to the great sanctity of our Fathers. But this is the hinge upon which so much error and heresy has been pushed for decades in the Church while souls have been lost: the Holy Bible does not require humility and piety, but only book knowledge. Then the Scripture can be seen as erroneous in need of correction.

Conclusion: Against the Tyranny of Theologians

This crisis will most likely not be resolved before my generation passes away. The theologians are too entrenched in their power throughout hundreds of universities throughout the world, and the Church has suffered, as Newman said of the Arian crisis a "temporary suspense of the functions of the teaching church."[149] And thus it is the laity who must rise up and put forth the saints as our guide with the authority of the oral Tradition and prior Magisterium. In order to do this we must read and pray. Read and pray. If you do not have time to do both, only pray. As we have tried to emphatically say in the first part of this work, it is prayer that is much more important than study. And in the devout reading of Holy Scripture, we must have the humility to say with St. Augustine:

> On my part I confess [concerning] those Books of Scripture which are now called canonical that I have learned to pay such honor and reverence as to believe most firmly that none of their writers has fallen into any error. And if in these Books I meet

---

[149] Newman, *The Arians of the Fourth Century*, op. cit., 254ff.

anything which seems contrary to truth, I shall not hesitate to conclude either that the text is faulty, or that the translator has not expressed the meaning of the passage, or that I myself do not understand.[150]

Brethren: *there can be no true error in Holy Scripture*. The actual words of our Lord Jesus Christ are truly contained in the faithful witnesses of the Gospels. If a copy error occurred in a manuscript, this is not a true error. This is what St. Jerome intended with his Vulgate revision and the subsequent editions of the same. If we do not understand any apparent contradictions, then there is some divine mystery present which has not been revealed to us. Or the translation has not been rendered fully, or, what is more common in our day, the translation is influenced by other motives. Let us, then, examine and evaluate further some of the Catholic English translations of the Holy Bible.

---

[150] Ep. lxxxii., i. *et crebrius alibi* as cited in *Providentissimus Deus*, 21

Part Three

Resources: Everything Else You Need

+

XI

LINGUISTIC ANALYSIS OF ENGLISH BIBLE TRANSLATIONS

As we stated above, beginning in the 19th century and early 20th, a number of new English translations were completed by Protestants (the RV and the ASV). These did not gain much popularity, however, and most Protestants continued to use the King James Version.

In the 1930s the English Catholic Bishops initiated a project to update the language of the Douay Rheims again, since some of the renderings were difficult to understand 200 years after the last revision by Challoner. For this project the English Bishops commissioned the learned scholar and Anglican convert, Msgr. Ronald Knox.

This new version ended up being an entirely new translation which followed a more "dynamic" translation philosophy. This meant that the English translation did not correspond word-for-word in the Greek or Latin, but included more elaboration for the sake of meaning. It was more a translation of "sense-for-sense." This type of translation philosophy, however, means that the translator has much greater control over the meaning of the text (see chart below).

A few years after *Divino Afflante Spiritu*, Msgr. Knox completed his Knox Bible in 1949 and received the personal recommended of Ven. Pius XII. The sub heading for the Knox Bible was "A Translation From the Latin Vulgate in the Light of the Hebrew and Greek Originals." It was meant to be read side by side with the Douay Rheims, which was a more "formal translation," meaning virtually each Latin word has an English equivalent. It is true that a number of verses in the DR are difficult. Thus Knox's translation was a helpful paraphrase translation which assisted with some meanings of obscure English phrases.

However, besides the dynamic translation, his work suffered from arbitrary choices, such as Lam. V. 13 in which Msgr. Knox chose to follow the Masoretic variant for no apparent reason other than the fact that the Vulgate and Septuagint reading is particularly gruesome. This suggests that Msgr. Knox was not following a principled approach, but one that was influenced by current ideas.

At the same time as this was happening, the Protestants were completing their newest revision of the King James Version, the Revised Standard Version, released in 1952. This version attempted to use the recent advances in ancient knowledge and biblical studies. But, just as the Protestants had done before, they imposed their 20th century opinions on Holy Writ by ignoring the Vulgate and the Septuagint in key areas, which we will cover below.

During the openness of the Second Vatican Council, a Catholic version of the Revised Standard Version was completed in 1966. They took the Old Testament from the Protestants untouched, added the deutero-canonical books, and made minor revisions to the New Testament. In addition, another Catholic translation was completed in America which was done in collaboration with Protestant heretics. This was the New American Bible which was completed in 1970.

The New Testament Misquotes the Old

All of these new translations suffered from imposing their modern opinions on the ancient text. Let's consider a very important text regarding the dogma of the Virgin Birth. This text is Isaias vii. 14. Originally, even Protestants and Catholics agreed on this verse. In the Douay Rheims *and* the King James Version, this verse reads:

> Therefore the Lord himself shall give you a sign. Behold a **virgin** shall conceive, and bear a son, and his name shall be called Emmanuel.

The key word here is "virgin." Now in comparing the Masoretic text as well as the Dead Sea Scrolls text, the word is not "virgin" explicitly but "maiden." There are two different words in Hebrew here, *betulah* ("virgin") and *almah* ("maiden"), but the oldest Hebrew (the Dead Sea Scrolls) accords with the Masoretic in using not *betulah* but *almah*. Thus the translators of the twentieth century reasoned, did not the original text say "maiden" and not "virgin"? Thus Knox has:

> The Maid shall be with child, and shall bear a son

But the Protestants reasoned, that because modern English does not use the word "maiden" anymore, it should be rendered as "young woman." Then the Catholic versions followed this.

The RSV (1966 Catholic) reads: "a young woman shall conceive."

The New American Bible (1970) initially had "virgin" but was revised in 2011 to be "the young woman, pregnant and about to bear a son"

In modern English, it need not be explained further that the term "young woman" completely changes the meaning of this verse and becomes an offense to the honor of our Lady.

Linguistically, it is incorrect to translate *almah* as anything other than "virgin" for a number of reasons. The first is that, as we have said, each word often had multiple meanings in every language. Therefore translation is an interpretation of the most important meaning of that word by selecting one and discarding the others. Therefore we need to consult the ancient translations of this text in order to understand how the word *almah* should be understood, as it was understood in ancient times. When the modern translators bypass these translations in favor of the "original text," they impose their opinions onto the ancient text and think they are more accurate.

What do the ancient translations say? The Aramaic Targum (2nd century A.D.) says "maiden." The Syriac Peshitta (2nd c. A.D.) says "chaste maiden." But the most prominent Greek translation, the Septuagint (2nd c. B.C.) says "virgin." Thus it is clear that from the ancient translations the sense of the word "young woman" was that she was a virgin. Why else would it be a "sign"? It would not be miraculous or significant if a young woman simply became pregnant.

What is striking, however, is that at least one Jew who made a different Greek translation of this verse in the 1st century departed from the standard Greek Septuagint and wrote "young woman" in Greek instead of "virgin." This was in the Aquila translation. In addition, St. Justin Martyr's second century dialogue with Trypho the Jew indicates that the Jews at that time were not interpreting this verse as "virgin," suggesting that the Jews were already departing from the earlier Jewish sense of "virgin" contained in the Septuagint.[151]

The other reason it is incorrect to translate *almah* as "young woman" is that the New Testament quotes this verse and says "virgin" in Mt. i. 23 and Lk. i. 35. A Protestant scholar illustrates this:

> It is unreasonable to say that the "true" text actually differs from what the early church believed it to be. ...The quotation from Isa. 7.14 in Mt. 1.23 makes this absolutely clear. Matthew says "virgin" in accordance with the Greek translation, whereas the Hebrew text uses the word "young woman." It would be pointless to rebuke the evangelist for using the "wrong" text. On the contrary, the "wrong" text gains a significance of its own by being used.[152]

Thus in both the 1966 RSV and the Knox Bible (and the 2011 NAB), the Gospel of Matthew misquotes its own text! If you are reading one these versions of St. Matthew and flip over to Isaias to check the reference, you will discover that the evangelist did not quote this text accurately. So these translations make a fool of the Gospel writer.

Finally, cultural and historical reasons make "virgin" the best possible translation as well. In ancient Israel, the term "young woman" was synonymous with "virgin." This used to

---

[151] See St. Justin Martyr, *Dialogue with Trypho the Jew*, ch. 71ff
[152] Mogens Müller, *The First Bible of the Church: A Plea for the Septuagint* (Sheffield Academic Press, 1996), 23

be the case also with the two words "maiden" and "virgin" in English. They both mean virginity, but one is more specific. Whereas in modern English, lamentably, "young woman" does not necessarily mean "virgin."

Another example of causing the Holy Bible to misquote itself regards the words of Jesus Christ Himself. Our Lord quotes Deuteronomy in Mt. iv. 4, Lk. iv. 4 against the temptation of Satan. In this passage he quotes the Septuagint: "not in bread alone doth man live, but in *every word* that proceedeth from the mouth of God." This verse has obvious Christological typology. The bread of the Manna that was given to Israel (itself a *typos* of the Sacrament) points yet deeper still to the Word which comes from God: the Word Which became flesh and dwelt among us.

But the RSV in that passage in Deuteronomy (viii. 3), quotes the Masoretic: "…but by *everything* [NAB: "all"] that proceeds from the mouth of God." This difference of one word may seem minor, but as we have seen with the Virgin Birth, entire doctrines can be drawn out from a single word, which is why the Fathers showed great reverence toward each word of Holy Writ.

But consider the implications of this translation choice. The Second Person of the Trinity is quoting the Holy Scriptures. If you are reading the RSV or the NAB, and flip back to read that Deuteronomy passage, you find He did not exactly quote that passage accurately! Is it not the height of folly to cause Jesus Christ to misquote the Holy Bible? But these modern translations, thinking themselves more accurate, actually depart from the standard of the New Testament itself and cause the Gospels and our Lord to misquote the Old Testament.

Revisions Since the 1960s

The Revised Standard Version Catholic Edition went through a number of revisions until the most recent edition was published in 2006. In this text the publishers advertise:

> This second edition of the RSV doesn't put the biblical text through a filter to make it acceptable to current tastes and prejudices...[it is the] only Bible translation that uses standard (non-feminist) English and is in conformity with the Church's translation guidelines found in the Vatican document, *Liturgiam Authenticam*.[153]

Here we must say a word about *Liturgiam Authenticam* and the struggle for the 3rd Edition of the Roman Missal. In 1969, under Pope St. Paul VI an official document was approved to guide the translation of the New Mass: *Comme le prevoit*. This document said, among other things, that some Latin texts of the Old Mass are "contrary to modern Christian ideas," and thus approved of their removal for the text of the New Mass, or of translating in such a way as to remove them from the vernacular.[154] Thus what texts Bugnini was not able to remove from the Old Mass (only 17% of prayers from the Old Mass remain in the New), he was able to remove by translation obfuscation.[155] This then, caused a series of translations

---

[153] < https://www.ignatius.com/Ignatius-Bible-RSV-2nd-Edition-P1126.aspx>. Accessed November 23, 2019.
[154] Concilium, *Comme le prévoit* (1969) <http://natcath.org/NCR_Online/documents/comme.htm>. Accessed November 23, 2019, 24
[155] Fr. John Zuhlsdorf, "2nd Sunday after Epiphany – liturgical unicorn," *What does the Prayer Really Say?* January 19, 2019 < https://wdtprs.com/2019/01/wdtprs-2nd-sunday-after-epiphany-liturgical-unicorn/>. Accessed November 24, 2019.

heavily influenced by modern philosophy, imposing modern ideas on the ancient Text. This was the origin of the blog by Fr. John Zuhlsdorf, *What Does the Prayer Really Say?* which compared these foolish translations with the actual text of the New Mass.

This approval given by Pope St. Paul VI caused such controversy that a coalition of priests eventually was able to convince Pope St. John Paul II to reverse this instruction and issue *Liturgiam Authenticam* in 2001.[156] This document said that the translations must be "free from all ideological influence," and follow a word-for-word translation, instead of the more loose "dynamic" translation from Paul VI.[157] This is the context for the new RSV's advertising its adherence to this document and its freedom from ideologies.

Thus in the new RSV translation the mis-translation of Isaias vii. 14 was corrected so that it now reads "virgin." Also the Epistles say "brethren," (translating the same Greek *adelphoi)* instead of adding "brothers and sisters" as the NAB lectionary does, altering the Sacred Text to fit modern ideas. Nevertheless, the RSV continued to cause Jesus Christ to misquote Deuteronomy.

The RSV 2006 also suffers from what appears to be an embarrassment about the Sacred Text in some of its hard sayings. For example, in Lk. XII. 46 and Mt. XXIV. 51 our Lord's parable says that the Master returns to the unworthy slave and separates him with the unbelievers. The Greek for

---

[156] For the full story of this struggle, listen to the lecture by one of these priests (from the organization *Credo*), Fr. Jerry Pokorsky, "Liturgiam Authenticam," *Institute of Catholic Culture*. Some countries, such as Italy and Germany, refused to obey John Paul II and change their translations, and Pope Francis gave them power to decide for themselves in *Magnum Principium* (2017).
[157] John Paul II, *Liturgiam Authenticam* (2001), 3

"separate" (διχοτομέω) is a rare word which means to literally "cut into pieces" or "cut with scourges." If the RSV translators had been consulting what the Vulgate received, they would have known that the sense of this violent language is an unalterable separation as the DR renders the Latin "separate." This, then, clearly points to the final judgment.

Instead, the RSV renders this word "punish," which is the most general sense of the Greek, but does not render the particular sense of a unique word (there are general Greek words for "punishment" such as ἐκδίκησις or κρίσις but this is a word with a specific action involved). They then include the explicit translation in each case in a foot note. This suggests a false principle of a dynamic paraphrase—saying words that do not adhere to the Greek—or else being influenced by modern sensibilities and thus the ideologies from which the RSV claimed to be freed.

The New American Bible, published in 1970 as we said to their credit, initially had "virgin" but this was later revised to say "the young woman, pregnant and about to bear a son" in 2011. It continues to cause the misquotation of Dt. viii. 3. Thankfully, in the NAB lectionary read at the New Mass, "virgin" is re-inserted into the Text.

The Importance of the Vulgate: Doctrine

As we discuss why every word of Holy Writ matters, this becomes particularly acute when we look at the Vulgate of St. Jerome. This will have a significant impact on our discussion of Catholic English Bible translations. There have been a number of Catholic doctrines which have been based on texts from the Latin Vulgate which do not appear in modern Catholic Bibles based on the Masoretic Hebrew or Protestant Biblical scholarship. As we have said, the Church has permitted variants, and some of these variants have been the source of doctrines. That is why an over-emphasis on an imaginary "original text" which does not exist can lead to doubting the Catholic faith since it can easily be asserted that these saints just had faulty texts and thus produced faulty doctrines.

The first is Isaias xi. 2-3. St. Jerome translated this from ancient Hebrew manuscripts now lost. This Hebrew was different than the Masoretic and the Dead Sea Scrolls but accorded with the Septuagint's Hebrew source. In this verse the seven gifts of the Holy Spirit are enumerated:

> Et requiescet super eum spiritus Domini: spiritus sapientiæ et intellectus, spiritus consilii et fortitudinis, spiritus scientiæ et pietatis; et replebit eum spiritus timoris Domini.
>
> And the spirit of the Lord shall rest upon him: the spirit of wisdom, and of understanding, the spirit of counsel, and of fortitude, the spirit of knowledge, *and of godliness*. And he shall be filled with the spirit of the fear of the Lord.

From this verse the Church understood that there are seven gifts of the Holy Spirit which perfect the virtues. St. Thomas discusses these in I-II q68, representing the Latin tradition on this point following also the Septuagint in this verse. These gifts of the Holy Ghost formed a fundamental basis for the spiritual life as expounded by Latin Christianity.

The Masoretic text, however, does not include the penultimate gift: piety (godliness), but rather simply repeats the "Fear of the Lord." Thus the gifts of the Holy Spirit are not enumerated the same way but this gift is excluded from the list according to the Masoretic. Thus even Jordan Aumann, an otherwise excellent Catholic spiritual writer, cannot understand where the Gift of Piety came from.[158]

Galatians 5:22 also enumerates the fruits of the Holy Spirit based on a Latin variant, counting twelve: charity, joy, peace, patience, benignity, goodness, longanimity, mildness, faith, modesty, continency, chastity. This is the list enumerated and explained by St. Thomas in I-II q70. But this appears to be an early commentary in the Latin Text, as this list of twelve does not exist in the Greek manuscripts, which only have nine. The modern Catholic English translations all reduce the number to nine. Thus it might be concluded that the whole Latin Tradition was wrong about the number of fruits of the Holy Ghost. But this is only possible if we assert that inspiration is restricted to the Text of the Holy Bible, and not the oral Tradition that governs it. Here was see how the oral Tradition and the original text overlap. Both must be accepted with piety.

Another example is Tob. viii. 9:

> And now, Lord, thou knowest, that not for fleshly lust do I take my sister to wife, but only for the love of posterity, in which thy name may be blessed for ever and ever.

> Et nunc Domine, tu scis quia non luxuriæ causa accipio sororem meam conjugem, sed sola posteritatis dilectione, in qua benedicatur nomen tuum in sæcula sæculorum (verse 10 in the Latin)

---

[158] See his classic text, *Spiritual Theology*, which is an excellent treatise on the doctrinal and practical aspects of the spiritual life.

But the new translations follow a different variant which says, "not because of lust but with sincerity [in truth]." This involves a controversy which began under Pius XI about the *Nouvelle théologie* thinkers hoping to re-order and re-define marriage. Pius XII condemned this in 1944 when he decreed that the primary end of marriage is children and the secondary end of marriage—the remedy for lust and the good of the spouses—can never be equated with the primary end, nor the primary subordinated to the secondary.[159]

Unfortunately the *Nouvelle théologie* thinkers were able to work ambiguity into *Gaudium et Spes* 48 which seemed to at least equate the two ends of marriage, or else subordinate procreation to the good of spouses. This led to ambiguity in the New Code of Canon law of 1983, which redefined Marriage and removed the traditional doctrines about Matrimony (in the wake of St. John Paul II's *Theology of the Body* which already challenged the traditional doctrine as we have noted). Thus the New Catechism 2361 quotes the "sincerity" version of Tobit, which supports the new ambiguity about Marriage.

But perhaps the most fundamental doctrine which is obscured today is Original Sin. St. Augustine drew evidence for this doctrine from a variant of Romans v. 12:

> Wherefore as by one man sin entered into this world and by sin death: and so death passed upon all men, **in** whom all have sinned.
>
> Propterea sicut per unum hominem peccatum in hunc mundum intravit, et per peccatum mors, et ita

---

[159] Decree of the Holy Office, April 1, 1944

in omnes homines mors pertransiit, **in** quo omnes peccaverunt.

The Council of Trent in its Fifth Session then issued an anathema on the dogma of Original Sin based explicitly on this passage:

> If anyone denies that infants, newly born from their mothers' wombs, are to be baptized, even though they be born of baptized parents, or says that they are indeed baptized for the remission of sins, but that they derive nothing of original sin from Adam which must be expiated by the laver of regeneration for the attainment of eternal life, whence it follows that in them the form of baptism for the remission of sins is to be understood not as true but as false, let him be anathema, for what the Apostle has said, by one man sin entered into the world, and by sin death, and so death passed upon all men, *in whom* all have sinned, is not to be understood otherwise than as the Catholic Church has everywhere and always understood it.

But the Protestants could read this anathema and laugh. They knew the Greek which could be translated this way:

> *Therefore as sin came into the world through one man and death through sin, and so death spread to all men because all men sinned* (Catholic RSV 2006).

The Greek manuscripts all have *eph' ho* which means "upon whom" or "in as much as." It was translated into Latin as two variants: *eo quod* (because of) or *in quo* (in whom). St.

Augustine obviously had the latter variant in the manuscripts he used, which was then confirmed by Trent.

But an over-emphasis on the "original text" can be used by heretics in this case to undermine Augustine and Trent. Did Augustine err because he was not consulting the Greek? Of course not. This verse, like every verse of the Scriptures, is governed by the oral Tradition. It "is not to be understood otherwise than as the Catholic Church has everywhere and always understood it."

Variant Passages in the Liturgy

Now we come to significant variants which are not single words but entire verses, stories or passages not contained in all manuscripts but received by the Church as authentic.

First we can consider what is known as the "Johannine comma":

> And there are three who give testimony in heaven, the Father, the Word, and the Holy Ghost. And these three are one (I Jn. v. 7).

This verse is a variant which appears in both Greek and Latin Manuscripts, which indicates that many different scribes considered the verse authentic. It concludes the responsories for Matins on Sundays traditionally and also appears in the epistle on the Sunday after Easter in the traditional Roman Rite.

It is certainly possible that these words were not written by St. John himself and yet, according to the inspired oral Tradition enshrined in the sacred *cultus*, they contain (at least) an authoritative commentary on the text from the earliest times. Therefore this profound verse is not to be rejected, but received by the faithful Christian.

Another example is the story of the woman caught in adultery, read on Saturday after the third Sunday of Lent. This passage is also quoted by many Fathers as authentic, confirmed as well by Trent. Thus this suggests an oral Tradition of our Lord that was not written down until after St. John's Gospel had been written and copied for some time. This would be similar to the saying from our Lord which is mentioned in Acts xx. 35. Perhaps St. John himself added it to the manuscripts after they had been copied, or perhaps one of his disciples added it in his name. In any case, the Church has received this story as authentic, and the speculations of theologians should not induce any soul to pridefully reject what our Fathers received.

Finally, the longer ending of St. Mark xvi. 9-20 is read on Ascension Thursday. Modern translations cast doubt on this being part of the original text because it does not exist in all manuscripts. Nevertheless this too has been received by the Church in the same way as the story of the woman caught in Adultery. Because the theologians reject oral Tradition, they cannot understand why some manuscripts would have these verses and some would not. Yet this story is true, it was passed down and remembered exactly by eyewitnesses and inserted into the Text by St. Mark himself, or another authority in his name. The Church has received this and calls it authentic.

Other Vulgate Features: Gender and Christ

Finally regarding the Vulgate, we already discussed above the use of the word *Christus* in the Old Testament. This appears in particular Psalms (Psalm II, LXXXIII) as well as the Song of Anna we discussed in Part II. Unfortunately this is one of the few areas where the Challoner revision of the Douay Rheims lost a great deal from the original Vulgate and Septuagint, founded on ancient Hebrew.

In the Vulgate, there are far more instances of *Christus* than appear in the Challoner revision. The original Douay Rheims retained these. For example, Ps. CIV says in the Latin, referring to Israel against her enemies: "Touch ye not my Christs, and do no evil to my prophets." This is a particularly remarkable prophecy since it anticipates Acts XI. 26: *at Antioch they were first called Christians*. Another example:

> After which David's heart struck him, because he had cut off the hem of Saul's robe. And he said to his men: The Lord be merciful unto me, that I may do no such thing to my master the Lord's Christ, as to lay my hand upon him, because he is the Lord's Christ (I Kngs. xxiv. 6-7).

Perhaps this is a mystery of the Jews and Gentiles rejecting or accepting Christ, just as David was received as King while Saul was rejected. These divine mysteries are hidden within the Text, but obscured even by the Challoner revision of the Douay Rheims.[160] When we begin to consider these instances we see how significant was the title of "Christ" and the coming of our Lord into His mission as the Christ.

Another aspect of this is gender. With the dominance of Feminism, we have already mentioned how the NAB adds the words "and sisters" to the Greek *adelphoi* (which means "brethren"). The NAB (required in American parishes) especially suffers from this (see the chart below). This type of

---

[160] Unfortunately the English of the original Douay Rheims is extremely difficult to read and the Challoner revision was absolutely necessary.

translating only serves ideological interests and lacks reverence for what the Word actually says. Modern man must conform himself to the Holy Scriptures, not the Scriptures to modern man. Nevertheless the translator must translate so that modern man can understand it, with the utmost reverence to the words as they appear.

Another example of this gender issue comes through the Latin concept of manliness. This translates the Greek words concerning courage and strength, reflecting traditional roles of men and women which are now under threat by Feminism and other ideologies. Thus does Ps. XXVI read in the Douay Rheims:

> Expect the Lord, do manfully, and let thy heart take courage, and wait thou for the Lord (14).

Or again I Corinthians XVI:

> Watch ye, stand fast in the faith, do manfully, and be strengthened. Let all your things be done in charity.

Such renderings show what the early Church understood about courage and strength, against the extravagance of prideful theologians today which deny that gender exists.

Finally, one particular verse illustrates the way in which the marital hierarchy has been removed with the influence of St. John Paul II and general Feminism. This is Eph. v. 33 which states in Greek and Latin: "let the wife *fear* her husband." St. Paul commands the husband to die for his wife, and the Feminists have no problem with that. But as a part of an overall shift in gender ideology, this verse gets softened to be "reverence" or even "respect" (see the chart below).

Archaic Language Confirms Oral Tradition

Finally, the use of archaic language—"thees" and "thous"—is absolutely essential. Why is this? Because it manifests the oral Tradition. People do not speak with archaic language in modern speech. Archaic language shows that this Text is a part of a long line of fathers passing this down to their children. It gives the Text a sacred character, since it is separated from all other kinds of speech (the word "holy" means "separate").

Archaic language immediately changes the tone of the words into a formal and reverent manner of speech. Archaic language communicates to the reader (or hearer) the obligation for humility and piety. We do not feel a sense of antiquity or mystery when we read a post on Twitter, and there is no reason why we should. At the same time, there is no reason why we should read the Holy Word of God with contemporary, modern English that is normal on Twitter. The language should immediately draw the hearer to the mystery of divinity, not the routine of everyday life.

	Douay Rheims	New Vulgate [161]	King James Version	Knox	RSV Catholic 2006	NAB 2011
Dt. viii. 3	"word"	"word"	"word"	"word"	"thing"	"thing"
Is. vii. 14	"virgin"	"virgin"	"virgin"	"maid"	"virgin" (corrected)	"young woman"
Lk. i. 28	"full of grace"	"Gratia plena"	"highly favoured"	"full of grace"	"full of grace"	"favored one"
Acts xvi. 4	"decrees decreed"	dogmata decreta"	"decrees ordained"	decrees laid down"	decisions reached	decisions reached"
Tit. i. 5	"ordain priests"	constituas presbyteros	"ordain elders"	appoint presbyters"	"appoint elders"	"appoint presbyters"
Is. xi. 2-3	7 gifts	6 gifts	6 gifts	7 gifts	6 gifts	6 gifts
Tob. viii. 9	"only for the love of posterity	"In veritate"	N/A	"only in the dear hope of leaving a race behind me."	"but with sincerity	"but with sincerity
Rom. v. 12	"in whom all have sinned"	"Eo quod"	"for that all have sinned"	"All alike were guilty men"	"because all men sinned"	"inasmuch as all sinned"
Gal. v. 22	12 fruits	9 fruits	9 fruits	12 fruits	9 fruits	9 fruits

---

[161] We include here also the New Vulgate (2nd ed. 1986), which was based mostly on the Masoretic but is ignored by most English Catholic translations.

	Douay Rheims	New Vulgate	King James Version	Knox	RSV Catholic 2006	NAB 2011
I Jn. v. 7	Included	Removed	Included	Included	Removed (shown in footnote)	Removed
Jn. viii. 1-8	Included	Included	Included	Included	Included	Bracketed
Mk. xvi. 9-20	Included	Included	Included	Included	Included	Bracketed
Ps. ii.	"against his Christ."	"adversus christum eius"	"against his anointed"	"against the King he has anointed."	"against his anointed"	"against his anointed one"
I Cor. xvi. 13	"do manfully"	"viriliter agite"	"quit you like men"	"play the man"	"be courageous"	"be courageous"
Jn. i. 4	"light of men"	"lux hominum"	"light of men"	"light of men"	"light of men"	"light of the human race"
Eph. v. 33	"let the wife fear her husband"	"uxor autem timeat virum"	"the wife see that she reverence her husband"	"the wife is to pay reverence to her husband"	"let the wife see that she respects her husband"	"the wife should respect her husband"
Archaic Language	Yes	n/a	Yes	Yes	No	No

Thus making a comparison in the verses we have discussed and their Catholic implications, only the Douay Rheims maintains a truly accurate translation which also supports the Catholic faith. In addition, the Douay Rheims retains all the variant readings which have been established liturgically in the

Church, even though it is possible they were not a part of the original text. This accords the best with the decree of Trent judging the Text by the *cultus*: "as they have been accustomed to be read in the Catholic Church" as well as the "books in their entirety and with all their parts." Thus the Douay Rheims represents a thoroughly Catholic translation suitable for reading, study and prayer.

Especially for academic purposes, the Church may approve another text (like the New Vulgate) which may represent another approximation of the "original text" according to the trends of modern scholarship (which, although fickle, are not without their merits). This text may even be more accurate in certain places.[162]

Still, since the Vulgate is confirmed by the Magisterium as without error in faith or morals, we can trust the Douay Rheims the most, as it is free from all ideology and represents a very Catholic translation (although it is not without its own defects). In particular in the Euro-American religious culture dominated by Protestantism, reading the Douay Rheims keeps our children safe from falling into the error of the Protestants (see chapter 13 on Protestantism).[163] As we have argued in this work, it is vital that we approach the Holy Text with fear of the Lord. The Vulgate is the Text used by all the saints and doctors, and forming the basis of our Doctrine, therefore even

---

[162] For example, there is a strong parallel between the 3,000 saved at the New Pentecost (Acts ii. 41) and the 3,000 slain at the First Pentecost (Ex. xxxii. 28). But this parallel only exists in some manuscripts, and does not appear in the Vulgate (which has the number slain at 23,000). The New Vulgate asserts that the correct verse in Exodus is "3,000." In addition, Acts XVI. 4 in the New Vulgate is "priests" and not "elders" as in the Vulgate of Jerome.

[163] I have known Catholics who have read the Holy Bible for the first time as teenagers or young adults and fallen away into a Protestant sect. It is hard to see how this is possible by reading the Douay Rheims.

though new editions can be reasonably approved, the Church does not reject the old and venerable.

XII

ANNUAL BIBLE READER ACCORDING TO THE TRADITIONAL OFFICE OF MATINS

It is pious practice to read the entire Bible every year. This annual reading plan was adapted from the traditional readings in the office of Matins in the Divine Office. Each year, most of the books of the Bible are read in this office. This custom is derived from the Rule of St. Benedict. However, these books are not read in their entirety nor is every book read.

As much as possible, this reader preserves the existing Matins cycle but adds the missing sections and missing books into an annual cycle which covers the whole Bible. Some books, such as I and II Esdras, have no place in the traditional cycle and were given a place based on thematic content. These are distinguished in the introduction by the phrase "The Church reads…" indicating the traditional office, whereas "Because of [this reason]" introduces a book's reading according to this arrangement.

The wisdom books of Proverbs, Ecclesiasticus and Ecclesiastes are traditionally read in the Fall but have been distributed instead into a daily reading on weekdays after

Pentecost to make room for the books left out, such as Paralipomenon.

In addition, this reading plan does not include the Psalms, since these are prayers and would normally be prayed weekly from the Divine Office. Finally, the Gospel cycle is loosely based on the New Lectionary, since there is no parallel which reads the entire Gospels throughout the year in the traditional cycle. (As an alternative, the reader can also follow the New Lectionary for the Gospels only, but he will need to also add in the parts of the Gospels that are missing.)

Depending on your reading style, this plan takes 15-20 minutes per day, six days a week. However, during Lent and Paschaltide (as well as around October and November) there are times when the reading is more lengthy. If there are any longer readings, they are usually placed on Sunday according to the custom of Matins. Also, because of the variable length of certain Church seasons, the reading schedule must shift in places where noted. For questions with Bible books and abbreviations, see chapter 16.

Advent

During Advent the Church reads the Prophecy of Isaias for its sublime prophecies concerning our Lord. Because Advent is the coming of Incarnate Wisdom, the Wisdom of Solomon is also read at this time. No Gospel is read otherwise than in the Missal.

Note: the fourth week of Advent is variable, so the plan is divided as if Christmas would fall on a Wednesday. The reader must read more or less per day during the O Antiphons (Dec. 17-24) in order to finish before Christmas.

	Sun	Mon	Tues	Wed	Thurs	Fri
I Advent	Is. 1-3 Wis. 1	Is. 4-6 Wis. 2	Is 7-9 Wis. 3	Is. 10-12 Wis. 4	Is. 3-15 Wis. 5	Is. 16-18 Wis. 6
II Adv.	Is. 19-21 Wis. 7	Is. 22-24 Wis. 8	Is. 25-27 Wis. 9	Is. 28-30 Wis. 10	Is. 31-33 Wis. 11	Is. 34-36 Wis. 12
III Adv.	Is. 37-39 Wis. 13	Is. 40-42 Wis. 14	Is. 43-45 Wis. 15	Is. 46-48 Wis. 16	Is. 49-51 Wis. 17	Is. 52-54 Wis. 18
IV Adv.	Is. 55-58 Wis. 19	Is. 59-62	Is. 63-66			

Christmas and Epiphanytide

Because Christmas manifests the union between God and Man in Christ's Incarnation, the Canticle of Canticles is read during the Octave of Christmas. This book is a mystical prophecy of the coming of Christ and His Church.

During Epiphanytide, the manifestation of Christ to the world, the Church reads the epistles of the Doctor of the Gentiles, St. Paul. The Gospel of St. Mark is also read at this time.

Note: because Epiphanytide varies, the reader will need to consider when Septuagesima starts and finish Hebrews and St. Mark before then. He can begin early if there is time between Epiphany and the 1st Sunday after Epiphany, or else finish these readings if the Sundays after Epiphany resume before Advent.

12/25	12/16	12/27	12/28	12/29	12/30	12/31
Cant. 1	Cant. 2	Cant. 3	Cant. 4	Cant. 5 Rom 1-2	Cant. 6 Rom 3-4	Cant. 7 Rom 5-6
1/1 Cant. 8 Rom 7-8	1/2 Rom 9-10	1/3 Rom 11-12	1/4 Rom 13-14	1/5 Rom 15-16	1/6 Epiphany	

After Epiphany	Sun	Mon	Tues	Wed	Thurs	Fri
I Sunday *Mark 1-3*	I Cor. 1-3	I Cor. 4-6	I Cor. 7-9	I Cor. 10-12	I Cor. 13-14	I Cor. 15-16
II Sunday *Mark 4-6*	II Cor. 1-3	II Cor. 4-5	II Cor. 6-7	II Cor. 8-9	II Cor. 10-11	II Cor. 12-13
III Sunday *Mark 7-9*	Gal. 1-2	Gal. 3-4	Gal. 5-6	Eph. 1-2	Eph. 3-4	Eph. 5-6
IV Sunday *Mark 10-12*	Philip. 1-4	Col. 1-2	Col. 3-4	I Thess. 1-3	I Thess. 4-5	II Thess. 1-3
V Sunday *Mark 13-15*	I Tim. 1-3	I Tim. 4-6	II Tim. 1-2	II Tim. 3-4	Titus 1-3	Philemon
VI Sunday *Mark 16*	Heb. 1-3	Heb. 4-5	Heb. 6-7	Heb. 8-9	Heb. 10-11	Heb. 12-13

Septuagesima and the Great Fast of Lent

The readings in Septuagesima and Lent are longer, as befits the penitential character of the season. Beginning in Septuagesima the Church reads the books of Moses beginning with Genesis, telling of the Fall of our first parents and the struggle of their just descendants with the wicked line of Cane. Exodus centers on the Paschal sacrifice of the Lamb of God. Leviticus on the purification from sin.

The Book of Numbers begins at Passiontide, as this book contains the story of Moses lifting up the serpent (a typos *of our Lord's Passion, Jn. iii. 14) and many other salutary stories. This book concludes the narrative of Israel's journey for 40 years as a* typos *of the Great Fast of 40 days.*

Passiontide also begins the Prophesy of Jeremias, which contains many typoi *of the Passion of our Lord. From Spy Wednesday through Holy Saturday, the Lamentations are read as at Tenebrae, as well as Baruch.*

	Sun	Mon	Tues	Wed	Thurs	Fri
Sept.	Gen. 1-5	Gen. 6-8	Gen. 9-11	Gen. 12-14	Gen. 15-17	Gen. 18-19
Quin.	Gen. 20-25	Gen. 26-28	Gen. 29-31	Gen. 32-34	Gen. 35-37	Gen. 38-39
Sexa.	Gen. 40-42	Gen. 43-44	Gen. 45-46	**ASH WED**	Gen. 47-48	Gen. 49-50
1 Lent	Ex. 1-5	Ex. 6-8	Ex. 9-11	Ex. 12-14	Ex. 15-17	Ex. 18-20
2 Lent	Ex. 21-26	Ex. 27-29	Ex. 30-32	Ex. 33-35	Ex. 36-38	Ex. 39-40
3 Lent	Lev. 1-3	Lev. 4-5	Lev. 6-7	Lev. 8-9	Lev. 10-11	Lev. 12-13
4 Lent	Lev. 14-17	Lev. 18-19	Lev. 20-21	Lev. 22-23	Lev. 24-25	Lev. 26-27
Pass.	Num. 1-4 Jer. 1-5	Num. 5-8 Jer. 6-10	Num. 9-12 Jer. 11-15	Num.13-16 Jer. 16-20	Num.17-20 Jer. 21-25	Num.21-24 Jer. 26-30
Palm	Num.25-29 Jer. 31-35	Num.30-33 Jer. 36-40	Num.34-36 Jer. 41-45	**Spy Wed** Jer. 46-52	**Holy Thurs** Lam1-3 Bar.1-3	**Good Fri** Lam4-5 Bar.4-6

Paschaltide

Because of its theme of return from exile, I Esdras is read during the Octave of Easter with its accompanying prophecy, Aggeus. This is then continued in Pentecost week with II Esdras and Zacharias.

During Paschaltide the Church reads the Gospel St. John, as the catechumenate has now entered the mystagogy, when the mysteries of the faith are expounded to the newly enlightened faithful.

For this reason too, the book of Deuteronomy is read, which retells the story of Exodus-Numbers before entering the battle against the Canaanites. Since the Gentile nations are typoi *of the seven deadly sins, Paschaltide now refreshes us before entering again into the rigor of spiritual combat. Thus continues the saga of Israel from Josue through Ruth before the time after Pentecost begins the story of David, the anointed typos of our Lord.*

During this time the Church also reads the book of Acts, as well as the Catholic epistles. The readings are more extensive through this time, as the faithful are refreshed with the joyous Alleluia of the Resurrection.

	Sun[164]	Mon	Tues	Wed	Thurs	Fri
Easter	I Esd. 1-2 Ag. 1:1-11	I Esd. 3-4 Ag.1:12-15	I Esd. 5-6 Ag. 2:1-9	I Esd. 7-8 Ag.2:10-19	I Esd. 9 Ag. 2:20-23	I Esd. 10
Low Sun	Jn. 1 Acts 1-2 Dt. 1-3	Jn. 2 Acts 3 Dt. 4-6	Jn. 3 Acts 4 Dt. 7-9	Jn. 4 Acts 5 Dt. 10-12	Jn. 5 Acts 6 Dt. 13-15	Jn. 6:1-15 Acts 7 Dt. 16-17
2 Sun after Easter	Jn. 6:16-21 Acts 8-9 Dt. 18-20	Jn. 6:22-59 Acts 10 Dt. 21-23	Jn. 6:60-71 Acts 11 Dt. 24-26	Jn. 7 Acts 12 Dt. 27-29	Jn. 8 Acts 13 Dt. 30-32	Jn. 9 Acts 14 Dt. 33-34
3 Sun after Easter	Jn. 10 Acts 15-16 Jos. 1-2	Jn. 11 Acts 17 Jos. 3-4	Jn. 12 Acts 18 Jos. 5-6	Jn. 13 Acts 19 Jos. 7-8	Jn. 14 Acts 20 Jos. 9-10	Jn. 15 Acts 21 Jos. 11-12
4 Sun after Easter	Jn. 16 Acts 22-23 Jos. 13-14	Jn. 17 Acts 24 Jos. 15-16	Jn. 18 Acts 25 Jos. 17-18	Jn. 19 Acts 26 Jos. 19-20	Jn. 20 Acts 27 Jos. 21-22	Jn. 21 Acts 28 Jos. 23-24

---

[164] It may be profitable to read the Sunday readings noted here on the Saturday before so that they do not distract from the proper Gospel readings appointed in the Missal for the Sunday Mass. This is also true for time after Pentecost.

	Sun	Mon	Tues	Wed	Thurs	Fri
5 Sun after Easter	Ja. 1-3 Jdg. 1-3	Rogation Ja. 4-5 Jdg. 4-6	Rogation I Pt. 1-3 Jdg. 7-9	Rogation I Pt. 4-5 Jdg. 10-2	**Ascension**	Jdg. 13-15
Sun after Ascension	II Pt. 1-3 Jdg. 16-7	I Jn. 1-3 Jdg. 18-9	I Jn. 4-5 Jdg. 20-1	II Jn. 1 Ruth 1-2	III Jn. 1 Ruth 3-4	Jude
Pentecost	II Esd. 1-3 Zach. 1-4	II Esd. 4-5 Zach 5-6	II Esd. 6-7 Zach 7-8	II Esd. 8-9 Zach 9-10	II Esd.10-1 Zach 11-12	II Esd.12-3 Zach 13-4

Time After Pentecost

During this time is read the Gospels of St. Matthew and St. Luke, and the Church reads the rest of the Scriptures, continuing the saga of Israel with David the King. Because the Christian soldier is in need of daily wisdom, the wisdom books are read daily through the 19th Sunday after Pentecost. At the end of the year the Maccabean saga is read with the Apocalypse and the final prophets, anticipating the Advent of Jesus Christ at the end of the world.

After Pentecost	Sun	Mon	Tues	Wed	Thurs	Fri
Trinity	Mt. 1-4 1Kngs 1-3	Mt. 5:1-12 Prov. 1 1Kngs 4-6	Mt5:12-19 Prov. 2 1Kngs 7-9	Mt5:20-26 Prov. 3 1Kg 10-11	Mt5:27-32 Prov. 4 1Kg 12-13	Mt5:33-37 Prov. 5 1Kg 14-15
2 Sun	Mt5:38-48 1Kg 16-19	Mt. 6:1-6 Prov. 6 1Kg 20-22	Mt. 6:7-15 Prov. 7 1Kg 23-25	Mt6:16-18 Prov. 8 1Kg 26-27	Mt6:19-23 Prov. 9 1Kg 28-29	Mt6:24-34 Prov. 10 1Kg 30-31
3 Sun	Mt. 7:1-5 2 Kg 1-2	Mt. 7:6-11 Prov. 11 2 Kg 3-4	Mt7:12-14 Prov. 12 2 Kg 5-6	Mt7:15-20 Prov. 13 2 Kg 7-8	Mt7:21-29 Prov. 14 2 Kg 9-10	Mt. 8:1-17 Prov. 15 2Kg11-12

	Sun	Mon	Tues	Wed	Thurs	Fri
4 Sun	Mt8:18-22 2Kg13-14	Mt8:23-27 Prov. 16 2Kg15-16	Mt8:28-34 Prov. 17 2Kg17-18	Mt. 9:1-8 Prov. 18 2Kg19-20	Mt. 9:9-17 Prov. 19 2Kg21-22	Mt9:18-26 Prov. 20 2Kg23-24
5 Sun	Mt9:27-31 3Kg 1-2	Mt9:32-38 Prov. 21 3Kg 3-4	Mt. 10:1-7 Prov. 22 3Kg 5-6	Mt10:8-15 Prov. 23 3Kg 7-8	M10:16-23 Prov. 24 3Kg 9-10	M10:24-33 Prov. 25 3Kg 11
6 Sun	M10:34-42 3Kg 12-13	Mt11:1-19 Prov. 26 3Kg 14-15	M11:20-30 Prov. 27 3Kg16-17	Mt. 12:1-8 Prov. 28 3Kg18-19	Mt12:9-37 Prov. 29 3Kg20-21	M12:38-50 Prov. 30-1 3Kg 22
7 Sun	Mt13:1-17 Eccl. 1 4 Kg 1-3	M13:18-35 Eccl. 2 4 Kg 4-5	M13:36-58 Eccl. 3 4 Kg 6-7	Mt14:1-21 Eccl. 4 4 Kg 8-9	M14:22-36 Eccl. 5 4 Kg 10-11	Mt15:1-20 Eccl. 6 4 Kg12-13
8 Sun	M15:29-39 Eccl. 7 4 Kg 14-15	Mt16:1-12 Eccl. 8 4 Kg16-17	M16:13-28 Eccl. 9 4 Kg 18-19	Mt17:1-21 Eccl. 10 4Kg 20-21	M17:22-27 Eccl. 11 4 Kg 22-23	Mt18:1-20 Eccl. 12 4Kg 24-25
9 Sun	M18:21-35 1 Para. 1-3	Mt19:1-15 Ecclus. 1 1Par. 4-6	M19:16-30 Ecclus. 2 1 Par. 7-9	Mt20:1-19 Ecclus. 3 1 Par. 10-1	M20:20-28 Ecclus. 4 1 Par. 12-3	M20:29-34 Ecclus. 5 1 Par. 14-5
10 Sun	Mt.21:1-22 1 Par.16-18	M21:23-32 Ecclus. 6 1 Par.19-21	M21:33-46 Ecclus. 7 1 Par.22-23	Mt22:1-14 Ecclus. 8 1 Par.24-5	M22:15-33 Ecclus. 9 1 Par.26-7	M22:34-46 Ecclus. 10 1 Par.28-29
11 Sun	Mt23:1-12 2 Par. 1-3	M23:13-24 Ecclus. 11 2 Par. 4-6	M23:25-39 Ecclus. 12 2 Par. 7-9	Mt24:1-14 Ecclus. 13 2Par10-12	M24:15-35 Ecclus. 14 2Par. 13-15	M24:36-51 Ecclus. 15 2 Par.16-18
12 Sun	Mt25:1-30 2Par19-21	M25:31-36 Ecclus. 16 2Par.22-24	Mt26:1-25 Ecclus. 17 2Par25-27	M26:26-46 Ecclus. 18 2Par.28-30	M26:47-56 Ecclus. 19 2 Par.31-33	M26:57-75 Ecclus. 20 2 Par.34-36
13 Sun	Mt27:1-23 Job 1-5	M27:24-31 Ecclus. 21 Job 6-8	M27:32-44 Ecclus. 22 Job 9-11	M27:45-66 Ecclus. 23 Jon 12-14	Mt28:1-15 Ecclus. 24 Job 15-17	M28:16-20 Ecclus. 25 Job 18-20
14 Sun	Lk. 1 Job 21-25	Lk. 2 Ecclus. 26 Job 26-29	Lk 3:1-22 Ecclus. 27 Job 30-33	Lk3:23-38 Ecclus. 28 Job 34-36	Lk. 4:1-30 Ecclus. 29 Job 37-39	Lk4:31-44 Ecclus. 30 Job 40-42
15 Sun	Lk.5:1-16 Tob. 1-4	L5:17-26 Ecclus. 31 Tob. 5-6	L5:27-39 Ecclus. 32 Tob. 7-8	Lk.6:1-16 Ecclus. 33 Tob. 9-10	L6:17-36 Ecclus. 34 Tob.11-12	L6:37-49 Ecclus. 35 Tob.13-14

	Sun	Mon	Tues	Wed	Thurs	Fri
16 Sun	Lk.7:1-17 Judith 1-4	L7:18-35 Ecclus. 36 Judith 5-7	L7:36-50 Ecclus. 37 Judith8-10	Lk.8:1-21 Ecclus. 38 Judit11-12	L8:22-39 Ecclus. 39 Jud 13-14	L8:40-56 Ecclus. 40 Jud 15-16
17 Sun	Lk.9:1-17 Esther 1-4	L9:18-36 Ecclus. 41 Esther 5-7	L9:37-62 Ecclus. 42 Esth 8-10	L10:1-16 Ecclus. 43 Esth 11-12	L10:17-24 Ecclus. 44 Esth 13-14	L10:25-42 Ecclus. 45 Esth 15-16
18 Sun	Lk11:1-13 1Mach1-3	L11:14-36 Ecclus. 46 1Mach 4	L11:37-53 Ecclus. 47 1 Mach 5	L12:1-21 Ecclus. 48 1 Mach 6	L12:22-40 Ecclus. 49 1 Mach 7	L12:41-59 E. 50-1 1 Mach 8
19 Sun	Lk.13:1-9 1Mach9-11 Ez. 1-3	L13:10-21 1 Mach 12 Ez. 4-6	L13:22-35 1 Mach 13 Ez. 7-8	Lk14:1-14 1 Mach 14 Ez. 9-10	L14:15-24 1 Mach 15 Ez. 11-12	L14:25-34 1 Mach 16 Ez. 13-14
20 Sun	Lk15:1-7 2Mach 1-2 Ez. 15-17	Lk15:8-10 2 Mach 3 Ez. 18-20	L15:11-32 2 Mach 4 Ez. 21-23	Lk16:1-13 2 Mach 5 Ez. 24-26	L16:14-18 2 Mach 6 Ez. 27-28	L16:19-31 2 Mach 7 Ez. 29-30
21 Sun	Lk17:1-10 2Mach8-10 Ez. 31-34	L17:11-19 2 Mach 11 Ez. 35-37	L17:20-37 2 Mach 12 Ez. 38-40	Lk18:1-14 2 Mach 13 Ez. 41-43	L18:15-30 2 Mach 14 Ez. 44-46	L18:31-43 2 Mach 15 Ez. 47-48
22 Sun	Lk19:1-27 Dan. 1-4 Osee 1-4	L19:28-40 Dan. 5-6 Osee 5-6	L19:41-48 Dan. 7-8 Osee 7-8	Lk20:1-18 Dan. 9-10 Osee 9-10	L20:19-26 Dan.11-12 Ose11-12	L20:27-47 Dan.13-14 Ose13-14
23 Sun	Lk. 21:1-9 Apoc. 1-2 Joel 1-3	L21:10-28 Apoc. 3-4 Amos 1-5	L21:29-38 Apoc. 5-6 Amos 6-9	Lk22:1-23 Apoc. 7-8 Abdias	L22:24-38 Apoc.9-10 Jonas 1-4	L22:39-71 Apoc. 11 Mich. 1-4
24 Sun	Lk23:1-12 Apoc12-13 Mich. 5-7	L23:13-43 Apoc14-15 Nahum1-3	L23:44-56 Apoc16-17 Hab 1-3	Lk24:1-12 Apoc18-19 Soph 1-3	L24:13-35 Apoc20-21 Mal. 1-2	L24:36-53 Apoc. 22 Mal 3-4

XIII

REFUTE PROTESTANTS IN FIVE MINUTES: THE FOUNDATIONAL GUIDE

Give Protestants True Charity: Convert Them

Before becoming Catholic, I spent many years in the Protestant heresy. By the grace of God, as the eastern rite of reception says, I was "delivered from deception." Eventually God brought good Catholics into my life to turn me away from error to Jesus Christ, and I am eternally grateful for them. If you live in the United States or Britain, you probably know some Protestants in your family or at your work. This short guide is designed to help you direct them to Jesus Christ in communion with His Mystical Body by using the Holy Scriptures themselves.

They are brothers because they are baptized in the Name of Blessed Trinity and call upon the Holy Name of our Lord Jesus Christ. But yet they are heretics, who deny Jesus Christ in His Body and His doctrine. Unless they repent of the sins of their fathers and return to the Body of Christ—the Roman Catholic Church—they have no sure hope to be saved.[165]

---

[165] Bl. Pius IX condemned the error that "we can have a good hope that non-Catholics will be saved" (*Syllabus of Errors*) and Vatican II stated

As such it is an act of true charity to refute our heretic brethren and warn them of the dangers of eternal damnation. These are the spiritual works of mercy of "instructing the ignorant" and "admonishing the sinner." But hear this: brother, *you must have charity*. If you cannot speak to your Protestant friends or family with charity, do not speak at all. As it is written, *Whosoever shall say, Thou fool, shall be in danger of hell fire* (Mt. v. 22) and again *If any man say: I love God, and hateth his brother; he is a liar* (I Jn. iv. 20) or again:

> Be ready always to give a defense to every one that asketh you a reason of that hope which is in you—
> But with modesty and fear, (I Pt. iii. 15).

It is imperative that you understand: if you cannot speak with *modesty and fear*, you should not speak at all. For *the tongue is a fire, a world of iniquity* (Ja. iii. 6). Catholics who speak without charity to Protestants do more harm than good.

---

this: "Basing itself upon Sacred Scripture and Tradition, [this Council] teaches that the Church, now sojourning on earth as an exile, is necessary for salvation. Christ, present to us in His Body, which is the Church, is the one Mediator and the unique way of salvation. In explicit terms He Himself affirmed the necessity of faith and baptism and thereby affirmed also the necessity of the Church, for through baptism as through a door men enter the Church. Whosoever, therefore, knowing that the Catholic Church was made necessary by Christ, would refuse to enter or to remain in it, could not be saved" (*Lumen Gentium*, 14). And this is also affirmed in the Creed of Pope St. Paul VI. An important distinction with this is Objective vs. Subjective, see < https://meaningofcatholic.com/2019/06/28/glossary-of-philosophical-terms/#objective>.

Be Sensitive to Their Attachments

From experience as a Protestant and knowing Protestants across the nation and the world, it is my estimation that among all their tens of thousands of sects, most of them boil down to one or both of these things: emotional or intellectual attachments. An attachment is something in your senses or soul which incline your intellect and will toward a certain created object. An attachment gives you a pleasure which addicts you and causes you to return again and again to get this pleasure.

These attachments are most easily seen in the Protestant worship services. They may consist of powerful sermons, songs or hymns which cause emotional highs in the worshipers (helping them satisfy their emotional attachments). Or perhaps long, intellectual sermons which fulfill an intellectual attachment. Or they may include both of these. Most Protestants that I've ever known measure the value of their worship based on its personal emotional or intellectual stimulation.

It must be noted that these attachments, though disordered, *do* call upon the Name of our Lord Jesus Christ. Thus it is *impossible* that they do not have some positive spiritual value to every soul (at least in potency). As it is written: *No man can say The Lord Jesus, but by the Holy Ghost* (I Cor. xii. 3).[166]

Nevertheless properly ordered Christian worship is *lifting the intellect and will to God in prayer*. This does not mean getting an emotional high—although it can include this. And

---

[166] I am passing over the fact that a soul in mortal sin cannot merit eternal life. Nevertheless it cannot be denied that a Protestant who seeks (by actual grace) the Lord Jesus is much closer to the truth than a Jew or Muhammadan.

it does not mean gaining more intellectual knowledge—although it can include this as well. Lifting the intellect and will to God means growing in charity, which is union with God.

This is a subject for a much larger treatment but the point to seize upon here is that Protestants generally have these attachments. Thus it is crucial that the Catholic have charity for the Protestant, and take all possible care to be sensitive to these things. That means praying to the Holy Spirit to give you the gift of Counsel to speak words for *this particular soul*, not just to win an argument. Do all you can by God's grace to speak with truth and charity, and trust not in yourself but in God, Whose instrument you are.

St. Thomas observes that we should not correct our brother if we know that a correction will make him worse (II-II q33 a6). If we insist on correcting him nonetheless, this is evidence of our own pride and lack of charity. Many Catholics just care about winning arguments, instead of the individual soul with whom you are speaking.

Instead, ask God for the grace to perceive where that soul is spiritually. If it is clear that a soul is obstinate and will not listen or become worse if you evangelize them, just offer prayers and penance for them instead.

We have to realize that disordered attachments also serve to darken one's intellect. Thus many Protestants will not understand you when you are speaking. If you find a Protestant who seems to have a sincere desire to understand, this soul is especially ready for you to focus on charity and truth. Give these souls as much of your time and energy as you can. But do not waste time speaking to obstinate, prideful Protestants—except to refute them for the benefit of others. Do not vainly hope to convert a fool, as the Holy Ghost says, *Rebuke a fool, and he will hate you. Rebuke a wise man and he will love you* (Prov. ix. 8).

Refute Them with the Holy Scripture

Once a man has true charity for the Protestant soul, it is very often helpful to ask questions. This allows the Protestant to come to his own conclusions and moreover, it is one of the favored methods of our Lord. It is also crucial that a Catholic use the Holy Scriptures to prove the Catholic faith, since the Protestants generally hold the Holy Bible to be authoritative.

All that is necessary is for Protestants to read the Sacred Scripture entirely and in context and they will become Catholics. I will never forget my astonishment when, as a Protestant, I learned about the verses we will discuss below. Since the Protestant sects were founded on heretical theologians, they were never taught how to read the Scriptures with humility as we have discussed in this work.

The important thing to note is that many Protestants either ignore important texts from the Scriptures or else rely on incorrect translations. To this point, these refutation methods will each utilize a small amount of Scriptures, as well as the original languages. Note: these refutations will not convince all, but only those whom the Holy Spirit has prepared.

Refutation #1: The Truth

Thus the first question to ask a genuine Protestant Christian is this: what does the Holy Bible hold to be the pillar and foundation of truth itself?

Your average Protestant would answer that question with the assertion that their Sacred Scriptures (that is, only 66 books in the canon of their bible) are the foundation of truth.

But what does the Holy Word itself say of this? From St. Paul's first letter to St. Timothy:

> But if I tarry long, that thou mayest know how thou oughtest to behave thyself in the house of God, which is the church of the living God, the pillar and ground of the truth (I Tim. iii. 15).

> Si autem tardavero, ut scias quomodo oporteat te in domo Dei conversari, quæ est ecclesia Dei vivi, columna et firmamentum veritatis.

> ἐὰν δὲ βραδύνω, ἵνα εἰδῇς πῶς δεῖ ἐν οἴκῳ θεοῦ ἀναστρέφεσθαι, ἥτις ἐστὶν ἐκκλησία θεοῦ ζῶντος, στῦλος καὶ ἑδραίωμα τῆς ἀληθείας.

Here we may point out a few things: the Church is here identified with two physical, architectural elements in relation to an abstract thing: truth. This metaphor would have immediately brought up a common sight to St. Timothy who grew up in Lystra in the Roman province of Galatia: the temple.

[167] Wikipedia Commons

It is not difficult for a modern man to see the foundation and the columns here. Temples of this sort were scattered all over the Roman Empire, but even the Second Temple at Jerusalem would have also included a foundation and columns as well.

What can we draw out of the meaning that St. Paul is discussing here with St. Timothy? The truth stands or falls with the Church in the same way that a temple stands or falls with its columns and foundation. In other words, the truth is *dependent* on the Church. And this makes sense when you consider the chronology we have discussed:

~250-150 BC: Septuagint Old Testament is translated and used by Jews across the Roman Empire

33 AD: The Church is founded. Uses the Septuagint as its primary Scripture and Apostles, oral Tradition as authority (Acts xv)

~33-100 AD: Church writes New Testament, quoting primarily Septuagint as Scripture

~90 AD: Pharisees and Rabbis who rejected our Lord create Rabbinic Judaism, start the Masoretic Old Testament (later Protestant Scripture)

The New Testament came *after* the Church. So it makes sense that the Church is the pillar of truth since we cannot have Christianity without truth. The Protestants assert that the foundation of truth is 66 books of their bible. But Christianity was founded before this bible existed. Thus the question becomes: *how can the Church be the pillar of truth without the 66 book Bible?*

Refutation #2: The Scripture

Most Protestants think like Muhammadans: they think that Christians are a "people of the book." For a Muhammadan, their "scripture" is claimed to have fallen from the heavens into the mouth of their "prophet" and was written down immediately. Protestants don't generally realize that their 66 book bible didn't exist until about the 16th century. How could Christianity exist for so long without its foundation?

Let's look at one of the common verses they cite in support of this man-made tradition, Sola Scriptura ("The Bible is the Only Authority"). This is their foundational doctrine. In their minds, the Holy Bible is the only authority from which we can take doctrine. But the Sacred Scriptures themselves declare that the *Church* is the "pillar and foundation of truth." But Protestants will usually cite this verse to support their man-made tradition:

> All scripture, inspired of God, is profitable to teach, to reprove, to correct, to instruct in justice: That the man of God may be perfect, furnished to every good work (II Tim. iii. 16).

> Omnis Scriptura divinitus inspirata utilis est ad docendum, ad arguendum, ad corripiendum, et erudiendum in justitia: ut perfectus sit homo Dei, ad omne opus bonum instructus.

> πᾶσα γραφὴ θεόπνευστος καὶ ὠφέλιμος πρὸς διδασκαλίαν, πρὸς ἐλεγμόν, πρὸς ἐπανόρθωσιν, πρὸς παιδείαν τὴν ἐν δικαιοσύνῃ, ἵνα ἄρτιος ᾖ ὁ τοῦ θεοῦ ἄνθρωπος, πρὸς πᾶν ἔργον ἀγαθὸν ἐξηρτισμένος.

Out of context, this verse appears to support the Protestant tradition that the Bible is the only authority. But consider the context: as before, St. Paul is writing to St. Timothy in the first century. When he speaks of "Scripture," he cannot be referring to his own letter, or the New Testament—which did not exist at that time. What was considered the Scripture at that time? The Greek Septuagint.

Why is the Septuagint the Christian Scripture?

The early Church accepted the Greek Septuagint, which includes the deutero-canonical books, as their Old Testament Scripture. Numerous Protestant scholars are willing to admit this. We have already quoted Morgens Müller, a Danish Lutheran theologian, in his book *The First Bible of the Church: A Plea for the Septuagint* (1996), in chapter 11. Another witness, the Protestant biblical scholar Brevard Childs writes:

> Why should the Christian Church be committed in any way to the authority of the Masoretic text when its development extended long after the inception of the Church and was carried on within a rabbinic Tradition?[168]

Another excellent scholar, this time a Methodist, comes to the same conclusion: William J. Abraham in *Canon and Criterion in Christian Theology* (Oxford, 1998). A further example is the evangelical scholar Craig D. Allert, *A High view of Scripture?* (Baker, 2007). Thus even the Protestants themselves admit that the Greek Septuagint was the Scripture

---

[168] Brevard S. Childs, *Introduction to the Old Testament as Scripture* (Philadelphia: Fortress, 1979), 89, quoted in Anderson, op. cit. 11

of the early Church, which contradicts the ideas of the Protestant Reformers.

2 Tim 3:16 Argues *Against* Sola Scriptura

Therefore it is abundantly clear that the Greek Septuagint was the normal Christian Scripture at the time when St. Paul wrote the words above. St. Timothy was half Greek from Asia Minor where the common language was Greek, and St. Paul's letter was written in Greek. He says to Timothy in the verse before this *you have been taught the Scriptures from your youth*. This would have been the Greek Septuagint.

St. Paul might as well have said: *All the Septuagint, inspired of God, is profitable to teach, to reprove, to correct, to instruct in justice.* It is completely out of context to use this text to support Sola Scriptura, since the 66 book Protestant Bible did not exist for another 1500 years. The Hebrew manuscript tradition had not become dominant at this time. So how did this discrepancy come about?

Destruction of the Second Temple

As we discussed in part II, after the destruction of the Second Temple by the Romans in 70 AD. (on the same calendar day when the First Temple was destroyed, Tisha B'Av), the Jewish community was shattered. The Saduccees, whose power base was the Roman alliance and the temple, were scattered. The Zealots were defeated by the Romans. The Essenes were self-exiled. Who was left to lead the Jews? The Pharisees.

The Pharisees took over the Jewish community and reinterpreted the Law of Moses in a new way, imposing their oral tradition which had been rejected by our Lord (cf. Mk. vii. 8). They created a new religion: Rabbinic Judaism.

As we said above, this Judaism was radically different from the Judaism of Moses, David, and the Apostles. This Judaism had no priesthood, no temple, and no sacrifice. Instead, the Pharisees said that their own man-made traditions were authoritative. These were eventually written down in the Talmudic texts along with blasphemous curses against our Lord and our Lady as we have said.

It was these Pharisees who started the Hebrew manuscript tradition. Centuries later in the 16th century, the Protestant revolutionaries stopped using the Christian Old Testament in favor of the Pharisees' Hebrew Scriptures. This is when the 66 book Protestant Bible was born.

The Pharisees' Old Testament still holds great value however (being the original tongue, albeit transmitted by the Jews). Thus St. Jerome used them as we have discussed. But the oldest Masoretic manuscripts we have now date to the 10th or 11th centuries AD. Whereas the Greek Septuagint manuscripts date from the 4th century AD. The Dead Sea Scrolls, unfortunately do not contain enough manuscripts to check the whole Bible, but they indicate that the Septuagint and the Masoretic form two very ancient Hebrew traditions.

In addition as we have said, when one digs deeper into the manuscript Traditions, not only in Greek and Hebrew and Latin, but Coptic and Syriac and other languages, one finds that there really is no definitive, whole original text of the Holy Bible. Certain verses continue to remain obscure. Even the oldest Septuagint is a copy of prior copies, which itself is a translation of ancient Hebrew manuscripts now lost. This is why Christians are not a "people of the book."

Even though St. Paul referred to the Greek Septuagint when he wrote to St. Timothy, there was also another source of revelation and authority which was tied in with the

Septuagint. And unlike the Pharisees who did not even claim that a prophet gave them the authority to create Rabbinic Judaism, the authority that St. Paul writes about was of divine authority. This was the authority that founded the Church and guided her before the New Testament was written.

Refutation #3 – Oral Tradition

We have already discussed the importance and authority of oral Tradition in the first chapter. Here we will discuss the most important verse for refuting Protestants on this point: II Thess. ii. 14 (*nota bene*: this is verse 15 in most Protestant bibles):

> Therefore, brethren, stand fast: and hold the traditions, which you have learned, whether by word or by our epistle.
>
> Itaque fratres, state: et tenete traditiones, quas didicistis, sive per sermonem, sive per epistolam nostram.
>
> ἄρα οὖν, ἀδελφοί, στήκετε, καὶ κρατεῖτε τὰς παραδόσεις ἃς ἐδιδάχθητε εἴτε διὰ λόγου εἴτε δι' ἐπιστολῆς ἡμῶν.

Now we have an explicit command from the Blessed Apostle to hold to oral traditions. However, if you mention this to a Protestant and he looks it up for himself, he may find his Protestant bible says something else. One of the most popular Protestant translations, the *New International Version* (NIV) erroneously translates the word παραδόσεις as "teachings." However, compare this to Mark VII. 9, when our Lord is condemning the Pharisees' tradition, the NIV translates the same Greek word as "tradition." Obviously a Protestant bias is removing all "good tradition" from their minds. But even if the word is translated "teachings," this argument still works like this.

You first need to establish some principles with a Protestant. Ask him: do you follow the Holy Bible? Do you follow the commands of Scripture? All faithful Protestants will say yes to these.

You can then ask them: are you following the oral traditions taught by St. Paul? Then discuss the verse above. The Blessed Apostle commands the Thessalonians explicitly to follow the oral traditions he taught them.

If the Protestant is able to say that yes, he will follow the Holy Bible and this verse, the question then becomes, what are the oral Traditions of St. Paul?

You can then help him to consider the fact that the Apostles traveled the globe preaching the Gospel, and only a few of them wrote books of the New Testament! Think about that. How did all these churches spring up from India to Turkey to Ethiopia to Spain without all these Apostles writing things down? How could the Church have been founded without writing anything down?

This is when they need to understand oral culture and how people remembered things back then. Remind them that Jesus Christ never wrote anything down either.

Once we've discussed this, then we can discuss the verse we also mentioned in Part I: *And the things which thou hast heard of me by many witnesses, the same commend to faithful men who shall be fit to teach others also* (II Tim. ii. 2).

Here we have a very clear reference to the handing on of oral Tradition through the office of the bishop. The Apostle Paul himself even confirms this action of passing down, as we have noted in part I, when he affirms *the things that I received I traditioned to you* (I Cor. xi. 23). Thus embedded in the New Testament is the oral Tradition and its guardian: the bishop.

The important point with Protestants is giving them the key to unlock the prison of their mind. Their mind is locked in Sola Scriptura. If you can do just enough to show that the early Church existed before the New Testament, founded on an oral doctrine about the Septuagint, the entire edifice of Protestantism falls.

This is why it is easy to refute Protestantism. Their errors are based on historical falsehoods and misconceptions. The difficulty is really in engendering humility and charity with them, as their objections usually have little to do with intellect and a lot to do with their attachments as we have said.

These few points are enough to bring down the entire Protestant heresy. But let's address two more important aspects of this which will often arise with Protestants.

Refutation #4 – Justification by Faith Alone

As stated above, Luther justified his actions by denying that he had free will. It's best not to bring up Luther's sordid deeds as these are more disputed in the history than the doctrine which was taught. Justification by faith alone according to Luther consists in these points:

1. Man does not have free will
2. Every action he does is sinful
3. Therefore, it is impossible that he should do good works that should contribute to salvation
4. Therefore God forces some to go to heaven, and some to go to hell irrespective of what they have done or not done

5. If Faith were an act, it would be a sin, since all acts are sins
6. Thus, faith is not an act of the will or intellect but a 100% passive reception of God's choosing you to go to heaven – this is what faith is
7. Thus, we are saved (forced into heaven) by faith (God chooses, we have no choice) alone

This is Luther's doctrine in a nutshell.[169] In all fairness to him, Luther did not receive a proper education on Christian dogma.[170] He never read the standard textbook at the time (Peter Lombard's *Sentences*) nor St. Thomas. He relied on the work of Ockham and his strange philosophical ideas (besides helping to create the office of "theologian" Ockham also was a *nominalist*). Luther did use Peter Lombard, however, for his idea of Original Sin.

Lombard's idea of Original Sin was that Original Sin was concupiscence. This word means a divided will, which knows to do good but is tempted to do evil. We all have concupiscence. It *is* an effect of Original Sin, but not the primary definition.

However, Luther asserted (against Lombard) that concupiscence was an actual sin itself. So when you are tempted but do not give in to the sin (according to Luther) — you have still committed a sin. This is false, since only an act of the will can be a sin. But Luther thought that having a divided will by concupiscence was already sinful.

---

[169] These doctrines are particularly contained in his work *The Bondage of the Will*.

[170] In this I follow the work of Lutheran convert William Marshner. He has a good lecture on these things from the *Institute of Catholic Culture*: "The Protestant Revolution"

How did he come to this conclusion? By reading the Holy Bible without the oral Tradition. In the Latin, the ninth commandment "Thou shalt not covet" reads in Latin as *Non concupisces*. So Luther actually thought that God was commanding man to do something that he could not otherwise do. Luther's idea was that "in every good work the just man sins."[171]

So when Luther read St. Paul's letters, he saw that St. Paul said things like Romans III. 28 which we have mentioned: *For we account a man to be justified by faith, without the works of the law*. We saw how Luther added to the word "alone" to this verse to make it teach his error. But the other mistake he made was that he understood "works of the Law" (and other similar phrases) as *good works in general*. Thus Luther concluded that St. Paul was teaching justification by faith alone. In order to be justified, good works were not necessary.

But St. Paul was not speaking about good works in general, since he says in another place:

> For in Christ Jesus neither circumcision availeth any thing, nor uncircumcision: but faith that worketh by charity (Gal. v. 6).

Or as St. James says,

> Do you see that by works a man is justified; and not by faith only? ... For even as the body without the spirit is dead; so also faith without works is dead. (Ja. ii. 24, 26).

---

[171] This is one of the errors contained in his bull of excommunication

So what did St. Paul mean when he said "without the works of the Law?" He meant the *works of the Law of Moses*. Many of St. Paul's letters are simply working to implement the Council's decision in Acts XVI. 4 which we have discussed: the Gentiles are not required to keep the Law of Moses. They are not required to become circumcised or refrain from eating pork. St. Paul was fighting against the heresy of the Judaizers who sought to impose the Law of Moses onto the Gentiles. This is the meaning of St. Paul when he is making this distinction between faith and "works of the Law." St. Paul was not arguing against good works in general.

Thankfully, a movement has arisen among Protestants that is willing to admit this and say that Luther and the Reformers misunderstood this concept. This movement is known as the "New Perspective on Paul." One prominent scholar in this movement is able to admit, "The Reformation tradition's approach to Paul is fundamentally wrong."[172] Ironically this is a part of a larger movement among Protestants called "The Great Emergence" which is attempting to go "back to the sources."[173] These Protestants are reading the Church Fathers and realizing that the "Reformers" did indeed misunderstand St. Paul.

When you talk to a Protestant about Justification by Faith alone, it is important to realize that their main problem is that they think Catholics are trying to "earn their salvation." In short, they think that Catholics are Pelagians (see chapter 15 for more on this).

---

[172] Francis Watson, *Paul, Judaism, and the Gentiles: Beyond the New Perspective* (Eerdmans: 2007), 1. The most popular writer in this regard is N.T. Wright.
[173] Some prominent writers in this movement are Brian McLaren and Phyllis Tickle

You can politely inform them that this heresy was condemned by St. Augustine (d. 430) and multiple councils since. Rather, the Catholic doctrine is that God Himself sends grace into our souls—which is divine power—in order to do works while maintaining our free will. As St. Paul says:

> For it is God who worketh in you, both to will and to accomplish, according to his good will (Php. ii. 13).

Or again:

> For we are his workmanship, created in Christ Jesus in good works, which God hath prepared that we should walk in them (Eph. ii. 10).

The Catholic doctrine is that God's grace does good works inside a Christian, while maintaining his free will (since he can choose to fall away from the faith), and then rewards His own work. St. Augustine summarizes it this way: "Your good merits are God's gifts, God does not crown your merits as your merits, but as His own gifts."[174] The best explanation of this is the Council of Trent Session 6.

The Virgin Mary

Perhaps the most difficult thing for Protestants to understand is the love and veneration that we have for our Blessed Mother. The most important thing to consider about this is that devotion to the Virgin Mary roots out all pride. All the proud have a problem with this veneration, because the

---

[174] St. Augustine, *On Grace and Free Will*, ch. 15

Virgin Mary is for the humble and is herself humble.[175] Thus Marian devotion is usually incomprehensible to Protestants, because they are proud.

If you find yourself talking to a Protestant who is open to understanding Marian devotion, it is important to center your explanation on Jesus Christ. For a Protestant, their chief concern is that the glory due to God is not obscured or diminished, which is a fair concern.

The Blessed Apostle declares to the Galatians: *as many of you as have been baptized in Christ, have put on Christ* (Gal. iii. 27). The word for "put on" is ἐνδύω which means to sink into clothing. In another place the Apostle, in his passage concerning Matrimony, states concerning Christ that *we are members of his body, of his flesh, and of his bones* (Eph. v. 30).

These mysterious sayings of the Apostle have been understood by the Church from the earliest times to express the *total* union with Christ through the Sacraments. The term "total" is applied here to contrast a *partial* union, which takes place in only part of you – for instance, your "heart" or "mind" or "soul" only. This is the type of union that the Protestants have. They do not claim to have total union with Christ.

The difference with *total* union is that it is a union with Christ which unites all of you with all of Him. In particular, the contrast becomes acute when we consider that our very *bodies* are also united to Him in the Sacraments, and not just our souls. In this way our bodies truly become the temple of the Holy Ghost (I Cor. vi. 19).

And so in Baptism we *put on Christ* in a way that changes our spiritual and bodily reality. Thus St. Paul considers the

---

[175] For more on this, please see my essay "Why Heretics Hate Mary, but We Should Love her More and More," *One Peter Five* (August 5, 2019). <https://onepeterfive.com/heretics-hate-mary>

fruit of this union to transcend the bodily realities of race, state, and gender (Gal. v. 28). Thus the bodily union with Christ in the Sacraments is a physical union which is actually physical and yet is *more real* than our physical reality we see. It does not destroy our physical nature, but unites it to him sacramentally.

It is thus that we must begin our discussion about Marian devotion, because Marian devotion comes straight from union with Christ. Marian devotion is a direct result of true union with Christ, and therefore lack of Marian devotion may be a result of lack of union with Christ.

It is important for Protestants to understand that for most Christians throughout history, loving Mary is a purely natural, freely flowing devotion to our Mother that any child would have.

For if union with Christ forms the cause of Marian devotion, we may identify another cause from the perspective of the commandments of God: the Fourth Commandment. For if we are truly united to Christ in a way that is physical yet is more real than our normal physical world, we are truly *in Christ* to the point that God is our Father and Mary is our Mother – just as is true for our Lord.

As it is written *he saith to the disciple: Behold thy mother. And from that hour, the disciple took her to his own* (Jn. xix. 27) and again *The dragon was angry against the woman: and went to make war with the rest of her seed, who keep the commandments of God, and have the testimony of Jesus Christ* (Apoc. xii. 17).

In this we see that Christians are called the seed of Mary in the same way as Christ is the seed of Mary and the Holy Ghost. Thus if we are truly united to Christ we must have Mary as our Mother. Otherwise, our union with Christ is not real.

Thus we have God our Father and Mary our Mother. In laying down the Ten Commandments, our God reserved the first three for Himself: no other gods, the hallowing of His Name, and the keeping of His Holy day. The first commandment which is justice to man is the virtue of piety contained in the fourth commandment: *honor thy father and thy mother*.

This is re-affirmed emphatically by the Law of Moses in the additional judicial precept *He that curseth his father, or mother, shall die the death* (Ex. xxii. 17). The justice of this penalty is re-affirmed by our Lord in Mark vii. 10 in his disputing with the Pharisees. This shows the importance of the Fourth Commandment and how serious an offense to God it is to break it.

Thus if Mary is our mother in a way that is more real even than normal physical reality, *then she is our mother in a way greater even than our biological mother*. And if God commanded us to honor our earthly mother and a curse against her warrants death, how much more our true, heavenly Mother Mary?

From these considerations you can bring a Protestant to understand why all Catholics love and celebrate Mary as our Mother. Most of all, her intercession can often open doors for you that you cannot unlock yourself by your own prayers. Pray to her for the graces to give Protestants the gift of charity: the truth.

XIV

TYPOLOGY - *ON PASCHA* BY ST. MELITO OF SARDIS

What follows is my translation from a Greek sermon by one of the pre-Nicene Fathers. Melito of Sardis was a Christian Bishop in Asia Minor in the second century A.D. He was numbered among a group of Christians known as the 'quartodecimans.' This group was named such because of their practice of celebrating Pascha (Easter) on the 14th day of the Jewish month of Nisan, which appears to have been taught by the Apostle St. John. This group was localized in the area of Asia Minor and their practice later came into conflict with the larger practice of the universal Church when Easter was formally established at the Council of Nicea.

Melito himself was a Jewish convert to the faith, and there is reason to believe that the people who heard this sermon might very well have shared similar origins.

On this note, it is important to understand Melito's usage of typology. As we have stated, the Christian Fathers used typology as a method of understanding what they called the 'Old Covenant' which was the Law of Moses. The Christians believed that the Law had been 'fulfilled' in the person of Jesus Christ. This does not mean that it was destroyed, but that it was a 'type' of the coming truth, Jesus Christ. I contrast two Greek words in my translation in order to bring out the meaning that Melito is delineating in his sermon. The first, *typos*, which I translated as "Type," refers in effect to an architectural rendering of a structure that is being built. The Type is absolutely vital to the guidance of the building and its precise construction, but this is contrasted with *aletheia*, translated "Truth." This refers essentially to the construction when it is completed, to which the Type "yields" because its purpose has been served.

The Type is played out in different things: the sheep, the people, the blood. It is not merely symbolism, and also not allegory. Symbolism is meant to illustrate a 'higher' reality, and the symbol is virtually worthless outside of its reality. But typology asserts that the efficacy and power of the reality itself is actually contained within the Type. Thus we see Melito suggesting that the Israelites were saved because the Pascha was the Type of Jesus Christ. Also, an allegory usually points to a philosophical or moral truth outside of its material instance. Typology points to a physical reality *inside* of its material Type. In other words, the physical existence of the Type also has meaning for the Truth.

Throughout the piece I translate *typos* always as "Type" and *aletheia* always as "Truth." I also capitalize key 'types' and 'truths' within theology of Melito. The same Greek word is always translated into the same English word. This becomes particularly clear in the closing portions of the passage. This text itself is only a section of a much larger homily. The Greek text used came from Whitacre's *A Patristic Greek Reader*. I employed his method of arranging the text for rhetorical sense and I am thankful for it. Further reading:

Cohick, Lynn H. *The* Peri Pascha *Attributed to Melito of Sardis: Setting, Purpose, and Sources.* Providence: Brown Judaic Studies, 2000

Stewart-Sykes, Alistar. *Melito of Sardis On Pascha.* New York: St. Vladimir's Seminary Press, 2001

Whitacre, Rodney A. *A Greek Patristic Reader.* Peabody, MA: Hendrickson Publishers, Inc., 2007

The scripture of the Hebrew Exodus has been read
    And the words of the mystery have been made clear
       How the sheep is sacrificed
       And how the people are saved
       And how Pharoah through the mystery is plagued
Therefore, O beloved, understand how it is:
       New and Old
       Eternal and Passing
       Perishable and Imperishable
       Mortal and Immortal
           This is the mystery of Pascha.
Old because of the Law
    But new because of the Word
Passing because of the Type
    Eternal through Grace
Perishable by the sheep's slaughter
    Imperishable by the Lord's life
Mortal by of the earthly burial
    Immortal by the resurrection from the dead.
Old is the Law
    But new is the Word
Passing the Type
    But eternal the Grace
Perishable is the sheep
    But imperishable the Lord
       Not crushed as a lamb
       But risen as God
For even if he was led into the slaughter as a sheep—
    He was not a sheep;
    And if he was silent like a lamb—
    He was not a lamb.
For as there once was a Type

So now the Truth has been found.
For in the place of the lamb there was the Son
    And in the place of the sheep the man
    And in the man Christ encompassing all things
So the slaughter of the sheep
    And the show of blood
And the writings of the Law go forth unto Christ Jesus
Because of whom all things in the older Law came to be —
    But how much more in the new Word!
For even the Law has become the Word
    And the old has become new —
        Coming together out of Zion and Jerusalem —
    The commandment has become Grace
    And the picture Truth
    And the lamb a Son
    And the sheep a man
    And the man God.
For as the Son has been born
    And the lamb led
    And the sheep slaughtered
    And the man buried
        He is raised up from the dead as God, in
nature being God and man
    He who is all things:
    Through him the Law judges
    Through him the Word teaches
    Through him the Grace saves
    Through him the Father begets
    Through him the Son is begotten
    Through him the sheep suffers
    Through him the man is buried
    Through him the God is raised up

He is Jesus the Christ
> To him be the glory unto ages of ages. Amen.

This is the mystery of Pascha
> Just as it is written in the Law
> As it was read before for a short time,

I will tell the events of Scripture
> How God commanded Moses in Egypt
> When He wished to blind Pharoah with plagues

And release Israel from the whip by the hand of Moses.
For lo, he said, you shall take a spotless lamb without blemish
And in the evening you shall slaughter it with the   sons of Israel,
> And at night eat it in haste
> You shall not break a single bone.

Thus, he said, you shall do
In one night you shall eat it according to your families and houses
> Girding your loins
> With staffs in your hands,

For this is the Pascha of the Lord,
> An eternal remembrance for the sons of Israel.

And taking the blood of the sheep
> Anoint the front doors of your homes

Placing it on the doorposts of the entrance
> The sign of the blood for persuading the angel.

For lo, I will strike Egypt
> And in one night she will be made childless from beast to man.

Then after Moses had slaughtered the sheep

    And in the night completed the mystery with the sons of Israel,
He sealed the doors of the houses
    To protect the people and persuade the angel
And when the sheep was slaughtered
    And the Pascha eaten
    And the mystery completed
    And the people gladdened
    And Israel sealed,
Then the angel came to strike Egypt—
    Uninitiated in the mystery,
    With no share in the Pascha,
    Not sealed with the blood,
    Unprotected by the Spirit,
    An enemy,
    Unbelieving—
She was struck in one night and made childless
The angel went around Israel,
    And seeing the seal of blood from the sheep,
He came upon Egypt,
    And painfully conquered stiff-necked Pharoah
    Clothing him not with a gray garment
        Nor with a torn robe
    But with all of torn Egypt itself—
        They mourned over their firstborns.

Such an event encompassed Egypt
    Suddenly she was made childless
But Israel was guarded by the slaughter of the sheep
    And baptized together in shed blood
And the death of the sheep secured a wall for the people
O strange and ineffable mystery!

The slaughter of sheep secured the salvation of Israel
And the death of the sheep became the life of the people
    And the blood persuaded the angel
Speak to me, O angel, what was it that persuaded you?
    The slaughter of the sheep or the life of the Lord?
    The death of the sheep or the Type of the Lord?
    The blood of the sheep or the Spirit of the Lord?
Surely you are persuaded:
    You saw the mystery of the Lord in the sheep
    The life of the Lord in the sheep's slaughter
    The picture of the Lord in the sheep's death
Because of this you did not strike Israel
    But only Egypt was made childless
What is this new mystery?
    Egypt dashed into destruction
    But Israel shielded for salvation
Hear the power of the mystery:
There is nothing, O beloved, that is said or done
    Apart from parable and design
All things that would be said or done receive parables
    What is spoken of gets a parable
    What is made gets a prototype
So that in fact what is made might be explained through
    the prototype
And what is spoken of is illuminated through the parable
So this happens during the preparation for construction
    The completed work is not yet raised up
For the greater thing is seen through the preliminary
    sketch
Through this it becomes a design of the coming thing
    Whether made out of wax or clay or wood
So that the greater thing to be raised up—

>   Greater in size
>   And stronger in power
>   And beautiful in form
>   And rich in its craftsmanship—
>   May be seen through this small and perishable design
> But when the work is raised up according to the Type
> Then the sketched image of that which is to come—
>   This is done away with since it has become useless
>   The sketch yields to its true nature
>   And then its value becomes worthless
>   Because its true worth has been revealed
> For each thing has its own meaningful time
>   The Type has its own time
>   The material has its own time
>   The Truth has its own time
> You make the Type and you want it
> Because you see in it the image of that which is to come
> You produce the material for the Type and you want this
>   Because the greater thing will be raised up through it
> You complete the work and you only want this and only
>   love this
> Because in it you see the Type and the material and the
>   Truth
> Therefore as in the perishable patterns
>   So also in the imperishable
> As in the earthly things
>   So also in the heavenly things
>   Both the salvation of the Lord and the Truth has been
> prefigured in the people
>   And the teaching of the Gospel was designed by the Law
>   Therefore the people became the Type of the design
>   And the Law became a parable

And the narrative of the Gospel became the completion of the Law
　　　　　And the Church the source of Truth
So the Type was valuable before the Truth
　　　　　And the parable was wondrous before its explanation
This is why the image of the people was precious before the Church was raised up
　　　　　And the Law was wondrous before the illumination of the Gospel
But since the Church has been raised up
　　　　　And the Gospel has come to be
The Type which passed on the power of the Truth has become empty
　　　　　And the Law which passed on the power of the Gospel has been completed
　　　In the same way that the Type that passes on the image
　　　　　Is emptied by the true nature
And the illuminated parable is completed by its explanation
　　　So even the Law has been completed by the explanation of the Gospel
　　　　　And the image of the people is emptied by the raising of the Church
　　　And the type has been done away with by the appearance of the Lord
　　　　　And today the precious things have become worthless
Since now the naturally precious things have been revealed
　　　For precious was the slaughter of the sheep
　　　　　But now it is worthless through the life of the Lord
　　　Precious the death of the sheep
　　　　　Now worthless through the salvation of the Lord
　　　Precious the blood of the sheep
　　　　　Now worthless through the Spirit of the Lord

Precious the silent lamb
    Now worthless through the unblemished Son
Precious the temple below
    Now worthless because of the Christ above
Precious was Jerusalem below
    Now worthless because of Jerusalem above
Precious was the exclusive inheritance
    Now worthless because universal Grace
For the glory of God rests
    Not just in one place or on a small piece of land
But His Grace is poured out
    Over all the ends of the whole world
And it is here that the Almighty God makes his dwelling place
    Through Christ Jesus
    To Him be glory unto the ages, amen.

XV

OVERVIEW OF THE TEILHARDIAN HERESY IN HISTORICAL CONTEXT

This first appeared in Catholic Family News *December 2019 as "The Pelagian Roots of Our Ecclesial Crisis: Importance of True Doctrine on Nature and Grace." It provides a larger context to the appearance of Teilhardianism in the history of theology.*

The Church's doctrine on *nature* and *grace*—terms intimately bound up with the reality of Original Sin and its effects on mankind—was formulated during the time of a great Western heresy in the early centuries of the Church. This doctrine has been foundational for the growth of the Roman Church, and its obscuring has led to nothing but confusion and error in our own time. This essay will trace the doctrine's rise, fall, and why we must recover it.

Pelagianism and the Augustinian Triumph

In the early 400s, a British monk named Pelagius was unhappy with a lack of Christian penance and began to preach against it. Like many heresies, there was some truth mixed in with his error; and in his zeal against laxity, Pelagius began with a good intention. Over time, however, his error became manifest when he began to teach that man could lift himself up to God without the help of divine grace.

Essentially, Pelagius taught that the sin of Adam afflicted man only by leaving him a bad example. As a result, man (according to Pelagius) is not fallen (wounded) in his nature but has the power to reach God by his own efforts. For Pelagius, "grace was within the natural capacity of man."[176] Christ, then, is not really necessary as a Redeemer but is simply a great moral teacher. According to Pelagius, "Christ's deed of Redemption consists above all in His teaching and in His example of virtue."[177] Sound familiar?

Related errors also spread during this time, for example, that "the primary desire for salvation proceeds from the natural powers of man." Some said the first moment of grace can be a result of man's own efforts, nor does he require grace for final perseverance.[178]

Against this heresy came the mighty pen of St. Augustine of Hippo (A.D. 354-430). One of the greatest doctors of the Christian West, Augustine emphatically stated, "I proclaim the grace of Christ, without which no one is justified."[179] The sin of Adam was not merely a bad example but a true corruption of nature, passed down "by propagation, not by imitation,"[180] to every single one of his descendants other than Our Lady, who was preserved "at the first instant of her conception, by the singular grace and privilege of Almighty God,"[181] and Our

---

[176] Ludwig Ott, *Fundamentals of Catholic Dogma* (Baronius: 2005), p. 240.
[177] Ibid.
[178] Ibid., 241.
[179] St. Augustine, *De Natura et Gratia*, 62, 73.
[180] Council of Trent, Session 5, Decree on Original Sin (D.H. 1513).
[181] Pope Pius IX, Bull *Ineffabilis Deus* (Dogmatic Definition of the Immaculate Conception) (D.H. 2803).

Lord, Who is the Second Person of the Blessed Trinity and thus immune from sin by virtue of His divine nature.

Practically speaking, the corruption of nature that resulted from Adam's sin equates to a darkened intellect, a weakened will, and an inclination to evil—all of which are encompassed by the term *Original Sin*. Our fallen nature, of itself, cannot achieve union with God without the supernatural power of grace. Thus, grace is freely given by God apart from merit on our part. It "transcend[s] the being, the powers and the claims of created nature."[182]

Augustine's doctrine, firmly rooted in Scripture and Tradition, was confirmed by local councils at Carthage in 411 as well as by the Third Ecumenical Council in 431 at Ephesus. The clearly defined truth about Original Sin served to affirm and strengthen a foundational axiom in the spiritual life: distrust of self and trust in God.[183] As a result, the Pelagian heresy was suppressed and the faithful were preserved from grave error—for a time.

The Greek Fathers

As previously mentioned, Pelagianism was a great Western heresy; thus, the precision of orthodoxy was likewise developed and confirmed in the West under Augustine. The Greek Fathers dealt with the great Eastern heresies and codified other points of orthodoxy (e.g., the Divine Personhood of Jesus Christ in two natures and two wills, the veneration of images, etc.). As such, the Greek Fathers, being concerned with other threats to the Faith, never developed a precise terminology in Greek for the orthodox doctrine on

---

[182] Ott, *op. cit.*, 238.
[183] Dom Scupoli, *The Spiritual Combat* (Scriptoria: 2009), Ch. 1.

Original Sin, nature, and grace. They certainly believed these things, but because there were no analogous Eastern heresies, their theological language did not attain the same degree of precision on this point that the Latins did.

For example, St. Maximus the Confessor, the great Greek defender of the Papacy, spent much of his ecclesiastical career combatting the heresy of Monothelitism—the false claim that Our Lord has only one will. As such, Maximus did not develop a great doctrine against Pelagianism as Augustine did. Because of this, his language on this point is vague. For instance, consider this statement:

> The state that comes from contemplating God and enjoying the gladness it gives is rightly called pleasure, rapture, and joy. It is called pleasure because the term means *that for which we naturally strive*.[184]

Here, St. Maximus states that the contemplation of God is that thing *for which we naturally strive*. But in what manner does St. Maximus speak of "naturally?" Surely, he would not claim with Pelagius that man can strive for union with God by his own nature alone. But the lack of precision in his words can cause them to be misunderstood in this manner.

The City of God Against the Pagans

In the Latin West, the Augustinian triumph over Pelagianism made the faithful press forward with the Gospel.

---

[184] St. Maximus the Confessor, *Ambiguum* 7. In *Ad Thalassium*, 60. Quoted in Nicholas J. Healy, "Henri de Lubac on Nature and Grace: A Note on Some Recent Contributions to the Debate," *Communio* 35 (Winter 2008), 539.

The knowledge that grace was absolutely necessary for nature only provoked a greater missionary zeal among our fathers, who strenuously labored to convert the barbarian tribes from the darkness of paganism to the light of Jesus Christ.

The doctrinal life of the Church reached its zenith in the Scholastic theology of St. Thomas Aquinas, who confirmed Augustine's doctrine against Pelagius:

> Man, by his natural endowments, cannot produce meritorious works proportionate to everlasting life; and for this a higher force is needed, viz. the force of grace. And thus, *without grace man cannot merit everlasting life*.[185]

St. Thomas further confirmed that the preparation for grace, repentance from sin, good works, and final perseverance are all works of grace, without destroying free will.[186] Thus, the greatest doctor of the second millennium confirmed and elevated the greatest doctor from the first in this fundamental truth: we must not place our trust in man, but in God.

By the 14th century, just a few generations before Columbus discovered the New World, the last vestiges of paganism were eradicated from continental Europe,[187] after which time the colonial period began. Even when Christendom was shattered by the Protestant revolt, our fathers were taking the Gospel to the ends of the earth, burning with charity for souls. Our Lord gave the commandment to "preach the Gospel to every creature" (Mark 16:15) and make disciples of "all

---

[185] ST I-II, q. 109, a. 5. Emphasis mine.
[186] Ibid., a. 6-10.
[187] The last European region to be converted was the region of Latvia in and around the 1300s.

nations, baptizing them in the Name of the Father, and of the Son, and of the Holy Ghost" (Matt. 28:19). Due to Original Sin and the absolute need for grace, man could not have any hope for salvation apart from Christ. Thus, the doctrine formulated by Augustine and confirmed by Aquinas continued to provide ample motivation for missionaries down through the ages. By the 19th century, large swaths of formerly pagan nations had converted and professed allegiance to Christ the King.

The Rise of Teilhardian Heresy and "Resourcing" the Greek Fathers

Tragically, in the late 19th and early 20th centuries, there arose in Christian Europe a movement which repudiated this sacred allegiance. Following the Protestant revolt of the 16th century, the secular revolutionaries sought to revive Pelagianism by denying Original Sin and placing all trust in the power of man. The popes continuously condemned these revolutionaries, who insisted they were not inclined to evil.

Despite these papal rebukes, and even after witnessing the horrors of two World Wars, men still arose to challenge the Augustinian-Thomistic doctrine. Notable among them was Fr. Teilhard de Chardin (1881-1955), a French Jesuit. This man was consumed with the errors of secularism and declared that Original Sin was not a dogma: "In our modern perspective of a Universe in a process of cosmogenesis, the problem of evil no longer exists." Thus, he concluded that through a process of evolution evil simply came about as a necessary byproduct.[188]

---

[188] Pierre Teilhard de Chardin, *Comment je vois*, Par. 29, Tr. p.39, *cit.* Jacques Maritain, *The Peasant of the Garonne* (New York: Holt, Reinhart and Winston, 1968), p. 265.

Dr. Dietrich von Hildebrand (1889-1977), the renowned German Catholic philosopher and theologian, condemned de Chardin since his philosophy obliterated the distinction between the natural and the supernatural. In his landmark book *Charitable Anathema*, von Hildebrand mentions how de Chardin "exclaimed violently" that Augustine was "an unfortunate man" who "spoiled everything by introducing the supernatural."[189]

Although it should be evident that Teilhard de Chardin was a heretic, he nevertheless created a "fascination...for an entire generation," in the words of the progressive Austrian Cardinal Christoph Schönborn.[190]

Enter the *Nouvelle Théologie*

Teilhardianism, as it has become known, was supported and propagated in the Church by members of a movement known as the *Nouvelle théologie* (French for "new theology"). Fr. Henri de Lubac (1896-1991), likewise a French Jesuit, was one of the leading figures in the movement and wrote multiple works defending his heretical confrere. As CFN's longtime editor John Vennari (RIP) noted years ago, it was de Lubac and others in the *Nouvelle théologie* movement who helped develop the Teilhardian error that "anything supernatural (sanctifying grace) that is in man ultimately comes from the nature of man himself."[191] The terrible result, of course, is that

---

[189] Dietrich von Hildebrand, "Teilhard de Chardin: Towards a New Religion" in *Charitable Anathema* (Roman Catholic Books, 1993), p. 179.
[190] Christoph Schönborn, *Change or Purpose?* (Ignatius: 2007), p. 142.
[191] John Vennari, "A Short Catechism on the New Theology" (http://www.catholicapologetics.info/modernproblems/modernism/newtheo.htm).

Original Sin is obscured and supernatural grace is made obsolete.

And this is where the Greek Fathers and their lack of precision concerning Original Sin come into play. De Lubac did a great deal to bring the Greek Fathers into Western theological discourse. In itself, this was a laudable pursuit, but without the Latin precision on the doctrine in question, the Greeks are vague, which is why de Lubac was accused by his contemporaries in the Thomistic camp of not acting in good faith. As Vennari pointed out:

> Writing in *The Thomist* (1950), Father David Greenstock warned that the only reason that the leaders of the New Theology overwhelm the reader with the Greek Fathers is in order to get around St. Thomas Aquinas, whom they actually disdain, no matter how much they pledge their devotion to him.[192]

De Lubac's ambiguities were condemned by Pope Pius XII in *Humani Generis* with these words: "Others destroy the gratuity of the supernatural order, since God, they say, cannot create intellectual beings without ordering and calling them to the beatific vision."[193] By using, in the words of Pius XII, "a certain vague notion...found in the ancient Fathers, especially the Greeks" de Lubac and the New Theology challenged the Magisterium of their day.[194] It created enough ambiguity so that the Teilhardian heresy could finally challenge the dominant Thomism as a larger influence over the Church. Thus, even reading de Lubac as sympathetically as possible,

---

[192] Ibid.
[193] Pius XII, Encyclical *Humani Generis* (Aug. 12, 1950), n. 26.
[194] Ibid., 18.

his teaching was perilously close to a contradiction of the true Augustinian doctrine and toward the Teilhardian heresy.

Fatima and Vatican II

This Teilhardian evolutionary optimism, which denies Original Sin (i.e., the true state of man after the Fall), runs completely contrary to the warnings given by Our Lady of Fatima in 1917. According to the historical record, Pope John XXIII opened and read the famed Third Secret of Fatima in mid-August 1959[195] – even though it was supposed to remain sealed until 1960[196] – but instead of publishing it, he kept the text hidden, choosing to focus on plans for a new Ecumenical Council, a venture he first announced on Jan. 25, 1959.

During his opening address at the Second Vatican Council (1962-1965), John XXIII stated, "We feel we must disagree with those prophets of gloom, who are always forecasting disaster, as though the end of the world were at hand." Instead of adhering to Our Lady's Fatima Message, he stood with Teilhard, claiming that "Divine Providence is leading us to a new order of human relations which, by men's own efforts and even beyond their very expectations, are directed toward the fulfillment of God's superior and inscrutable designs."[197]

---

[195] See Congregation for the Doctrine of the Faith, *The Message of Fatima* (June 26, 2000).

[196] See Frère Michel de la Sainte Trinité, *The Whole Truth About Fatima* Vol. III: *The Third Secret* (Buffalo: Immaculate Heart Publications, 2001 ed.), pp. 470-479, 489.

[197] "*At Nobis plane dissentiendum esse videtur ab his rerum adversarum vaticinatoribus, qui deteriora semper praenuntiant, quasi rerum exitium instet. In praesenti humanorum eventuum cursu, quo hominum societas novum rerum ordinem ingredi videtur, potius arcana Divinae Providentiae consilia agnoscenda sunt, quae per tempora succedentia, hominum opera, ac plerumque praeter eorum exspectationem, suum*

Thus, the Council was dominated by a naïve optimism which implicitly denied the reality of fallen human nature and man's need for grace.

Concerning this Teilhardian thrust, Cardinal Joseph Ratzinger (the future Benedict XVI) would later write:

> The impetus given by Teilhard de Chardin exerted a wide influence [on the Council]. With daring vision it incorporated the historical movements of Christianity into the great cosmic process of evolution from Alpha to Omega. ... The Council's 'Pastoral Constitution on the Church in the Modern World' (*Gaudium et Spes*) took the cue; Teilhard's slogan, 'Christianity means more progress, more technology,' became a stimulus in which the Council Fathers from rich and poor countries alike found a concrete hope.[198]

The obvious problem with such "concrete hope" is that it is not *theological* hope (trust in God and the power of His grace), but rather a foolish trust in the so-called "evolution" of modern man and his natural power to overcome his evils. Forsaking Augustine, Aquinas, and even the Queen of Heaven herself, the Council Fathers forged ahead toward their fanciful springtime of renewal.

---

exitum consequuntur[.]" Pope John XXIII, Address *Gaudet Mater Ecclesia* (Oct. 11, 1962). Full English translation found in Walter M. Abbott, S.J. (Gen. Ed.), *The Documents of Vatican II* (New York: The America Press, 1966), pp. 710-719.
[198] Joseph Ratzinger, *Principles of Catholic Theology* (San Francisco: Ignatius Press, 1987), 334

The Road to Assisi and P-chamama

In reality, such excessive optimism led directly back to the error of Pelagius, namely, that union with God is within the natural capacity of man. As a result, the Church's missionary impulse was profoundly weakened since, according to the logic of the revived Pelagian error, other religions contain "seeds of the Word"[199] and are thus more or less good. In other words, the urgency to convert the nations was all but lost. As Marshall adroitly puts it:

> Rather than striving to convert all nations and peoples to Christ in the Catholic Church through baptism, Catholics would now accompany all people in their spiritual journeys. The Catholic Church became a pilgrim church calling not for conversion but for conversation.[200]

This optimism fit perfectly with the secularist revolutionaries who had been denying Original Sin since 1789.

---

[199] Vatican II, Decree *Ad Gentes* on the Missionary Activity of the Church (Dec. 7, 1965), n. 11. The phrase "seeds of the Word" is often attributed to St. Justin Martyr (d. ca. A.D. 165), although the actual phrase he used in his *First Apology* is "seeds of truth". Read in context, however, the sainted Church Father is arguing *against* the sufficiency of pagan "seeds of truth" and the dependence of all men on Divine Revelation: "For Moses is more ancient than all the Greek writers. And whatever both philosophers and poets have said concerning the immortality of the soul, or punishments after death, or contemplation of things heavenly, or doctrines of the like kind, *they have received such suggestions from the prophets* as have enabled them to understand and interpret these things. *And hence there seem to be seeds of truth among all men*; but they are charged with not accurately understanding [the truth] when they assert contradictories." (*First Apology*, 44, emphasis added – http://www.newadvent.org/fathers/0126.htm).
[200] Taylor Marshall, *Infiltration: The Plot to Destroy the Church from Within* (Manchester: Crisis Publications, 2019), p. 138.

In the 1960s, it was the vision of the United Nations, which foolishly believed they could achieve peace on earth without the Prince of Peace. Pope Paul VI removed his tiara and placed his hope in the United Nations with a "solemn moral ratification of this lofty Institution" since, as he told them and the world, he was "convinced that this Organization represents the obligatory path of modern civilization and world peace."[201]

If the effects of Original Sin are minimized, and the capacity of man's nature for grace is maximized, a secular organization then becomes the "obligatory path" of world peace. The dominion of Christ the King can be relegated to the eschaton, as the New Mass has done by relegating the Feast of Christ the King to the last Sunday of the liturgical year (thus associating it almost exclusively with the Second Coming). After all, as John XXIII said at the beginning of Vatican II, "men of themselves are inclined to condemn [their own errors]."[202]

Pope John Paul II also embraced this optimism wholeheartedly, affirming:

> If all men and women, whatever the differences between them, cling to the truth, with respect for the unique dignity of every human being, *a new world order* – a civilization of love – can be achieved.[203]

Because of this hope in humanity, John Paul II created what Archbishop Marcel Lefebvre and Bishop Antonio de

---

[201] Paul VI, Address to the United Nations (Oct. 4, 1965).
[202] *Hodie homines per se ipsi ea damnare incipere videantur.* John XXIII, op. cit.
[203] John Paul II, Address at Monument Dedicated to Gandhi (Feb. 1, 1986, emphasis added).

Castro Mayer called an "immeasurable, unprecedented scandal."[204] At Assisi in 1986, he allowed false gods to be worshipped inside a Catholic church. He justified this firmly on the error of Pelagius, that man's nature was striving for God, which allowed him to exonerate the wicked men who have created false religions down through the ages:

> ...every quest of the human spirit for truth and goodness, and in the last analysis for God, is inspired by the Holy Spirit. The various religions arose precisely from this primordial human openness to God. At their origins we often find founders who, with the help of God's Spirit, achieved a deeper religious experience. Handed on to others, this experience took form in the doctrines, rites and precepts of the various religions.
>
> In every authentic religious experience, the most characteristic expression is prayer. Because of the human spirit's constitutive openness to God's action of urging it to self-transcendence, we can hold that 'every authentic prayer is called forth by the Holy Spirit, who is mysteriously present in the heart of every person' (*Address to the Members of the Roman Curia*, 22 Dec. 1986, n. 11; *L'Osservatore Romano* English edition, 5 Jan. 1987, p. 7).
>
> We experienced an eloquent manifestation of this truth at the World Day of Prayer for Peace on 27

---

[204] 1986 Declaration of Archbishop Lefebvre and Bishop de Castro Mayer.

October 1986 in Assisi, and on other similar occasions of great spiritual intensity."[205]

He repeated similar gatherings in 1993 and 2002.

Ratzinger, to his credit, tried to moderate this excessive optimism when he said in *Dominum Iesus* that the Church "must be primarily committed to proclaiming to all people the truth definitively revealed by the Lord, and to announcing the necessity of conversion to Jesus Christ and of adherence to the Church through Baptism."[206] Nevertheless, he too participated in an Assisi gathering while Pope in 2011 and repeated the same secularist dream on the first day of that same year:

> Religious freedom is an authentic weapon of peace, with an historical and prophetic mission…May all men and women, and societies at every level and in every part of the earth, soon be able to experience religious freedom, the path to peace![207]

Thus, it is very clear that when Pope Francis says, "The pluralism and diversity of religions…are willed by God,"[208] he is following the same underlying optimism of Teilhardian errors. Indeed, his only innovation is that he is the first Roman Pontiff to reference Teilhard de Chardin in an official papal document.[209] Therefore, the faithful should not look upon Francis as the primary issue to overcome, but rather upon the decades of error which have obscured the Augustinian and Thomistic doctrine on nature and grace. Is it any wonder, after

---

[205] John Paul II, General Audience (Sept. 9, 1998).
[206] Congregation for the Doctrine of the Faith, *Dominus Iesus* (2000), n. 22.
[207] Benedict XVI, Message for World Day of Peace (Jan. 1, 2011).
[208] Document on Human Fraternity (Feb. 4, 2019).
[209] See *Laudato Si'* (May 24, 2015), footnote 53.

all these years, that idols were worshipped at the Amazon Synod?

The Way Forward

How do we face this? First, the faithful must confess the true doctrine that man, afflicted by Original Sin and devoid of divine grace, must be converted. Next, they must stand firm in their allegiance to Christ the King and reject any sort of false peace that excludes His divine prerogatives.

But how can we stand for Christ in this wicked and adulterous generation? It begins at home: enthrone the Sacred Heart of Jesus as King over your family. In the enthronement ceremony, a child learns from the earliest age that he must not trust in himself but in Jesus Christ the King of kings, outside of whose reign there can be no true peace. It is here, in our children, that the next generation will grow and pledge their undying loyalty to Christ the King. It is they, or perhaps their children, who will finally see the triumph of Our Lady's Immaculate Heart, and with it the liberty and exaltation of Holy Mother Church.

Let us place our trust not in the power of man, corrupted by sin, but in the grace of Jesus Christ our Savior. Let us pass down the Faith to our children. Let us confess Christ the King, so that at our death we may receive the reward of everlasting life.

XVI (Appendix)

ROMAN NUMERALS, NAMES OF BOOKS AND ABBREVIATIONS

In this text we have used the normal way of citing Scripture from Catholics before Vatican II: Roman numerals. This practice preserves the sacred character of the Text, but unfortunately it has fallen out of use since the Council. To aid readers to acclimate to Roman numerals, here is how it works.

Each numeral has a numeric value which is added to all others when placed to the right of a number:

I = 1
V = 5
VI = 6

Then, when a numeral of lesser value is placed *before* a numeral it subtracts from it:

IV = 4

This principle holds for all the larger numbers:

X = 10
L = 50
C = 100
XL = 40
XC = 90

After a subtraction such as this, other numerals can be added:

XLVII = 47
XCII = 92

I hope that helps with any readers finding difficulty with the citations.

Below is a chart of all names of books and abbreviations.

Douay-Rheims	Also Known As	Abbreviation
Genesis	-	Gen.
Exodus	-	Ex.
Leviticus	-	Lev.
Numbers	-	Num.
Deuteronomy	-	Dt.
Joshua	-	Josh.
Judges	-	Jdg.
Ruth	-	Rth.
I Kings	I Samuel	Kngs.
II Kings	II Samuel	
III Kings	I Kings	
IV Kings	II Kings	
I Paralipomenon	I Chronicles	Para.
II Paralipomenon	II Chronicles	
I Esdras	Ezra	Esd.
II Esdras	Nehemiah	
Tobias	Tobit	Tob.
Judith	-	Jud.
Esther	-	Est.
Job	-	Job
Psalms	-	Ps.
Proverbs	-	Prov.

Ecclesiastes	-	Eccl.
Canticle of Canticles	Song of Songs	Cant.
Wisdom	-	Wis.
Ecclesiasticus	Sirach	Ecclus.
Isaias	Isaiah	Is.
Jeremias	Jeremiah	Jer.
Lamentations	-	Lam.
Baruch	-	Bar.
Ezechiel	Ezekiel	Ez.
Daniel	-	Dan.
Osee	Hosea	Os.
Joel	-	Joel
Amos	-	Amos
Abdias	Obadiah	Abd.
Jonas	Jonah	Jonas
Micheas	Micah	Mich.
Nahum	-	Nah.
Habacuc	Habakkuk	Hab.
Sophonias	Zephaniah	Soph.
Aggaeus	Haggai	Agg.
Zacharias	Zechariah	Zach.
Malachias	Malachi	Mal.
I Machabees	-	Mac.
II Machabees	-	
Matthew	-	Mt.
Mark	-	Mk.
Luke	-	Lk.
John	-	Jn.
Acts	-	Acts
Romans	-	Rom.
I Corinthians	-	I Cor.

II Corinthians	-	II Cor.
Galatians	-	Gal.
Ephesians	-	Eph.
Philippians	-	Philip.
Colossians	-	Col.
I Thessalonians	-	I Thess.
II Thessalonias	-	II Thess.
I Timothy	-	I Tim.
II Timothy	-	II Tim.
Titus	-	Tit.
Philemon	-	Philem.
Hebrews	-	Heb.
James	-	Ja.
I Peter	-	I Pt.
II Peter	-	II Pt.
I John	-	I Jn.
II John	-	II Jn.
III John	-	III Jn.
Jude	-	Jd.
Apocalypse	Revelation	Apoc.

XVII (Appendix)

LIST OF FURTHER READING AND RESOURCES

Approved Commentaries

Catena Aurea by St. Thomas Aquinas. *This is the essential collection of patristic commentary on the Gospels. Free on the iPieta App.*

Haydock's Bible commentary (free on the iPieta App) – *covers entire Bible*

Lapide Commentary of the New Testament – *online* catholicapologetics.info/scripture/newtestament/Lapide.htm

Neale's Commentary on the Psalms (4 volumes, free on archive.org) – *this is the work of an erudite Anglican who brings together multiple patristic and liturgical sources. The best overall commentary on the Psalms*

St. Augustine's commentary on the Psalms – *online* newadvent.org/fathers/1801.htm

St. Robert Bellarmine's commentary on the Psalms – *online* ecatholic2000.com/bell/psalms.shtml

St. Thomas' Commentaries – *online* https://aquinas.cc/la/en/~ST.I

Other works of the Fathers on individual books – *online* newadvent.org/fathers/. Ctrl+F and enter a book of the Bible

Online Resources
    Catechismclass.com
    NewSaintThomas.com
    InstituteofCatholicCulture.org

The Protestant Heresies

The Catholic Controversy *by St. Francis De Sales.*
https://archive.org/stream/catholiccontrove00sain/cath
oliccontrove00sain_djvu.txt
On the Roman Pontiff *by St. Robert Bellarmine.*
Available only in print from Mediatrix Press.

On the Historical Reliability of the Holy Bible

K.A. Kitchen, *On the Reliability of the Old Testament* (Grand Rapids: Eerdmans, 2003).

James K. Hoffmeier, *Israel in Egypt: The Evidence for the Authenticity of the Exodus Tradition* (Oxford: Oxford University Press, 1996).

James K. Hoffmeier, *Ancient Israel in Sinai: The Evidence for the Authenticity of the Wilderness Tradition* (Oxford: Oxford University Press, 2005).

Craig Blomberg, *The Historical Reliability of the Gospels.*

Craig Blomberg, *The Historical Reliability of the New Testament.*

Principe. Sainte Trinité.